OLD ENOUGH TO SAY WHAT I WANT

OLD ENOUGH
TO SAY WHAT I WANT

AN AUTOBIOGRAPHY

DAVE BROADFOOT

with Barbara Sears

To the memory of Frank Shuster

National Library of Canada Cataloguing in Publication

Broadfoot, Dave, 1925-
Old enough to say what I want : an autobiography /
Dave Broadfoot ; with Barbara Sears.

ISBN 0-7710-1656-5 (bound). – ISBN 0-7710-1657-3 (pbk.)

1. Broadfoot, Dave, 1925-.   2. Comedians – Canada – Biography.
I. Sears, Barbara   II. Title.

PN2308.B76A3 2002   792.7'028'092   C2002-902359-9

We acknowledge the financial support of the Government of Canada through the Book Publishing Industry Development Program and that of the Government of Ontario through the Ontario Media Development Corporation's Ontario Book Initiative. We further acknowledge the support of the Canada Council for the Arts and the Ontario Arts Council for our publishing program.

Typeset in Minion by M&S, Toronto
Printed and bound in Canada

McClelland & Stewart Ltd.
The Canadian Publishers
481 University Avenue
Toronto, Ontario
M5G 2E9
www.mcclelland.com

1 2 3 4 5   07 06 05 04 03

CONTENTS

FOREWORD

by John Morgan

What can you say about Dave Broadfoot that hasn't already been said. However, this is no time for recriminations.

For fifteen years Mr. Broadfoot was a cornerstone of Air Farce and a font of comedic lore. Combine a cornerstone with a font and you're halfway to recreating a historical horse trough.

It was from this trough that we Farceurs drank deeply of Mr. Broadfoot's vast compendium of comedy wisdom. Who can forget his great "Mots Justes," or, as we say in English, "Just Moe":

"Never accept an engagement in a place called the Moose Room in Dryden."

"If you're hired for the Grandstand Show in Lloydminster by a guy in two-tone shoes, get the cheque up front."

"If he wants you for the Stockman Hotel in Kamloops, let him know Gordie Tapp can do a better job."

Living by precepts such as these has ensured that Mr. Broadfoot is a survivor. Survivor, hell. He has beaten down all that has stood in his way to reach his present pinnacle.

Who can forget the cherished characters Mr. Broadfoot has created, such as Big Bobby Clobber, one of hockey's legendary mouth-breathers. Living proof that undergoing a lobotomy doesn't mean you can't live a meaningful life.

Carping social critics may point out the natural advantages Mr. Broadfoot possessed that enabled him to create the Clobber character. But Mr. Broadfoot is immune to the pin pricks of such critics, for he knows many of the pins personally.

Sergeant Renfrew of the Royal Canadian Mounted Police is also one of his creations, and one that will stand proudly in the pantheon of great Canadian comedic characters. The carpers say that Mr. Broadfoot's creation was motivated by considerations other than comedy, and point to the fact that, during the countless years he has been portraying Sergeant Renfrew, he has never once received a speeding ticket from a member of the RCMP. That, again, is missing the point.

In creating his popular political figure, the Member of Parliament for Kicking Horse Pass, Mr. Broadfoot was well aware that, ever since Confederation, Canada has produced many great statesmen, men of courage, vision, and wisdom. The Member for Kicking Horse Pass is none of these. He is a politician who treads the fine line between adequacy and apathy. He speaks for the "average" Canadian.

Another facet of the man whose life lies before us is that, unlike most working in comedy, he does his research. Who can forget his pondering the conundrum, "If a cat always lands on its feet and toast always lands butter-side down, what happens if you attach a piece of toast butter-side up to the back of a cat and throw it out a window?"

We can attest to Mr. Broadfoot's many attempts to solve this dilemma, notwithstanding the lack of humour displayed by the SPCA at the subsequent inquiry.

Mr. Broadfoot's rise to the pinnacle of his profession has not been without some trauma. The unexplained word that haunted the life of Charles Foster Kane was "Rosebud." With Mr. Broadfoot, the word is "Norwegian." Many years ago, he was the target of a heckler, who, for reasons unexplained, used only this one word, "Norwegian." It was a non sequitur of awesome proportions, and to this day, Mr. Broadfoot, on occasion, wakes up screaming "Norwegian." More than once he has had to ask for understanding from Air Canada flight attendants who naturally assumed he was flying with the wrong airline.

Mr. Broadfoot once took the Air Farce team to visit his birthplace, a small clapboard house in North Vancouver. We were so moved by the experience, we asked the owner about attaching a small plaque to the building. The owner may have misunderstood. The only words we could make out of the shouted response were "defacing" and "police."

Yes, the man whose life we witness between these covers has truly earned his spurs, paid his dues, and been an adornment to his profession.

Stephen Leacock is no doubt looking down on the contents of this publication and nodding his head sagely. He will see in Dave Broadfoot a soul brother, someone who takes the grist from the daily mill and points out its absurdities.

Yes, I'm sure Mr. Leacock is sitting up there enjoying a fine single malt and chuckling. And we all know where he's sitting. Right next to a Norwegian in the Moose Room of the Stockman Hotel in downtown Valhalla.

July 2002

ACKNOWLEDGEMENTS

Many of the better pieces I have performed over the years, have been co-written. That is to say, others did a first draft of a piece, and then I took it from there. Or, conversely, I did the first draft and then others made their contributions. Either way, the end result was a better piece of comedy than I would have produced on my own.

This way of creating comedy material began, for me, with input from Jack Fulton in the 1950s and 1960s, then with input from the Air Farce team throughout the 1970s and 1980s and continues today with input from Nicholas Pashley and Jim Foster. My thanks to each of them for allowing lines in the comedy pieces collected here that may well have originated with Gordon Holtam, Rick Olsen, John Morgan, Roger Abbott, Don Ferguson, Nicholas Pashley, and Jim Foster.

My thanks also to those who were helpful in other ways ... people such as Mavor Moore, Bryan Hill, Walter Ikeda, Cedric Smith, Paul Simmons, Bob Johnstone, David Gardner, Don Cullen, Araby Lockhart, Edith Toop, and Ruth Blight. Also to my beautiful, tolerant wife, Diane Simard Broadfoot. Then there is Barbara Sears, without whom my story never would have reached print, and McClelland & Stewart's Pat Kennedy, who condoned the whole enterprise from Day One.

INTRODUCTION

And now, Ladies and Gentlemen, introducing a comedian who, over the years, has walked off with many of the country's top awards.

Nobody reported them missing, so he kept them.

A comedian who ended a performance in a seniors' hospital ward by telling the patients, "I hope you get better," and they replied, "You too!"

The very next day, in another hospital, he left the recovering invalids clutching their sides. They were hernia patients.

What have the critics been saying of this performer?

"We didn't want him to leave," said an inmate of a federal prison not far from Montreal. "He made us feel he was one of us."

They are referring to a comedian who has appeared in front of the Queen, the Prince, the President, and some cheaper hotels that must remain nameless.

Here he is, celebrating fifty years of crusading for comedy. Dave Broadfoot.

Chapter 1

ST. DAVE, THE BAPTIST

I would have preferred to have been born into a family of fun-loving atheists, but that is not how it turned out. I was born into a family where fun was not a priority, and religion was the centre of life. We were a mixed family – Anglican and Regular Baptist, with my mother, Beatrice, providing the Baptist influence. She believed in the literal truth of every word of the Bible. "It's so important to be ready," she would say, which meant ready at any time for death. For a devout Baptist like my mother, it's when you are dead that life really begins; but if you aren't "ready," if you haven't accepted Christ as your personal saviour, and live and witness for Jesus non-stop, then death means burning in Hell forever, if not longer.

My father, Percy, was the Anglican influence in the house. He was as religious as my mother, but in a different way. In truth, he was a bit of a fanatic. Percy Broadfoot, who was British to the core, firmly believed that the English were one of the lost tribes of Israel. All his life, he observed many of the Mosaic dietary laws; he never touched pork or shellfish. He was absolutely convinced that eating pork was about the worst thing you could do. It would give you cancer, he told anyone who was interested in listening.

Percy had come to Canada from England in 1903, at the age of twenty-one. Born in the Punjab, he lived there until he was twelve, when his father, a sergeant-major in the British Army, moved from

1

Meerut to Coventry in England. Percy's other passion in life (besides religion) was cricket, and he was very good at it. One day, he saw an advertisement in a Coventry newspaper: "Forming British eleven to tour Canada. If you are young and a skilful player, you may be qualified to join this cricket team. Please send your application to the above address with information as to where and when our team scout can observe you in action on a cricket field."

Percy had visions of playing cricket against the North West Mounted Police Eleven and winning. With great excitement, he sent in his application along with his game schedule. A few weeks later, he received a letter from the tour promoter, announcing that a talent scout had seen him in action and approved his membership. All he had to do now was send a deposit, which would cover half the return fare to Canada. He struggled to raise the money, with donations from his family and his friends at the bicycle factory where he worked. This, plus savings from his wages, gave him enough for the rest of the fare, and for spending money to get him through the tour. He was given big send-off parties by his family and his fellow workers, and set off for the docks at Southampton, with cricket bat and baggage in hand, eager for the trip.

At Southampton, to his dismay, he discovered there was no ticket waiting for him. There was no ship. There was no cricket team. There was no tour organizer. There was no tour. In stunned disbelief, Percy realized he had been scammed. There he was, with several other young men who had also been scammed by the same con artist. What should they do? Some were able to deal with the humiliation, and made their way back to their homes. But not Percy. He could not face the embarrassment of going back to family and friends, so he used all the money he had saved, plus what he got from selling his cricket gear, and bought a one-way ticket to Canada. Percy Broadfoot never went home again. He lived all of the rest of his long life in a country he never really liked, because he couldn't bear the thought of losing face. When asked if he was Canadian, he liked to say there was no such thing. "I'm much bigger than that," he would declare, then add, "I'm British."

My father arrived in Canada in the middle of the boom years of the early part of the twentieth century. He took whatever work he

My mother, with my eldest sister, Dorothy, 1917

could find, and eventually settled in Winnipeg, a town of some fifty thousand people and growing fast. He started out working in the offices of the Canadian Beamish Bag Company, which made paper bags that were used for everything from groceries to heavy industry. Slowly, he worked his way up the corporate ladder.

He met my mother, Beatrice Chappell, in 1914. She was working for the gigantic new Eaton's store on Portage Avenue, the pride of Winnipeg. Percy always said that he was attracted to the Eaton's girl wearing the stunning white blouse. They married in 1915, my oldest sister, Dorothy, was born the following year, and in 1917, they all three moved to Vancouver.

When they first reached the coast, they lived in the splendour of the Hotel Vancouver. By this time Percy was president of the Canadian Beamish Bag Company, and things were going extremely well for him, until a jealous employee manufactured a rumour that he could not be trusted with company funds. The rumour spread quickly, and when it reached my father he was crushed by the idea that anyone would question his honesty. "An Englishman's word is his bond," he liked to say. In his case, it was true, his word was his bond, and the blow to his pride was beyond endurance. It was not in his nature to fight back. He promptly resigned. The rumour-starter, no doubt, was on his way to the top. My father was on his way, if not to the bottom, to an endless struggle to stay afloat. He and Beatrice and Dorothy moved out of the Vancouver Hotel, and into North Vancouver, where my mother and father settled for the rest of their lives.

*Not yet three, yet furious at having my picture taken –
an obsession I eventually overcame*

North Vancouver was then a small community on the hill overlooking Burrard Inlet. It had begun life as a lumber settlement called
Moodyville back in 1862. By the time my family arrived, Moodyville
was long gone, the lumber mill was gone, and the waterfront was
dominated by a huge grain elevator and two shipyards. The North
Vancouver homes and sidewalks at that time were mainly made of
wood. The roads were mainly made of gravel. It was not a wealthy
area. By the time I made my appearance in the world, to join my
older sisters Dorothy, nine, Edith, six, and Betty, three, the family
was living in a small frame house, in the backyard of a real house,
at 335 East Eighth Street. This is where, at exactly 8:20 a.m., on
December 5, 1925, I was born for the first time. I was later told that,
when the doctor slapped me, I didn't cry. Of course I didn't – being
a Baptist, I knew the slap was deserved. With six now in the family,
we needed more space. We moved again, to a slightly less tiny house
on Keith Road.

My mother had passed on her religious enthusiasm to all of my
sisters. Even as children they were quite saintly. I was the only boy,
destined to be guarded over by three female would-be angels, all
determined to save my soul, although my earliest memory relates
more to their treatment of my body. I was one and a half, on the
front porch of our new home, and, with their friend Pat Matheson,
they were tossing me stark naked into the air on a blanket. For all
the world to see. I felt mortified, exposed, vulnerable, and helpless.

My sisters, Dorothy, Edith, and Betty.
That's me, in the middle.

Only one and a half years old, and the Dave Broadfoot personality was already in trouble.

At the age of two, I encountered more good punishment. I began limping and, in October 1928, was diagnosed with "hip disease," which meant six months in the Crippled Children's Hospital (they were more blunt about names in those days) at Marpole, near the Fraser River. My legs were placed in plaster casts from toe to groin, and I stayed immobile in bed, with nothing much to do but look out the window at a bugle band practising nearby, and play – as much as I *could* play – with a small fire truck that someone had kindly given me. I told a visiting reporter, who probably came in looking for a Christmas human-interest story, that I wanted a trumpet for Christmas, and proudly announced that the following Wednesday was my birthday, and that, no matter what, I was going to get a cake. "Luckily David is not in any pain, or his situation would be unbearable," the reporter wrote in true sob-sister style. "As it is, lying there, day after day, with only four walls to look at, nice though they are, is but poor compensation for running about on his own chubby legs." (She was exaggerating about the walls, and she didn't say how she knew my legs were chubby. They weren't. Still aren't.)

Dave Broadfoot, boy cripple, was now the poster child for the "Mile of Dimes," a campaign to raise money for the Marpole Hospital. My sister Dorothy, at the tender age of twelve, got busy in her spare time collecting for the hospital, on her way to becoming a leading fund-raiser. My mother often came to visit, and everyone was so nice that I never felt abandoned. I spent six months away from home before the age of four – an accomplishment that few others of my age could boast. It was the beginning of a lifelong habit of spending too much time out of town.

Once I was back home, and the "hip disease" had healed, I had three new ambitions: I was going to be a bugle player, and a fireman, and a medical missionary. I felt so happy to be home, that walking along the street one day with my three-year-old neighbour, I put my arm around her and kissed her. Suddenly, I looked up to see faces in the windows all laughing hysterically at the little boy kissing the little girl. Not yet four years old, and more psychological bruising. It would be a long time before I would kiss another neighbour in public.

Our lives changed dramatically on Christmas Eve, 1930. While we were at church, some coal in our Quebec heater exploded, set our Christmas tree on fire, and our little rented house went up in flames. As the Depression was well under way, it wasn't hard, if you had work as my father did, to find an empty house, since a good many had been abandoned. A much larger house was found on Sixth Street East, and through the kindness of friends, we were able to gather together enough furniture to make it livable.

I was delighted to find, after five years of being surrounded by girls, that our next-door neighbours had four boys, Lorne, Keith, Glen, and Roy MacDonald. Roy was my age and became a firm friend, initiating me into fishing, swimming, and going to the movies. The MacDonalds were different from us. I spent Friday nights at the Baptist church gatherings, where I saw colour slides of missionaries at work in Africa. It wasn't exactly Hollywood. Roy spent Saturdays with his friends going to see whatever movie was playing at the Lonsdale Theatre. Roy always invited me to come along, and I found it hard to say no. My parents never went so far as to say that movies were the work of the devil, but I was sure they would not approve. Roy kept telling me movie stories, and when he asked me to come to see *Alice in Wonderland* with him, I found it impossible to resist.

I went to see my mother, and launched into full-scale whining about needing a dime. I lied about what I needed it for – I can't remember what I said, but I certainly knew that telling the truth was out of the question. I was impressed with how smoothly I pulled it off. Later, I was amazed to find my mother had known I was lying from the very first whine.

My first movie. What a thrill! I was particularly intrigued with the young girl, Charlotte Henry, who played Alice. The all-star cast included W. C. Fields, Cary Grant, Gary Cooper, and a man who later became a favourite performer of mine, the ultimate deadpan man, Leon Errol. After watching *Alice*, I was sure that movies were magic.

When I got home, my father was digging in the garden. He looked up at me, and went into a rage. "Your mother tells me you went to a movie," he thundered. I couldn't deny it. "How dare you?"

"I wanted to be with the other kids," I said, lamely.

"You speak to me about these things in the future," he said, and went back to his digging. I was glad the shovel had remained in the ground while we were talking, otherwise I might have been even more divided than I already was. Much later, I was stunned to find out that the reason he was so enraged with me was not because I had gone to a movie. It was because I hadn't asked *him* to take me.

That was a side of my father I didn't often get to see – a side that loved show-business. He had once seen Charlie Chaplin in person at the Walker Theatre in Winnipeg, with the Fred Karno troupe, doing his greatest comedy routines. He knew all the old British music-hall songs, and loved to sing them. I knew that sometime, long ago, he must have had very different interests. But now, I would see him come home and, unlike my friends' fathers, he would not read the newspaper, he'd get out the Bible. Every day. "It's important to understand what's coming," he would say. "Read Isaiah. 'And they shall ride up on their horses through the valley of Jehoshaphat.'" What did that mean? I tried to tell him they didn't have horses in wars any more, they had tanks, but it made no impression.

His great love, all his life, was cricket, a game in which I had absolutely no interest. He played until he was seventy, and once captained a B.C. team that challenged the famed Marylebone Cricket Club. He took me to games at the Brockton Oval in Stanley Park a few times, but I would rather have been somewhere else, which must have been a disappointment to him. All the teams seemed to speak with English accents, wear white flannel, and drink tea. Whenever a player did well on the field, his performance was greeted with a very subdued "well played" and scattered, polite applause. "What am I doing here?" I asked myself. I felt like a misfit. The whole British ambience seemed alien and condescending.

The church and cricket: that was my father's world. He worked as a book-keeper and later as a manufacturer's sales agent for men's and women's clothes. He took great pride in what he did, but working for $25 a week for the Sam Vickers Ladyswear wholesale business and doing Sam's books must have seemed a tremendous comedown from being the president of a corporation and living in the Vancouver Hotel. Of course, my father never said anything about it; he never complained. I guess, in the midst of the Depression, he felt fortunate to be one of the men who were lucky enough to actually have a job. But he would often come home from work and raise hell, about small things he thought were not right. "What's going on?" he'd yell at my mother. "Why is this fire out?" She bore the brunt of his anger. There were not many laughs with my father. On the rare occasion that he let his guard down, he could be fun. But it didn't happen often.

My mother, Beatrice, was loved by everyone. She was soft-spoken, and unlike my father, never ever abrasive. She was born in England, in Basingstoke, of a family that was Huguenot in origin. They had come to Canada when she was still in her teens. One sister settled in Montreal, another in Winnipeg, a brother in Fort William, and another brother and sister in North Vancouver. All through my child-hood, my mother struggled to make do on my father's infinitesimal salary. I never had new clothes, mainly hand-me-downs from the son of Sam Vickers. We were just scraping by, but dressing as well as we could. Not acting poor, that was important, although that is what we were. I think they call this "genteel poverty." There was no fur-niture on the top floor of our house, and we didn't have a car. We did have enough to eat, but there was little to spare.

What was clear to me, even as a child, was that we were not unusual. All around me, as I grew up, were signs of the Depression. Unemployed men would come to our door. For just a sandwich, they'd chop a whole cord of wood, and my mother would give them what she could. Our family was only a little better off. It was a common sight to see my Uncle Ernie out on the gravel roads, working with a rake and shovel to maintain the grade. That way he earned enough to pay his house taxes, which guaranteed he would not lose his home.

My mother spent all her spare time knitting, sewing, and making clothing for people she felt were worse off than we were. She was utterly selfless – loving, generous, and responsible, always thinking of others, never herself. There were little boxes around the house in which we put money to help missionaries in the Sudan and China.

I have never met anyone more dedicated to the church than my mother. It was her whole life. As a child, I would sometimes help her fill the tiny communion glasses with Welch's grape juice. That juice always seemed a curious anomaly to me. Every Regular Baptist I knew took the Bible very literally. To them, nothing in the Bible was a metaphor, it was all the literal Truth. I combed through the Bible, from Genesis to Revelations, yet I could find absolutely no reference to Welch's grape juice.

Sundays at our house were monumentally boring for a growing boy. I'd get up at eight, get dressed in my Sunday best, and then the round would begin. First there was Sunday School at ten. Then a church service at the First Baptist Church on 12th Street. In the afternoon, it was off to the Brethren Gospel Hall at Lonsdale and 17th Street, and in the evening, my father would take me to the service at St. John's Anglican Church at 13th and 8th streets. There were no discussions about whether or not I wanted to go. I went. That was it.

The capper was the Brethren Service, which lasted from one to three Sunday afternoon. They were a very severe, dour group, the Brethren. There was a big pendulum clock in the Gospel Hall, and I'd sit there listening to it going *doink-doink-doink-doink*, measuring every second of the time passing. The preacher, who had a

Scottish accent, was deadly, and the service was made even more deadly than the others by the fact that there were no musical instruments, no organ or piano to liven things up. They did sing hymns:

> Man of sorrows, what a name
> For the son of Man who came
> Ruined sinners to reclaim . . .

We ruined sinners would sit there, and the preacher would launch into his mind-numbing drone, interspersed with *doinks* from the clock. *And thou shall go unto their villages and lay waste their fields and dwelling places.* I don't remember much of what was talked about, but it often seemed to involve villages being burned down. Burning villages. I'd think about it, and it seemed to be okay, because the burning instructions had come from God. *Another hour or two*, I'd think, *and I'll be out of here.*

Once out of there, though, things weren't really much better, as I wasn't allowed to *do* anything. "What can I do?" I'd ask my mother. "Take a nice walk," she would say, meaning to be helpful. A nice walk? What fun was there in that? I felt a little better about it later when I read that Robert Service used to ask the same question and got the same consistent response: "Take a nice walk to the cemetery." At least my mother didn't suggest the cemetery. She knew it wasn't within walking distance. It was probably the same for thousands of other kids – we were not allowed to make a noise, swim, play games, or do anything physical. We just did a lot of Sunday-afternoon walking, which Dorothy, Edith, and Betty seemed to enjoy, as a time to be with their friends.

Sunday evenings things improved a bit. Evenings meant the Anglicans, and they were great. They'd been doing those prayers out of the prayer book for so many generations. *As-it-was-in-the-beginning-is-now-and-ever-shall-be-world-without-end-amen.* It came out all slurred together, all in the same tone. I used to marvel at that monotone: they seemed to have no idea what they were saying at all. It just went on and on – they did it last Sunday, they'd be doing it next Sunday, and the Sunday after that. No changes, no surprises. For a kid, this was perfect, because you could take a good, long nap.

The lighting in St. John's was always dim, and I would curl up by my Dad and go into never-never land. To me, the Anglicans never seemed to take their faith too seriously. Often, they'd been out drinking the night before. You could be sure that wasn't the case with the Regular Baptists.

At the age of eleven, I was born again, which was part of my sister Dorothy's plan for me. Dorothy had always been the one to watch over me when I was younger. Right from the start, she was my protector and guardian, and I liked her a lot. At seventeen, Dorothy went off to Bible School in Alberta. Worried about my everlasting soul, she asked a friend from Bible School, Howard Moss, to keep an eye on me while she was gone, which Howard sure did. Howard was always asking me to come out for the afternoon. I knew Dorothy had arranged this, and I wanted to please her, so I went. Howard and I would go down to Stanley Park and take a walk. Howard kept walking and talking about Jesus, about how important it was to give your life to Christ. On one of our walks, Howard told me it was time to make the decision, to make a commitment. I began to feel put upon, and quite literally cornered. It was pouring rain, and we were in a phone booth for shelter, near the North Vancouver ferry dock. What harm could it do? I thought I might as well please them all.

Betty, Dorothy, me, and Edith. Still outnumbered.

So that was where I took Christ into my life as my personal saviour. The persistent Howard had triumphed, and no doubt went on to sell life insurance.

Sister Dorothy was delighted with my rebirth. Much later, after I had given up religion and taken up show business, Dorothy remained intensely concerned about my soul. "Dave, I want you to know I'm praying for you," she said to me shortly before she died. "If the prayers are about me giving up comedy, forget it," I replied. "Listen," she added with great intensity, "you are mine. There were three of us girls, and I wanted a brother, and I prayed and prayed and prayed for a baby brother. When you came along, you were mine." That was how my big sister had always thought of me. For the short period of two years that I remained born again, she was happy. It didn't last long, though, and it took a lifetime for me to recuperate from my second birth, to claw my way out from under the mountain of guilt. Who could have known that, one day, I would have a thick file of comic sermons, delivered by me as an evangelist.

A question I have been asked more than once: "If God made us in his own image, why did he give us so many rules?" The answer, my friends, is because, being human, we cannot live without rules.

Look with me at Deuteronomy 22.

It is specific.

Listen: "Thou shalt not plough with an ox and an ass together."

I know very few people who have the courage to admit they have committed this sin.

Ploughed with an ox and an ass in the same harness. You may have done it unconsciously, when you were preoccupied. Or you may have done it only in your heart.

I know it takes courage in a large mixed audience like this to raise your hands in public admission of your sin, but I'm asking you to do that now. Let's see those hands. Oh. I was afraid of this. No courage.

Here in Deuteronomy is the penalty that awaits you guilty ones who are unwilling to admit the truth. "The Lord shall smite thee with consumption and with fever and with inflammation and with extreme burning." Ohhhhhhhh, I've had that! "And with blasting." I think I've had a bit of that. "And with mildew."

Maybe you can cope with consumption and fever, and inflammation and burning and even blasting. But I don't believe there's a person alive who is ready to deal with personal mildew.

And after the mildew. Listen to Deuteronomy. "The Lord shall smite thee with the botch of Egypt and with emerods."

Admittedly, being afflicted with emerods is not nearly so frightening since the advent of Preparation H. But getting the botch of Egypt would be no less tragic than getting stuck with a bad tattoo. I want a show of hands on this. All those who have endured the Egyptian botch. Exactly. No one knows how painful that can be. We can only imagine.

But these are not all the penalties. There are more. Listen to this from Deuteronomy. "Thine ass shall be violently taken from before they face." I can't even imagine that. There's more. "Thou shall eat the fruit of thine own body." There's the bottom line. If you can't overcome your urge to plough with a team that's half ox and half ass, you're going to have to eat your kids. The fruit of thy body.

"Oh," you say, "it doesn't bother me. My kids are adopted." Think again. Listen to Deuteronomy. "He that is wounded in the stones or hath his privy member cut off, shall not enter into the congregation."

"Wounded in the stones" does not refer to tripping over a rockery. We know what this means. And you know who you are. I'm not going to ask for a show of hands . . . or anything else . . . I am going to ask for a blessing on those of you who know in your heart, that you will never plough this way again.

Let me say in closing, "The road to hell is paved." That's why it is so attractive to people who live out of town.

School took me into another world. Ridgeway School, in North Vancouver, was a very ordinary public school, but the kids were great. Even the richest kid in class, the son of a bank manager, was a pleasure to be with, although it was a puzzle to me how he could be so wealthy and still be so much fun. I knew he was wealthy because I had been to his house, and his was the only home I had ever been in that had a maid.

All the kids at Ridgeway seemed so much more liberated than I was – they weren't going to church three times on Sundays, or to prayer meetings in the middle of the week, or to Friday-night meetings with missionaries. These kids were normal. I, however, went to school with a badge on my sweater that read, "Christ died for me." I wore it every day, and looking back, I'm surprised how tolerant my schoolmates were of me, because I was on my way to becoming a religious fanatic. I was really concerned about what might happen to them, that they would burn in Hell if they were not born again. Howard Moss had taught me well.

I hadn't been at Ridgeway long before I developed a massive ambivalence about my religion. They were showing movies at

Ridgeway School's embryonic military might. I'm second from right, in the second row.

school, but I didn't go to them, because I didn't want to displease my family. I didn't go to the parties either, or to any of the school dances. I wanted to, I truly wanted to be part of it, but I would then have to face my parents. My sisters never ever went to any of these things, and to the end of their lives they were loyal to their Baptist ideal. They never learned to dance.

Feeling that I was different from others, and yet not really wanting to be, led to a lot of turmoil and frustration. I didn't want to be in school, and I was a troublemaker. The person who bore the brunt of my bad behaviour was the math teacher, Mr. Darwin, a veteran who had lost an eye and a hand in World War One, and whom unfortunately I chose to harass. I was openly hostile to him and provided endless provocation. "A disruptive influence in the classroom," was how Mr. Darwin described me. Mr. Darwin thought I was uncooperative, that I didn't try, and that I was a general nuisance. Mr. Darwin was right. It got so bad that I was eventually banned from math class. When I started to walk in one day through the back door of the classroom, Mr. Darwin charged down the aisle toward me and broke his pointer over my head. When it happened a second time, I realized he was trying to tell me something.

I had less of a problem in other classes, probably because I was more interested in the subjects. I liked history and geography, and particularly English, as taught by the unforgettable E. R. Chamberlain, who would act out pieces of literature for us, bringing them alive. Early on, music was also a favourite subject. When I was twelve, the music teacher took us to the Orpheum Theatre in Vancouver, to see a Saturday-morning rehearsal of the Vancouver Symphony Orchestra. What an experience. I fell in love with the music, the musicians, the Orpheum, and the music teacher (there was only a nineteen-year difference between us, but she had other plans). That trip was the beginning for me of a real and lifelong interest in music. A year later, when a North Vancouver Schools Band was forming, I heard that a friend of our family, who owned a trumpet, had left town: his trumpet might be available. I was able to borrow it, and for a year practised every day. Then the trumpet-owner returned and wanted his trumpet back. That was the end of my career as a trumpet player, as there was no Dave Broadfoot Trumpet Foundation to fund me. I regret having given up so easily.

Charlie Murphy, who was in my class, became my closest school friend. His parents were both part-time teachers, and his dad also worked in a restaurant, reading teacups. That was one of the things that made Charlie's family different from mine. Another thing was that they had a gramophone. Charlie introduced me to different types of music, modern classical and jazz. He played me recordings of Aaron Copland's *El Salon Mexico*, and Jack Teagarden. These were a revelation to me, because the only music I really knew was church music. Soon Charlie and I started sneaking off to the Beacon Theatre in Vancouver, where we heard, among others, Jack Teagarden, Jimmie Lunceford, Lionel Hampton, and Duke Ellington. Without realizing it, I had become an ardent jazz fan.

Charlie was on the verge of being eccentric. Maybe that's why I liked him so much – he was a bit of a misfit, too. He wasn't interested in sports, like all the other boys. Charlie couldn't have cared less who played for the Leafs or the Canadiens, and he didn't listen to "Hockey Night in Canada." Charlie liked *architecture*. He was particularly interested in Frank Lloyd Wright. He loaned me several books on Wright's life and ideas, which gave me another lifelong interest. On my visits to Charlie's home, I was amazed to see the immensely detailed architectural drawings he had done, without any training at all.

A bunch of us now started going regularly to the movies on Saturdays, to see whatever Hollywood fare the local movie theatre had on offer. *North West Mounted Police*, with Gary Cooper, Paulette Goddard, Madeleine Carroll, and Robert Preston left a particular impression. The title was wrong, of course; the Mounties hadn't been called the North West Mounted Police since 1904 (they had been the Royal Canadian Mounted Police for nearly twenty years), but Hollywood liked the old name better, so they stuck to it. The new name, they felt, was too Canadian. The plot was a bit improbable: Gary Cooper had come up from Texas to volunteer his American know-how to the Force. Watching Gary Cooper play a Mountie you had the impression that a tragic accident, a fall from his horse perhaps, had left him mentally challenged.

We school chums had worked out a plan that would let us all into the movie theatre, with only one of us paying. Our secret scheme involved just three things: the theatre fire-escape door, silence, and timing. Thirty seconds after the start of the movie, the fire-escape door was silently opened by whichever one of us had paid to get in. The outsiders then quietly slipped into empty seats close to the exit. We carried on happily that way for a while, until one day, between the short and the feature, the manager came and sat down next to me. "Would you mind telling me how you entered the building tonight?" he asked politely. By then, my neighbour had slipped me the only ticket stub we had. I held it up, and said, "I came in through the front door, the same as everyone else."

I got away with it, but for me that was the end of the free movies. I could never do it again. I felt terrible, because the manager had been so polite. I decided I had to have an income, and within days had a job as a paper boy for the *Vancouver Sun*, my first smart career move. I saved money for a bicycle, which made doing the route easier, then I bought my mother a washing machine, on the install-ment plan. She was thrilled.

We were friends, my mother and I, and as a young boy I loved it when she took me with her on her errands about the city. It was on one of these trips that I saw for the first time how widespread the effects of the Depression really were. Going from the North Van ferry dock to Water Street, you had to cross the CPR tracks, and it was here that I saw hundreds of able-bodied men milling around – either waiting to jump a train or just arrived from the East in search of a job. Vancouver in the 1930s was a magnet for the unemployed men who rode the rods across the country looking for work. It was clear these men had no jobs, but what I couldn't understand was why there were no jobs for them to have. I asked my mother what it was all about, but she didn't really know either. She wasn't politi-cal, and was never one to bluff if she didn't understand something. One day those men left the track area, and went marching through the streets of Vancouver, smashing store windows out of frustration. It was a sobering sight for a young boy.

Later, in 1938, my mother and I were in the Vancouver Post Office a few times during the month when the unemployed staged their big sit-in there. I remember seeing the men, many of them asleep on the floor, others talking to the post-office customers as they came in to buy stamps. Vancouver seemed to sympathize with the strikers – people brought them sandwiches, tins of food, and coffee. The whole thing was remarkably peaceful, and my first real encounter with political protest. The morning after our first visit, when my mother came to wake me up, she found me asleep on my bedroom floor, fully clothed. It was my demonstration of solidarity with the protesters. Later, when I heard that the RCMP had used tear gas, riot whips, and clubs to force the men out of the building, I was terribly upset. It seemed such an excessive thing to do to hungry people whose only crime was that they couldn't find a job. This was the beginning of my long, ongoing political education, an education that continued when these unwanted men were all suddenly wanted and welcomed into the army shortly after the outbreak of World War Two in September 1939.

Another part of my early political awakening centred around my friend Walter Ikeda. I had met Walter at the Burrard Inlet Bible Camp one summer. My sister Dorothy's boyfriend, Eric McMurray, was a counsellor there, which was how I ended up attending. I wondered how Walter knew about the Bible camp, as he was of Japanese background, but there he was. I learned from him that Baptists had established a mission on Franklin Street, an area where quite a number of Japanese people lived, including the Ikeda family. The man in charge of the mission, Walter Ridgway, later married my youngest sister. Walter Ikeda was very short, and I was very tall, and we instantly clicked. For the four weeks of camp, we did everything together, which mostly consisted of learning hymns, taking Bible instruction, and doing a little bit of woodcraft and swimming. When camp was over, Walter and I stayed friends. Though he was only a young boy, Walter, filled with religious fervour, had gone out on the street with his Bible, preaching, trying to save the lost souls from his part of Vancouver. I never actually had the nerve to do that.

Walter would come to my house, and I would go to his. I was fascinated by the atmosphere there, by the foods they ate, and by the Japanese-style bath they had. Walter had two brothers and a lot of sisters. Maybe that's another reason why we got on as well as we did.

He would help me with my paper route and, when it was done, we would go fishing on the waterfront, taking fish right out of the water, with no fear of their being contaminated. Then suddenly, one day in 1941, Walter disappeared.

I found out what had happened driving back into Vancouver from a visit to the Fraser Valley with my favourite uncle, Billy. It was shortly after the Japanese had bombed Pearl Harbor, and coming back along Hastings Street, we passed the Pacific National Exhibition buildings. I could see a lot of faces peering out of the small windows. "What are all those people doing in there?" I asked Uncle Billy. It seemed odd, because it wasn't the time of year for the Exhibition. "It's the Japanese," he said. "They're going to be shipped inland." Just like that. I couldn't understand. Then I thought, *Where's Walter? Is he there? Is he still home?* I was puzzled by it. It was hard to grasp the whole thing. Why lock Walter up? What had Walter done? I later learned that the internment of Canadian citizens of Japanese descent was one of the most shameful episodes of our history. At the time, all I knew was that I had lost one of my best friends. It would be thirteen years before I found him again.

Me at 14, not yet able to finance my desire to be a snappy dresser, but determined to make the best of it.

Halfway through Grade 9, in 1940, the principal at Ridgeway Junior High called me into his office to make me an offer. "You can either leave," he said, "or you can be expelled. It's up to you." I decided to expel myself, which was a great relief to the principal and everyone else. So there I was, a high-school dropout, aged fifteen, with no idea what I really wanted to do in life. My sisters had all delighted my parents by becoming missionaries, Dorothy and Edith in China, and Betty in Bolivia. I knew that wasn't for me. Little did I know then that I would later become a different kind of missionary, producing as many converts to comedy as they did to Christianity, in a crusade that still carries me into the impenetrable suburbs of darkest Canada.

For now, my friend Charlie Murphy gave me the best idea. He had already left school and was an apprentice carpenter at a North Vancouver shipyard. I decided that I would join him there, not as a carpenter, but working on production of corvettes, minesweepers, and ten-thousand-ton freighters for the war effort. I knew the war was going badly for the Allies, and that someday I would probably have to come to their aid.

Chapter 2

U BOATS, ME SHIPS

Northorth Vancouver Ship Repairs employed several thousand workers, including David James Broadfoot, all engaged in the building of ships for the Allied war effort. Every day I set off with my lunch pail, on the bus down Lonsdale Avenue to the waterfront. My first job at the yard was in the freighter section and involved marking out the position of rivet holes on the ship's beams. Other teams marked out corresponding holes on the steel plates of the ship's hull. Fortunately, our holes lined up with their holes, the rivets went through, and not one ship fell apart, which is more than can be said for some of our neighbour's efforts. Across the border, the Henry Kaiser Corporation of Seattle was building ships with no rivets at all. "All-welded hulls," they called them. Several fell apart. In mid-ocean.

I soon graduated to the machine shop, where the foreman took one look at me and decided I was best suited for the graveyard shift. It was here that I discovered the shipyard wasn't quite the safe place it seemed. I was working at my lathe one night, when a flicker of light caught my eye. I looked up, and through a crack in the wooden floor of a small room high above my head, I saw sparks flying, as if coming from a welder's torch. "That's odd," I thought. "There's no one up there." I ran and told one of the machine-shop managers, who took one look, sounded the fire alarm, and called out our own Air Raid Precautions department. Seconds later the little wooden room above me burst into flames, and in minutes a huge fireball swept along the entire inside wall of the massive building. We spent the rest of the night trying to put out the fire. Working the hoses, we managed to contain it to the one building, but by morning that building was an empty shell. When the day-shift workers arrived, even though we were exhausted and soaked to our skins, they looked askance at us, as if we were the cause of the disaster.

Working at the shipyard was fine, but I knew it was only a matter of time before I would be conscripted. If I had had my choice, I would have preferred to serve in the navy, but when I inquired about that possibility, I found there were only about twenty thousand other young guys ahead of me. My chances for the navy were zero, and, as the army and the air force had no appeal, it occurred to me that there might be another way to serve at sea: the merchant navy. Before I could join, I was obliged to spend at least six months on a coastal ship, in order to qualify for deep-sea service. That was how I came to be a messboy on the passenger ship *Princess Alice*.

The *Princess Alice* almost ended my naval career before it had begun. There was a particularly objectionable officer in charge of us, who took a particular objection to me. He put me on the graveyard shift cleaning toilets. One day, after we were finished unloading and loading, and were ready to depart, I was not on board. I had deserted, or at least that's what they put on my discharge slip. Determined that this would not cut short my life at sea, I went into

Photo on my merchant-navy identity card. The determination to bring about the downfall of Hitler is obvious.

action, working very slowly and carefully, with a precious bottle of high-quality ink remover (no longer available in stores). By the time I had finished, the slip read simply "left ship."

I next found myself serving on the ss *Chilliwack*, a small freighter that carried cargo to all the ports along the mainland coast, the Queen Charlotte Islands, and both coasts of Vancouver Island. I was sixteen years old – the youngest on board, and green as they come – but I quickly learned the ropes. I learned to drink beer, I learned to drink wine, and most important, I learned how to stay upright. I also had a golden opportunity to study the language of the seasoned mariner. One morning I saw a deckhand having trouble with a winch. I asked if I could help. "The goddamn fuckin' son-of-a-bitch fuckin' winch don't have no fuckin' steam in the fucker for the third fuckin' time so . . . fuck it," he said. Having no linguistic talent, I was pleased at how quickly I was able to interpret what he had said. "No, thank you."

However, although I was the youngest on board, with virtually no experience, I still had to go on duty alone. My rating was "fireman," and my main task was to maintain the correct level of water in the ship's boilers. As we rounded Cape Scott and headed down the west coast of Vancouver Island, the waves were more than twenty feet high. The boiler gauges kept going from zero to extra full with every roll of the ship. As it hit extra full, I stared at the gauge transfixed. This boiler is going to explode, I thought. And I don't know what to do about it. At first, I was just plain terrified. Gradually, as time passed, I got used to the terror, calmed down, and learned the job. I knew that if I found myself lying flat on my back with something soft under me, I was not in the engine room. I was in my bed, having a nightmare.

Six months of coastal qualifying time, and I was ready to go "deep sea" as a full-fledged merchant seaman. Down I went to the shipping master's office, filled in the form that asserted I was seventeen, had myself fingerprinted and my mugshot taken, and got my Merchant navy identity number, 27457. It was August 1943, and I was about to set out on a four-year career in the Merchant Marine.

My first deep-sea ship was the *Brentwood Bay Park*. The *Brentwood Bay Park* was one of a fleet of "park" ships, built by the Canadian government, manned by Canadian seamen, and operated by Canadian shipping companies. The *Brentwood Bay Park* was operated by Imperial Oil. Throughout the Second World War, these ships carried cargo to ports all over the world, from Murmansk in the far north of Russia to Sydney, Australia. This vital part of the war effort was dangerous, as we were often sailing through U-boat-infested seas. Many, many of our merchant ships were sunk, and fifteen hundred of our seamen lost their lives. But, as with everyone else in those years, we seamen took our jobs as something that simply had to be done. If we were alive when it was all over, that would be a bonus.

The *Brentwood Bay Park* was a brand-new tanker. It had a bright young crew. Over my time at sea, I would learn that the younger the crew, the easier the voyage. The younger guys didn't care about traditions. They didn't get upset by trivialities, as some of the older guys seemed to. They took everything in their stride. We did a few trips carrying oil from Martinez, California, to Ioco in British Columbia, before proceeding south, through the Panama Canal, to begin a series of runs from the Orinoco River in Venezuela to Portland, Maine, which was the terminus of the pipeline to Montreal.

The Venezuela run could be daunting. A convoy of forty tankers passing through thick fog was not a happy place to be. Coming off duty from the engine room, walking along the main deck to the stern railing to get a bit of air, I would be quite unnerved to see suddenly, through the fog, the bow of the next tanker behind us, almost hitting our stern. Because our cargo was so volatile, we were as concerned about tanker collisions as we were about German torpedoes. If the tankers collided, it was an automatic catastrophe. In minutes a ship could become a raging inferno.

On that first voyage up the Orinoco, once we were docked and I was off duty, I went ashore to discover that what we were tied up to wasn't just a wharf. At the far end, there was a beer hall. There we were in the middle of the jungle, with nothing else around but ships and oil, a wharf, and beer. I walked into the beer hall to find it was already packed with seamen from our ship – and from two American tankers docked alongside. An all-out brawl was just getting underway. I watched as the big round tables loaded with bottles and glasses were being tipped over, one after the other. The floor was awash with beer, the depth of beer exceeded only by the breadth of broken glass. Fights were in full swing between the crew members of the various ships, and I was surprised to see our chief engineer (my boss) and a chief from a U.S. tanker, crawling through the broken glass, taking great mouthfuls of beer from the bottles that hadn't yet been smashed, then spurting the beer all over each other. They looked exactly like two great whales squirting each other from their blow-holes. It's almost impossible to describe such an outrageous scene. You had to be there. Unfortunately, I was. The next day, as we made our way back downstream toward the Atlantic, one of our deck crew was making his way by stretcher and train to Caracas to have seventeen stitches sewn into his back. Flowing away with his blood were my illusions that Canadians were better behaved than Americans. That experience made me realize it isn't your country that determines your conduct, it's the time of day you start drinking.

On the return journey to Maine, travelling in convoy, as we always did, and making our way north from our assembly point off Guantanamo Bay, Cuba, we received an order from the commodore to break up the convoy and hug the coast. That could only mean one thing: U-boats in the vicinity. The commodore clearly thought we had inadequate naval escort to handle the situation, but we didn't stick around to find out. I would never have believed a ten-thousand-ton tanker could move that fast, if I hadn't seen it. The engine-room deck plates were bouncing off their beams, and by morning we were hugging the coast – ten-thousand-ton hugs. Fortunately, we made it to Portland, Maine, safe and sound.

I did the oil run several times before an accident put me out of action. We were anchored off City Island, New York, waiting to join a convoy heading south, when I managed, in a remarkable piece of timing, to wrench my right ankle. There was nothing for it but to pay me off and give me leave to seek proper medical treatment in Manhattan. I attended a U.S. naval hospital three times a week for treatment of what the doctors called "tenosynovitus." To this day, in any comic situation where I can't think of what to call a disease, out comes "tenosynovitus." I found a small, cheap hotel at 6th Avenue and 47th Street, and stayed there for the month and a half that I received treatment.

The ankle wasn't that much of a problem – the biggest thing was the loneliness. As a civilian, I wasn't invited to stay at the nearby U.S. naval base, where I could have met people and made friends. In the hotel, I met no one. I spent hours talking to the desk clerk. The upside of my accident was that I got to see New York for the first time. For someone coming from a Baptist background, it was great to see so much sin.

The United States Service Organization made free tickets to New York shows available to all visiting Allied service people, and so courtesy of the U.S.O. I had my first real introduction to American show business. I saw *Oklahoma*, Radio City Music Hall, several Broadway plays, Cab Calloway and his big band, Perry Como, the Longines Symphonette, and a Harry James concert at Madison Square Garden. It was during the Harry James concert that I met three delightful girls from Brooklyn, who took me along with them after the concert, as they wended their way across Manhattan, stopping off anywhere a band was playing. At one of the hotels, Lawrence Welk gave me his autograph. I didn't ask for it. He just gave it to me.

A phone call from Montreal ended this brief introduction to big-city entertainment, and I was soon on my way south to report to a Canadian tanker at Newport-News. The tanker was a disgrace. The moment I set my newly healed ankle on her deck, my stomach began to turn. The *Vancolite*, was not, as its name suggests, a B.C. beer. It was an ancient, depressing, filthy Imperial Oil tanker, utterly unlike the *Brentwood Bay Park*. The main cabin, where the crew gathered, was reminiscent of the poorhouse scenes from *Oliver Twist*. It was dark, grimy, and had not seen a fresh coat of paint since Leif Ericsson returned to Norway.

The ship was in dry dock when I arrived, and it remained there for a month, giving me time to get to know the crew. They were all from Cape Breton, and their attitude toward me was one of refreshingly overt suspicion combined with a fair degree of resentment. Thankfully, they showed no curiosity. As I sat in the mess, listening to stories about people disappearing into thin air while walking down the street, and ghosts appearing who could be touched, two questions came into my mind: What did I do to deserve this? and

How am I going to get out of here? It didn't help that my cabin-mate liked to lie naked on his bunk, grabbing his genitalia, putting on a show as if I had paid admission. The problem was, he was ahead of his time. Fifty years later, two Australian lads perfected this style of entertainment and captured the world with a production called *Puppetry of the Penis*. Unlike my Cape Breton cabin-mate, the Australians had imagination.

In Newport-News, meeting the black members of the dry-dock team was the one thing that made the experience bearable. They were full of fun and music, and in the off time, they taught me how to jive and boogie. After watching them dance, I decided to check in to a dance studio on the main street in Newport-News and take some lessons. By the time I left town I wasn't what anyone would call a dancer, but my hips had learned a thing or two.

A month in dry dock, and the ship was ready to sail. The second engineer informed me that I would be one of a party leaving with the captain for Norfolk, Virginia, where we would sign the ship's documents. I rebelled. Putting it as subtly as I could, I told him there was no point in me going to Norfolk, as there was no way I would ever sign on as a crew member of such a pathetic rust bucket. The second mate was as determined as I was, and demanded that I go. In Norfolk, under the watchful eye of the captain and chief engineer, the shipping master wrote the appropriate details on the ship's register, then handed the pen to me. I silently handed it back to him. There was an audible gasp. Can this be the first time this has ever happened? I wondered. Have they forgotten that merchant seamen are civilians? Is it possible that they equate being young with being stupid? I was totally prepared to give my life to slow Hitler down, but there was absolutely no possibility of me going to sea in this rusting tragedy that should have been put out of its misery long ago. If nothing else, I wanted to die with dignity.

So I paid my way back to Montreal, and checked in at the Place Viger, an old railway hotel that had become a merchant-navy manning pool. I signed on in my category – the engine room – and waited. It wasn't long before I joined my first freighter, ss *Noranda Park*. We were headed for India, through the Mediterranean, with a cargo of military equipment. What I didn't realize was how fortunate

Convoy

my timing was. Casualties in the merchant navy through the early part of the war, when the German U-boats were cruising the Atlantic in packs, were very high. Entire convoys were sunk. By the time I was crossing the Atlantic, in September 1944, those German wolf-packs had themselves been devastated, and all we had to deal with were torpedoes from individual U-boats. Years later, I would use my experiences and those of my shipmates in a monologue by an old mariner.

Tiny Anderson, ex-merchant seaman:
My daughter only lets me work in her travel bureau part-time. But I'm telling yuh, if you folks are going on a cruise, you should try and get yourselves onto a freighter. It's nothing like the big cruise ships. You've only got eleven other passengers to get on your nerves.

I still remember my first freighter. We were in convoy. Carrying food and lumber and military stuff to Liverpool. We were just three days out when, over in the next row of the convoy, I see this freighter burst into flames. A direct hit from a U-boat. Only two lifeboats got away before she headed for the bottom. Then, over on our port side, I see another ship in flames. A tanker. A raging bloody inferno. No doubt about it. We were up against a wolf-pack!

Our navy escorts were doing their damnedest. Dropping their depth charges. But our ships were getting hit left, right, and centre. The one right next to us was hit amidships and went down like a stone. All hands lost. Then it was our turn. We got hit twice. We were trying to get a lifeboat away from her when she lurched over on her side and in no time was heading for the bottom.

I was dragged under, but damned if I didn't surface again. I swam over to a wooden crate that had come loose from our deck. I got a grip on that crate and hung on.

There was crude oil everywhere. In my hair. In my eyes. In my mouth. When the sun came up, some guys on a raft spotted me and pulled me on board. Just in time. We got strafed a couple of times. So when we were picked up five days later by a British corvette, we were not at our best.

That was the Atlantic. But, I'll tell yuh, I felt sorry for those guys on the Murmansk run. That voyage wasn't so easy.

Anyway, I gotta go. I'm only here part-time . . . You folks have yourself a nice cruise.

The crew were a mixed bunch, some of them seasoned graduates of His Majesty's penitentiaries, some of them equally seasoned drinkers. Pop Reilly was the oldest crew member; Hughie, the most feared crew member; Murray, the most brilliant alcoholic; Scotty, the reddest-haired alcoholic; and Paul, who was only a semi-alcoholic, held the record for doing the most time in a federal prison. Joe MacVae, the radio operator, was normal. Owen, a religious youth, and member of the Brethren Church, was there to remind me of home. We all had nicknames – I was "Spider," I guess because of my legs. As always we had our regular complement of Canadian navy gunners aboard. They took one look at the rest of us and kept to themselves.

We set off from Montreal on a beautiful September morning and were only a few hours out when I realized that something was amiss.

We had stopped at Pointe-au-Père to drop off the river pilot and wait for the convoy commodore, when I noticed a group gathered on the main deck, up near the bow. I could see they were very tense. "The son-of-a-bitch is selling our food," one of the deck crew said. We hadn't left Canada and the chief steward was already selling our provisions over the side. When challenged, he denied it, and turned the accusation on the crew. According to him, we were the ones doing the stealing. For the rest of the voyage, we watched him like a hawk.

From Pointe-au-Père we headed for New York City, where we were to wait for an eastbound convoy. During this short stop, I was able to get to the Paramount Theater on Times Square, to see Frank Sinatra in person, and get an early lesson in timing. I can still picture the upstage archway, the outline of Frank Sinatra's hands holding the archway curtains tightly closed. The sixty-piece Raymond Page Orchestra struck up the tune Sinatra had written, "This Love of Mine," then as that tune segued into the new hit song, "Come Out Wherever You Are," a voice announced, "Ladies and gentlemen, Frank Sinatra." The curtains flew open and there he was, running from the archway all the way to a downstage-centre microphone, arriving there on the exact beat of the first word of his opening song. His timing was impeccable, and I never forgot it. The crowd went wild. The screaming was so intense, he had to stop several times to ask the audience to calm down. "An awful lot of people paid an awful lot of money to be here today," he said, "and I don't think they came to hear you." All with a slightly rueful smile that gave grace rather than an edge to the remark. It was not long after he had left the Tommy Dorsey band, and yet, as a solo performer, he was already an absolute master.

Back on board, we were on our way to India, and I was getting to know my *Noranda Park* shipmates. Four or five of them were hard-core drinkers. There was no alcohol on board these merchant ships, so whenever and wherever we docked, the heavy drinkers vanished. They'd get as far as the nearest bar or bootlegger, and wouldn't be seen again until they crawled back up the gangplank just in time for the ship's departure. One drinker particularly intrigued me. Murray Kane drank even more than the others – yet once at sea, after his hangover had subsided, you couldn't ask for a better seaman or more interesting person. He was fun, respectful, and was reading all the time. He could read, talk to you, listen to the radio, and play cards, all at the same time. When it was over, he would have won the card game, told you the story of the book he'd just read, and list off the tunes we'd been hearing on the radio.

I was really excited about going ashore in India for the first time. One day I foolishly revealed my enthusiasm to another member of the crew. "I hope we'll have the opportunity to meet some Indians," I said.

"Indians? What the hell are you talking about?" he asked. "There's no Indians in India."

"There aren't?"

"Of course not," he said, "Indians are in North America. People who live in India are Hindus."

"Wait a minute," I said. "How would you like to be called a Hindu if you were a Sikh or a Muslim or a Buddhist?"

He looked at me in silence. "How would you like a punch in the mouth?" he said.

"It's too soon after lunch," I replied. "But thanks for the offer."

As soon as we docked in Bombay, I set out to see as much of the city as I could, knowing that I would never be back there again. There were many beggars – children with broken arms and deformed legs, lepers dressed in black to identify themselves, men and women with missing limbs. The begging was extremely persistent, a part of the way of life, and like everyone else, I quickly became inured to it. I was walking along the street, in busy pedestrian traffic, and saw a man, lying naked on the sidewalk, his genitals all raw and infected. He was almost dead, and not one single person stopped. Not even me, and I had no excuse. Almost equally upsetting were the colonial attitudes of the British residents I ran into. I felt oppressed by them. They were types that now you would say are caricatures, but then they really existed. Arrogant as could be in their perfectly pressed short khaki pants.

After we left Bombay, our next port of call was Calcutta, where I wandered into a British service club and found a British sailor exquisitely playing a Chopin piece on the piano. It's a piece Americans call "No Other Love," and the British call "Deep Is the

A typical merchant seaman's club, in Halifax

Night." Canadians call it "one of Chopin's études." Recognizing the tune, a British sailor who had just walked in went over to the piano, stood by it, and sang the entire song, in a glorious tenor voice. As I listened, I asked myself, "Could this be happening in a Canadian service club?" Myself had the sense not to answer. When I left the club at the end of the evening I was feeling so euphoric that I hailed a rickshaw, put the driver in the passenger seat, pulled him at a run all down Chowringhee, Calcutta's main drag, and back to the club. I gave him a handsome fee plus a handsome tip. He thought I was insane. I wasn't even drunk.

From Calcutta, we were sailing down the Hooghly River and into the Bay of Bengal, heading for Ceylon (Sri Lanka), when our radio engineer, Joe MacVae, fell ill. By the time we reached Colombo in Ceylon, Joe was in very bad shape, suffering with rashes, swellings, and a high fever. Colombo doctors were ushered on board, but were unable to diagnose Joe's illness. Two days later, after being taken by stretcher, liberty boat, and ambulance to a local hospital, Joe was dead. When the doctors determined that what had killed Joe was smallpox, they wasted no time. The officers and crew of our ship were all vaccinated in a hurry. The next day, it was my turn on the stretcher. I was taken from the ship and driven to a hospital in a jungle setting, far away from Colombo. I wasn't sure if I was being placed in quarantine, or carted off to die. At the hospital, I found out from one of the nurses that the area had just recovered from a smallpox epidemic, which made it even more difficult to understand why the doctors had had so much trouble figuring out what was wrong with Joe.

The day after I arrived, one of the nurses informed me that there were two more patients from the *Noranda Park* in the hospital. Everybody – the hospital staff and our shipmates – assumed we were all headed in the same direction as Joe MacVae but, as it turned out, we recovered. We had simply reacted badly to the vaccine. While I was recuperating, every day one of the nurses came and read to me. I grew fond of my caregivers, and they of me, and when it came time to leave, there wasn't a dry eye in sight. Shortly before I left the hospital, I slipped down into a green valley nearby, where I had seen a row of white grave markers. There was a fresh grave at the end of the row, with Joe's name on it. I took a leaf from the new wreath, for his mother, and could only think, as I got ready to go back to the ship, how easily that marker could have had my name on it.

We headed home the way we had come, back across the Indian Ocean, through the Red Sea and the Suez Canal. On our way through the Mediterranean to join a convoy that would take us back across the Atlantic, we almost extended the war single-handedly. An ominous Italian U-boat slowly began surfacing off our starboard bow. We were all ready for action stations, when someone remembered – just in time – that the Italians were no longer the enemy. They had surrendered.

Out on the Atlantic, on the last leg of our journey, when we were all excited at the prospect of getting home, our speed was nowhere near what it should have been. We were holding back all the other ships in the convoy. Longing to get home, we were not exactly thrilled when a destroyer from our escort pulled alongside and over its very loud PA system announced, "The *Noranda Park* will leave the convoy and head to Horta in the Azores." We spent ten long days lying at anchor off Horta with no shore leave. Engineers came aboard to fix our engine, and off we set again, to join another convoy. We hunted but couldn't find it. All we could find was floating wreckage. There was nothing for it but to head back to Horta. A week passed, and we heard about yet another convoy heading to North America. We managed to find this one, sailed into position, and were happy to be under way at last. In less than half an hour, when we had once again slowed to a crawl, an escort vessel pulled alongside, and a familiar message rang out: "The *Noranda Park* will leave the convoy and head for Horta in the Azores." I looked up at the bridge and saw the captain slumped on a bench, his head in his hands, the picture of humiliation and despair. Yet another team of engineers was brought on board.

It turned out that the engine problems of the *Noranda Park* could not be solved. We were afraid we might have to spend the rest of the war lying at anchor in Horta, so it was a huge relief when we finally received a message that a special convoy of crippled ships was heading across the Atlantic. Even moving at our pathetic speed, this was a convoy we were able to join.

In early May 1945, we finally limped into the harbour of Saint John, New Brunswick. My first long ocean voyage was at an end. It had taken just under eight months, I had survived it, was back in Canada, and the war in Europe was moving to its close. Victory in Europe was proclaimed while I was on the train to Vancouver. Since it was a Canadian train, the celebrating of VE day was fairly restrained.

In the short three weeks I spent at home, I caught up with my sister Dorothy, who had returned from China where she, her husband, and their two small daughters had been interned by the Japanese. They had been repatriated through the International Red Cross, and were staying with our parents in North Vancouver. One day, Dorothy brought a young friend, Ruth Jordan, back to our house from the immigration building, where she was being held in transit. Ruth had been interned with Dorothy, and was on her way to England. I had never met anyone quite like her – she was gracious, charming and bright, with a very pleasant, gentle way of speaking. I was a little bit smitten. But it was just one meeting, and then I was off on another ship, this time, the ss *Salt Lake Park*. Destination: Australia.

This was a non-convoy voyage. Things were obviously progressing for the Allies. Of all the ships I sailed in, the *Salt Lake Park* carried my favourite crew. No ex-cons, no alcoholics. Just upbeat, hardworking young men, who were a pleasure to go ashore with. What seemed to be a constant with all the ships I sailed on was the problem of chief stewards and the disappearing food. I brought the matter up at our first ship's meeting, and was instantly elected ship's delegate.

My job was to represent the crew to the captain. I was determined to do something about this endless thievery of our provisions. Our living conditions on board had been gained through long, hard union negotiations. To have that hard work undermined by crooks in our own crew was to me an outrage. All through the voyage, I kept a keen eye on the chief steward.

I fell in love with Australia. I loved the unpredictability. Hurrying to a hospital in Melbourne, to get a damaged knee looked at, I looked both ways, and then crossed a street before waiting for the light to turn green. Out of nowhere, a police officer appeared and slowly walked toward me until his nose was touching mine, and, in an indulgent tone that one might use speaking to a mentally challenged child, he asked, "Why did you walk against that red light?"

"I'm from Canada," was all I could think to say. In turned out to be a perfectly satisfactory explanation.

Midway through unloading our cargo in Sydney, the stevedores came across a dead snake in one of the holds. Immediately, as Australian stevedores had a strong tendency to do, they went on strike and headed out to the dog races. Dead snakes were not in their job description. I was curious about these Aussie dock workers and their powerful union. One of them spelled out his political philosophy to me. "There should be no such fucking thing as a fucking Henry fucking Ford, mate," he said. Ideally, I thought, this philosophy would be set to music. Possibly Aaron Copland's "Fanfare for the Common Man." Thanks to the dead snake, our two-week stay turned into six weeks and cost our employers a fortune. It was the best shore leave I ever had.

I was in Sydney when, on August 14, 1945, Japan announced its surrender. The Second World War was over. Sydney was euphoric. I headed down to Sloane Square in the heart of town and watched a sea of singing, dancing humanity. It was the most joyful, exuberant night I can ever remember. No vandalism, just sheer, unadulterated joy and relief. Not long before, the Japanese had been pounding at the doors of Darwin. Now the nightmare was finally and completely over.

As we headed home across the Pacific, I knew the time had come. I had to do something about the conduct of our chief steward. In

Melbourne and Sydney, I had done some sleuthing and discovered he was selling our food supplies. Our meals were now edible, but meagre, and most of our non-perishables had been stolen and sold in port. I discussed the situation with the crew, and everybody agreed that this sort of behaviour had to be stopped. So when we arrived back in Vancouver, I went down to the union office, and got the shore rep to come to a meeting.

As I opened the meeting, I looked out at the room full of crew members, and there, sitting right at the back, was the chief steward himself. I had no right to ask him to leave. He was a paid-up union member. I steeled myself for the moment, and tabled a resolution condemning him. It was greeted with absolute silence. Not one person would support it. The union rep was sitting there, and no one spoke up. It was a really bad moment. I asked for a show of hands in favour of a reprimand. As I looked around the room, I realized that the only raised hand was my own. I was stunned. Everyone who had been so adamant when the steward wasn't in the room, backed off when he was there. That was the day I learned the value of a secret ballot.

Overcome with humiliation, I quickly signed up for more. I joined another "Park" ship, the ss *Temagami Park*, bound for Manchester, England. Like almost all the other ships I sailed in during my merchant-navy years, half the people I was sailing with were French Canadians. I could be called on at any moment to give my life for them, or they for me, but I had grown up in a cultural environment that had denigrated them – had denigrated Quebec, Quebeckers, the Roman Catholic church, the French language, and French-speaking people in general. Yet when I looked at my Quebec shipmates, I saw people who were no different from me. It was quite a jolt to realize that I had been misled by people like my own father, whose attitude toward Quebec was suspicious, if not outright hostile. I started to question everything I had ever been taught. Particularly all the fundamentalist Baptist ideas I had been so steeped in.

If Christians die and go to heaven and live forever with no suffering, where does that leave a Baptist for whom suffering is an essential part of life?

Why did the Creator create Satan?

When the Creator looks at what he created in just six days, does he ever wish he'd taken a bit longer?

If the Trinity is three persons in one, does that make the Father and the Son the same age?

If Christianity exists because of a crucifixion, can a Christian be against capital punishment?

Jesus said, "In a little while, you will see me." Isn't two thousand years a big while?

Why would people who insist they are going to live forever when they are dead, be so unbelievably boring while they're alive?

How can eternal life not be boring when in just one lifetime one has seen the return of brush cuts eight times?

In Genesis it says "the earth was without form and void. And God said, 'Let there be light.' Who heard him say that? Which language did he say it in? And after the light came on, was the earth visible but still void?

Our ship, the *Temagami Park*, had been tied up at the Salford docks, near Manchester, for just three days when several Manchester Police arrived on board, with our chief steward in handcuffs, and our chef under police escort. In what I now realized was a time-honoured tradition, the chief steward had been selling our food on the local black market. This time, the police had caught him red-handed. Our chef, they said, was also implicated but not under arrest. The chief steward was placed in isolation and remained there all the way to Vancouver. The chef was another matter.

As we sailed south, heading for the Panama Canal, our meals became worse and worse. Our mess was receiving desperate items from the galley like "surprise pie" – hash with a crust on it. After a meeting with the crew, I went to see the chef. I told him "surprise pie" was not acceptable food in a ship that was stocked with the finest provisions obtainable. I told him we were angry. I told him we were angry we had been served "surprise pie" twice in four days. I told him that, if we were served it again, it would be tossed overboard and he would be lucky not to be tossed with it. He grabbed his sharpest knife from the galley counter, held it close to my face, and said, "Get out of my galley!" "Sure," I said, "let's get out of your galley so everyone can watch this. Bring the knife." He didn't budge. I left, and arranged a meeting with the captain to tell him about the anger building in the crew.

The next day, for supper, what did we get? "Surprise pie." It was all tossed overboard. A crew meeting was held, and a carefully worked-out plan was conceived, so that no one could be accused. At exactly 2:30 a.m., while I was on duty in the engine room, a man who was also on duty, plus two who had supposedly not yet been wakened to go on duty, quietly made their way into the chef's cabin and taught him a lesson. Unfortunately, it was the only kind of lesson that would register on his mentality.

The next day, with his blackened eyes, and bloated nose, the chef decided to meet with the captain. An unscheduled stop was arranged at the island of Aruba in the Caribbean. After that, we dined on steak, lamb chops, spaghetti and meatballs, cake, fruit salad, ice cream – you name it, we had it, all the way to Vancouver. The chef's learning experience was the only physically violent act I was ever involved in, and it haunted me for years. The irony is that, months after the incident, I met the chef on the street in Vancouver. He greeted me as if I was his bosom buddy, with lots of hugs, and even a kiss on the cheek.

My ongoing dream was that somewhere, somehow, someday, I would find an honest chief steward. On my very last voyage, there he was. I was told that the prime reason for this extraordinary manifestation was fear. Apparently, this chief steward had been thoroughly briefed on the arrest and incarceration of his predecessor and the rudeness we had shown to our Surprise Pie Chef.

In all, I spent just over four years at sea. On my final voyage as a merchant marine, there were three members of the deck crew who kept to themselves. They seemed different, diffident, and not very friendly. They were, it turned out, the vanguard of the Seafarers' International Union. Our union, the Canadian Seamen's Union, had kept our ships sailing throughout the war without a single strike. Despite this, the federal government under Louis St. Laurent decided that the CSU, which was Communist-controlled, had to be smashed. In its place, they welcomed the mobster Hal Banks and his Seafarers' International Union from the United States.

Using goons, bicycle chains, baseball bats, and a DO NOT SHIP list, Hal Banks destroyed our union. He added a refined technique of his own to the basic goonery – the "elevator treatment." If you were summoned to his office and he didn't like what you had to say, when you left and entered the elevator, a couple of men entered the elevator with you. By the time you got to ground level, you had been truly taken care of. It was like visiting a faith healer, but in reverse. You arrived walking, and you left in a wheelchair.

When the SIU arrived, people who had sailed under the CSU were blacklisted and could no longer go to sea. Banks destroyed a clean union and put a totally corrupt one in its place. His SIU eventually had to be put under trusteeship while a Royal Commission looked into the criminal activities of Hal Banks, who fled back to the United States in his big shiny white Cadillac, apparently unnoticed by the guards at the border. A very lucky crook.

There were some beneficiaries of all this nautical destruction. There were the bicycle-chain manufacturers. The baseball-bat makers. The SIU goons. But not Dave Broadfoot, card-carrying member of the CSU. With Hal Banks's goons in, I decided it was time for me to move out and find another way of making a living. The funny part of my life should be getting under way pretty soon.

Chapter 3

I CAN GET IT FOR YOU, RETAIL

My sisters had all found their vocation early in life, but it seemed that, after four years at sea, I still had no clear idea of what I wanted to do. My first job back on land was with a contractor specializing in finishing store interiors. He wanted a worker who could move like a demon. I was, at that time, just below tortoise speed. I didn't last long in the store-finishing business.

After making a few more attempts at finding employment as a misfit, I decided that, since I liked the clothing business, I should help my father. He, I reasoned, was less likely to fire me than anyone else. At that time, he was a manufacturers' agent representing three clothing companies. He travelled to Toronto and Montreal four times a year, to pick up sample garments from the manufacturers. Then, with his lines of men's suits and sports clothes, women's dresses and coats, he crossed the country, with his trunks full of samples, demonstrating his wares to interested store buyers. Unfortunately, he never took me along on these trips – which was where I might really have learned the business. Instead, I stayed in the office in downtown Vancouver, and felt boredom taking possession of me.

Rather than sit around waiting for something to happen, I decided to set out on a tour of my own, covering towns in the B.C. interior and Vancouver Island. This attempt to drum up extra trade was a stunning failure. Despite this, my father still had high hopes that I would carry on in the business. For my part, I was bored enough to consider going back into the merchant navy. I'd been reading about New Zealand, and decided I wanted to see it. The only way for me to get there was to go back to sea, so I went back down to the manning pool and let them know that, if there was a freighter headed for New Zealand that needed a crew, they could count me in. In a week or so, I got notice that there was a ship leaving in fifteen days.

Excited at the prospect, I was telling the receptionist in our office building, when she mentioned that her boyfriend was looking for a temporary worker in his menswear store. She had told him about me and had put in a good word. I felt the least I could do was go to see the man, and as soon as I walked into the store, I loved it. There was a warm, western, casual feel to the place. I phoned the manning pool, begged off the New Zealand trip, and started work at Richards and Smith the next day. My father was desperately disappointed that things had not worked out with him, but he understood.

I was twenty-one, and spent the next four years of my working life selling men's clothes. I liked being with the public, meeting people all day, and I wasn't a bad salesman. I quickly learned that having a genuine respect for fabric and an enthusiasm for tailoring was very helpful in making sales. I went from Richards and Smith to Finn's Ltd. to Dick's Ltd. and then to Woodwards department store, where I sold clothing for three years and loved every minute of it.

One evening, after leaving work, I went to watch a talent contest at the Denman Auditorium. It was an event that changed my life. Partway through the second half, I recognized one of the contestants. His name was Jack Cairns, and he was a neighbour. Jack performed a soliloquy from *Richard III* – "Now is the winter of our discontent" – and he held the audience spellbound. "How can someone who lives two blocks from me be this good?" I thought. That thought was followed by "If he can do this, maybe I can." I had no background, I knew absolutely nothing, and if I hadn't seen Jack that night, who knows, I might never have tried. It was just that I knew Jack so well – and I was utterly, totally, completely flabbergasted at the way Jack Cairns from 13th and Lonsdale could hold an audience.

It took me almost a year to work up the courage to join an amateur theatre group. When I finally did join the North Vancouver Community Players, I felt I had to keep it secret, at least until I knew how it would work out. I did not tell a soul. I particularly did not tell anyone in my family, who, even if they did not think of the theatre as a place of sin, did not hold it in particularly high regard. If I had been totally open with them, I knew I would have run into feelings and misgivings that I simply could not afford.

While I was waiting for the role of Richard III to come my way, I was cast as an awkward farm worker in a one-act play, *The Truth About Clementine*, written by a local playwright, John Richards. In one scene I had to kiss the girl from the next farm, then pull away, and say, "Pretty good suction, eh?" The dialogue was not Shakespeare, but I was dumbfounded at the laughter it brought. It may have been a long way from *Richard III*, but I, too, was holding the audience. For someone who had never been on stage before, the response seemed remarkable. Every entrance I made, every exit, each punchline, elicited laughter. I was funny.

My first-ever stage performance, in
The Truth About Clementine

And there was a bonus laugh. The set had both a practical door and a decorative door. At one point, I made a quick, unscheduled exit through the decorative door. The one with no hinges. Lying there, half-dazed on the floor, hearing the glorious sound of laughter, did something to me. The door did something to me, too, but I got over that. I never got over the sound of laughter. With it came the uncanny sensation that I had come home. For the first time in my life, I felt comfortable. I felt a sense of being exactly where I belonged. This is what I am going to do, I thought. This is where I want to be. Of course, I didn't stick my neck out and *tell* everyone, that would have been to set myself up for embarrassment and public failure. But I went at it, at breakneck speed, trying to make up for what I felt was lost time. After all, at twenty-one, I was already old.

All my spare time and energy was now devoted to theatrical comedy. I joined three more theatre companies: the Vancouver Little Theatre, Totem Theatre, and the United Jewish Peoples Drama Workshop. The question of circumcision did come up – but only in a comic context. They knew I was desperate for comedic experiences, and they accepted me as temporarily Jewish. By working in four different companies, I was able to manoeuvre my way into doing nothing but comedy. A serious actor, I wasn't. I appeared in *Charlie's Aunt, You Can't Take It with You, This Happy Breed, Our Hearts Were Young and Gay, Father of the Bride, Born Yesterday*, and many other plays whose names now escape me. *Are You a Mason?*, which nobody remembers today, was a nonsense comedy play, funnier, I think, than *Charlie's Aunt*, about a young man who wants to marry a young woman whose father is – or appears to be – a mason. I played the young man, who lies to his intended father-in-law that he is a mason, not knowing that the father-in-law is also lying. We were well rehearsed by the director, who sent us off in twos and threes to work on our own. We'd come back, try things out on him, and he'd either like it or he'd let us know how to fix it. I've never seen a director work that way since. He gave us the latitude to use our imaginations, and it saved time. We never had enough time.

By day, while selling menswear, I had my script at the ready in my pocket, learning lines between customers. At Woodwards, I was surrounded by career salesmen, all older than me, all on commission.

(Top left) With Betty Farquharson in This Happy Breed, by Noel Coward. North Vancouver Community Players, 1949. I built the fireplace, so I got the part. (Top right) North Vancouver Community Players, Our Hearts Were Young and Gay. (Below) In Born Yesterday, Vancouver Little Theatre, 1951. I'm fifth from the left in the back row.

It was a great department with a terrific manager, whom I remember buying up Eisenhower bomber jackets by the carload from the Victoria Cap and Leather Company (which, as should be obvious from the name, was located in Winnipeg) and selling them in the same volume. I enjoyed working for him and I was good enough at what I did that I was put on a course to become a manager. That was fine, but the focus of my life was now elsewhere.

Amateur theatre was flourishing in Vancouver in the late 1940s. There was little in the way of professional theatre, so anyone who was interested in acting either left town or did what work they could as an amateur. Amateur standards then were incredibly high. I met many amateurs who cared intensely about the quality of what they were doing, more than some professionals I later worked with. Director Ian Dobbie, then working for several theatre companies, was one. He kept casting me in play after play, keeping me working and passing on an amazing amount of theatrical knowledge in a very short time. Ian was not a man to explain himself. Once he gave me a stage move which I couldn't figure out. "I don't understand," I said. "After you've done it, you will," he replied. I did it – and I understood. A great director – not a wasted second. I trusted Ian, even when he cast me in a role for which I was entirely unsuited. *Three Men on a Horse* was a very funny comedy set at the racetrack. Ian asked me to play the villain. "Dave, this is not your role," he said. "But I want you to do it as a favour to me." He had the show cast and ready to go, but couldn't find anyone – except me – to play the heavy. I tried to get into it. On the page, the character looked nasty, so I played him nasty. I learned from Ian that you can't play the villain as "nasty" in comedy. Think of him as loud and hollow, was Ian's advice. Those words helped me understand instantly that this big gangster was both loud and a bit thick. The villain in comedy has to be funny, not frightening.

Another standout from that time was Marc Howard, a Toronto comedian who had moved to North Vancouver. Marc was just one of those funny people. When he smiled, his eyes twinkled, and he made everyone else want to smile. It was Marc who launched me on the road to sketch comedy, using me in what became an annual revue, *Rowboat Follies*. Marc produced and directed the first of these revues, in which I did a sketch based on Paul Revere's ride, which I wrote myself, basing the idea on a sketch I had first seen at the Tivoli Theatre in Sydney, Australia. It worked, and Marc subsequently invited me to do some banquet performances with him. This was my first exposure to a world that would subsequently become a very large part of my professional life.

I was still living at home when, one morning, I walked into the kitchen and found my mother lying on the floor, helpless, unable to move, and trying to call out for help. She had fainted, fallen backwards, and hit her head on the sink. I ran next door to fetch our neighbour (who was a doctor) and he helped me carefully lift her and put her on her bed. Gently, he proceeded to examine her. By the time the ambulance arrived, he had discovered she had broken her neck.

I watched in horror as the paramedics, handling her with the greatest of care, placed her on the stretcher and loaded her into the ambulance. They set off, and I followed on in a cab. In the back of the ambulance, one of the crew held his hands around my mother's neck, keeping it rigidly in position throughout the long ride from North Vancouver over the Lion's Gate Bridge to the Vancouver General Hospital.

There, the doctors went to work to try to save her life. There was nothing I could do, so I went down to Woodwards, told them what had happened, and then came back to the hospital and waited. When I was finally allowed to see my mother, I was totally unprepared. The sight of her that afternoon, lying in her hospital room, was the most devastating shock of my life. She was on a rack, her face bloated beyond recognition, her head shaved and covered in iodine, and bolts were fastened to her skull to keep her neck perfectly aligned. Every twenty minutes, the rack was turned; first she was right side up, then upside down, back and forth – to prevent fluid buildup in her lungs. Looking at this horrific contraption and my mother helpless in it, it was everything I could do to prevent myself bursting into tears. Somehow, I managed. I sat down beside her, and quietly talked to her, and read to her from a newspaper I found in my coat pocket. My mother hung there in agony.

Four nights after the accident, the surgeon who had operated on my mother took me aside and quietly warned me that he did not expect my mother to survive. With this type of injury, few did. I sat in her room, trying to comprehend what I had just been told. I tried to take comfort in what I knew about my mother's character. My mother was tenacious. She was, in her own quiet way, a fighter. A few years earlier, she had dealt with breast cancer, had a mastectomy, and had survived. The breast removal had damaged the nerves at the top of her left arm. Another doctor who was treating her referred to her breast surgery as "butchery." The way she dealt with the results of that surgery showed remarkable courage and persistence. She unceasingly exercised her left hand and arm until she had regained their full use. Now she was once again showing an overwhelming determination to stay alive. "God . . . help me get through this," I heard her quietly pleading. "Spare me."

My father, when he heard the news of the accident, cut short his quarterly sales tour and came home. He stayed for a few weeks, and it was only when my mother's condition slowly began to improve that he felt able to go back on the road and try to rescue what was left of his spring tour. I then moved into the YMCA, so that I could be nearby and spend time with her every day. Watching her recover, it was astounding to me that a person who was so soft-spoken and very gentle could have such incredible stamina. She was in hospital for over two months, but eventually, slowly but surely, she made a full recovery. The whole incident only increased my love and admiration for her.

On my second evening at the Y, as I was walking along the hall, I heard the happy sound of someone playing jazz piano, in the style of George Shearing. In a break between tunes, I introduced myself to the young man who was producing the great jazz. His name was Arthur Mawson, a visitor from England. He didn't consider himself a jazz musician – he was a surveyor by trade – and had just worked his way across the country. Arthur was a thinker with a sense of humour, and I thoroughly enjoyed his company.

Whenever we could, Arthur and I got together, heading off to jazz concerts, or to hear whoever was playing at the Cave, a Vancouver nightspot. When we found out that the CBC was going to broadcast

On Granville Street, 1949.
No wonder I was accused of
being an undercover cop.

a live concert with Sammy Davis, Jr., and Mel Torme, Arthur and I
were there in the audience. Somewhere, there is a photograph to
prove it: Arthur Mawson and Dave Broadfoot, together in the same
shot as a very young Sammy Davis, Jr., and Mel Torme. We were also
there on the night when the Lionel Hampton Band played the Cave.
The band marched through the audience, the trumpets going up one
side, the trombones the other, the saxophones through the middle,
and when they joined together at the back of the room, in behind
them came the Seaforth Highlanders Pipe Band, playing Hampton's
signature tune "Flying Home" in unison with the entire Hampton
band. Between the surprise and the sound, the excitement was almost
too much. The audience was ecstatic. These were just two of the
many events Arthur and I saw together, but eventually, Arthur had to
return home to England. Over time, as men do, we lost touch.

In the early 1950s, Vancouver had a semi-professional theatrical
company, Theatre Under the Stars, which played all summer, every
summer at the Malkin Bowl outdoor stage in Stanley Park.
Specializing in operetta and musicals, Theatre Under the Stars was
extremely popular with Vancouver audiences – as many as 3,500
people would see a TUTS show. James Johnston, an actor-director

with the company, saw me in one of the North Vancouver
Community Players' productions, and offered me, unbeknownst to
the producer, the lead role in the musical *Roberta*. He knew I had
limited experience but thought I could pull it off. We rehearsed
twelve days, and had the show moving really well, when we did a run-
through for the producer, Gordon Hilker. When the run-through
was completed, Gordon called James over.

"Who's this kid?" he asked.

"Dave Broadfoot," James told him.

"He's not going to play that part," said Hilker.

"He's not?" James was clearly surprised.

"No, he's not."

"Who is going to play it?"

"You are." I overheard the whole exchange. So did everyone else
in the cast. There was no arguing with the producer. And that was
that – the end of my starring role, the end of my budding career.
Everyone I knew within the Greater Vancouver area had heard I was
going to open in *Roberta*. Explaining what had happened to each
and every one of them was more than I could handle, so I changed
the departure date of a planned trip to New York, Montreal, Ottawa,
and Toronto and headed for the bus depot. Like my father, who quit
his job rather than defend himself, I had no interest in hanging
around for the humiliation.

When I returned to Vancouver, I threw myself into my amateur
roles with even greater determination. "Someday I'll show Hilker,"
I thought. Ian Dobbie continued to cast me in Vancouver Little
Theatre productions. I knew that if I was going to stick to performing comedy, I would have to have an "act," and a substantial
repertoire of comedy material that I could perform solo. So I set
about developing this "stand-up" material with a vengeance,
begging for ideas, borrowing one-liners, cribbing, stealing, anything
to build up material. I listened to other comedians on the radio. I
loved Wayne and Shuster, Allan Young, Sid Caesar, Bob Hope,
Groucho Marx, and Fred Allen, but as an influence, no individual
comedian stood out. I went to see any comedians who played in
Vancouver – Tommy Trinder, the British comedian, made a real
impression. I went to see his show three times and was absolutely

bowled over by his rapid-fire delivery. Not to mention his timing. Timing, I was beginning to realize, was key.

By 1951, I had developed my first "act." It consisted of a lot of one-liners plus three characterizations: a teenage girl on her way to school on the bus and driving the bus driver crazy; a young man reading aloud postcards from his vacationing girlfriend (the postcards tell him that she has lost all interest, but he doesn't get it); and the caretaker of a children's summer camp, who is the victim of the children's endless practical jokes. I performed whenever and wherever I could. Working at Woodwards turned out to be a big help at this time. All the departments held annual banquets, and to hone my act, I performed at these as a volunteer entertainer.

I was also getting paid for the occasional one-nighter at banquets and outdoor variety shows, but it wasn't until July 1952 that I got to work in a real nightclub. The Sirrocco, in Victoria, B.C., was very sedate and well run, with none of the raucous heckling I would later have to endure when playing rowdier nightclubs. The pay was minimal, but it was experience in front of an audience and that was what counted.

As the teenaged girl on the bus, one of my first characters, Burlington, Ontario, 1952

I had been doing amateur theatre and one-nighters for three years when Marc Howard took me aside and said he thought I had the talent to make it as a professional comedian. "You'll starve for a while," he said. "So while you're starving you might as well be in Toronto where you'll be surrounded by opportunity." I thought about it, long and hard. I would probably have taken the chance anyway, but it was Marc saying this that gave me the push I needed. The night I made the decision, I was standing on the boulevard in North Vancouver, near a cricket field, with the lights of the city twinkling in the distance. I decided I would try for it – and if it didn't work, it didn't work, but I was going to try. I wanted to be the best English-speaking comedian in the country. I never thought about New York or Los Angeles at all. My focus was Canada. That was the way it was then, and it still is.

I made a deal with myself. I would take two years, work hard, try to get something going, and, if nothing substantial happened in those two years, I would return to Vancouver, and hope Woodwards would take me back. I told everyone I was going to Toronto. I just didn't tell them what I was going to do when I got there. By not advertising it, I wouldn't feel an abject failure if it didn't work out.

In September of 1952, I got on the bus with my ticket and one hundred dollars in my pocket. Four days later, I got off the bus with my pathetic bit of luggage at the Toronto bus terminal. "Terminal" was an apt description of the Toronto bus depot at that time. By asking around, I found a cheap, gloomy room on nearby Grosvenor Street. As I waited for sleep to come, watching the flickering light-bulbs of Toronto's twenty-five-cycle alternating current system, I wondered what on earth I had done. "What am I going to do, and where will I go to do it?" I asked myself.

I knew no one in the city. No one. I didn't have a clue who I should call for help, but I knew this: I was prepared to do anything – as long as it didn't involve a lot of heavy lifting or store-interior finishing. As a comedian, the venues for me in the early 1950s would be mainly banquets, conventions, and club dates. Comedy clubs had yet to be invented, and revue theatre was just on the rise. For a comic actor, the opportunities in Toronto at that time were extremely limited. In fact, professional theatre in Toronto was still in its infancy. British and American touring companies came into the Royal Alexandra Theatre or Maple Leaf Gardens, while the New Play Society and the Jupiter Theatre were struggling to establish professional theatre in the city. As in Vancouver, what theatre there was, was mostly amateur. Actor David Gardner, who began his professional career in 1950, told me that when he sent in his first tax return, his travel expenses were allowed, but there was no classification for actors. His designation was David Gardner, "travelling salesman."

The natural fit for me would be to join the comedians, magicians, ventriloquists, vocal groups, acrobats, jugglers, dancers, and singers on the banquet circuit. The big venue in the city then was the Royal York Hotel. There, on a Saturday night, the four ballrooms would all be busy with entertainment for large companies holding their annual conventions. A typical night's entertainment might feature a comedian as master of ceremonies, a novelty act, dancers, and a headline singer, and run for about an hour. I was interested in getting this kind of work. I was also interested in performing on television and radio.

The morning after I arrived, I got up and went over to the CBC radio building on Jarvis Street. It looked very, very old, very dingy, and fairly depressing. "This can't be the main centre of Canada's English-language broadcasting," I thought, but it was. I could hardly believe that this was where Wayne and Shuster worked, where Andrew Allan and Esse Ljungh produced their radio plays. I walked in and looked around. That's all I did, look around. No one was about to employ a total stranger from North Vancouver. Nearby was the new television building, a plain brick box, six storeys high. It was literally the day before the start of television broadcasting in Canada, and things were in a state of flux. Performers were rehearsing, getting ready for the big day, anxious for the new opportunities of television, but nervous of making the adjustment from radio.

I asked around and found out that the top producer in television variety, in charge of the CBC's new flagship variety show, "The Big Revue," was Don Hudson. He was the one I needed to approach. But I knew better than to bother any of the producers that particular day – they had other things on their minds.

I set off to look for a day job and a permanent place to live. An ad in the *Toronto Star* led me to my first room-and-board accommodation. It was in the home of a pleasant enough common-law couple, with a thirteen-year-old-daughter. "These living conditions are peachy keen," I wrote to my parents. "It was quite a shock to come into this room, open the top bureau drawer, and actually find something in it! A New Testament and a dozen pencils. The pencils I'm using." I soon discovered the living conditions were less peachy keen than they at first seemed. The thirteen-year-old daughter was bursting with hostility. I never did find out for sure whether the hostility was generalized, or whether she had a specific hatred of me. "That man," I heard her say to her mother with venom, "picked up our telephone." I couldn't charge the landlord with false advertising, since there was no classified column for "room with hostility," but I spent every waking minute looking for a room with no board. "This isn't working out," the girl's mother said to me one day. "It sure isn't," I responded, and left at the end of the week.

Luckily, I ran into a fellow actor from Vancouver, Wally Marsh, and we set out looking for new digs together, walking along Suffolk Street, near the CBC. One of the homeowners was out working on his garden, and I asked if he knew of any rental accommodation. That was how I met my future landlord, Henry Schultz, and his wife, Simone, whose lodgings were to become my home away from home. They did not have room for Wally, who found digs off Spadina Avenue, but for the next five years I stayed mainly at the Schultz house. Henry was from Manitoba, Simone from Quebec, and I couldn't have found better landlords. Henry was a barber by day, and a hotshot gambler by night – he was rumoured to have paid off his mortgage with his winnings at the tables. Simone was sociable and kind, and I think she knew that I didn't always have enough to eat. I'd be working away in my room, and there would be a knock at the door, and Simone would be standing there with a big bowl of stew. She was an extraordinary cook. Sometimes they'd invite me to sit down to dinner with them. Henry liked to give the impression of gruffness – which was an act, because he wasn't gruff at all. "What do you think you'd pay for a meal like this in a restaurant?" he would demand. Before I could answer, he'd continue, "You can't get this kind of food in a restaurant." It was a routine he went through, every time. It was his backhanded way of complimenting Simone on her cooking.

I got a day job at Simpsons, in the menswear department, and began my campaign to break into Toronto show business. From the Yellow Pages I made a list of agents. There were a fair number booking club dates and variety in the city at that time, and I set off to see them all. At the Mart Kenney Agency I saw Paul Simmons (who later became my business manager); I saw Norman Harris and Doug Widdess, who booked clubs; Helen O'Connor, who put together variety one-nighters; George King, who booked the college circuit; Ian Reid, George Taggart, Stanley St. John, Dave Bossin – I met every one. Everywhere I went the answer was the same. "Let me know where I can come and see you work," they said. All I could do was keep on trying to find that one first gig. It was a perpetual dilemma. Agents have to be able to see exactly what it is you do in your performance. They couldn't get you a booking until they'd seen you perform with an audience, and you couldn't perform with an audience until you got a booking. You couldn't get a booking if you weren't in the union, and you couldn't join the union if you didn't have a booking.

It occurred to me that, if I couldn't get professional bookings, I could at least perform for free. I'd do the rounds of the Navy Club, the War Amps, and the 48th Highlanders. I'd wander in ahead of time, knowing that it was ladies' night or that there was a function on. I'd go up to the manager and say, "If you're doing any variety, I can do a few minutes if you want." "Sure," they'd say. "How bad can you be?" So, I'd get up and do my act. After I'd done this once, I'd go back to these same clubs, and they would say, "Hey, Dave, come on up." They'd be *asking*, little knowing that the only reason I was there was to get up and practise my stuff, because I didn't think it was fair to try out material on a paying audience. I felt, to get paid, you had to know in advance that every line was going to work. The club patrons thought they owed me for the entertainment, but I always felt I owed them for giving me priceless experience.

Soon I began to get work that paid – not much, $20 to $25 – but it paid. The work came in through some of the agents I had seen, and in those early days the jobs were mostly out of town. Places like

At an early club date,
Burlington, Ontario, 1953

Belleville, Whitby, and one memorable trip to Shannonville, where I was a great hit with the audience, who came mostly from the local reserve. I'd travelled there by bus, and found myself packing up at one in the morning, walking back out to the highway, and luckily hitching a ride back to Toronto on a transport truck.

There were times in those early days when I was hungry, times when a small box of raisins did for three meals a day. It didn't help that, before leaving Vancouver, I'd taken out a mortgage and bought my parents a house. They had lived in six different houses in North Vancouver, with one landlord after another giving them notice, and I was determined that they would never have to move again. I knew that my father, although he was still working, did not have enough for a down payment on a house. So I'd saved enough money for a deposit from my Woodwards salary, and by taking out a hefty mortgage had managed to buy a small modern home on Grand Boulevard for them. I was responsible for the mortgage payments, and keeping up with them wasn't easy. My letters home were full of apologies for the late cheques.

Simone, my landlady, knew I was struggling and, in addition to feeding me, never pressured me for rent payments. Paul Simmons, I later found out, also knew. "You know what was amazing about you, Dave?" he once said. "You never said, 'Please get me a job. Anything.' I heard that from lots of other performers, but you never did it. You always came in with a smile on your face." Paul did not really know me well then. He does now. He's been my business manager for thirty years. If he had known me then, he would have known that I could never plead for work. It's not in my nature. To me, it defeats the whole purpose. If you are begging for work, how could you get up in front of an audience? The lack of confidence would show. I also never wanted to give in to self-indulgence and feel sorry for myself. I found, right from the very beginning, that when things were really bad, if I went into my room and started working on material, trying to build a better act, the phone would start ringing with bookings. I don't know why, but it always seemed to happen that way.

So I sat in my tiny room at Henry and Simone's, with its bed, dresser, table, and hotplate, and wrote. I saw agents. I worked on publicity. I watched other comedians on television. I went to see Wayne and Shuster perform their radio show – many times. When the money ran out, I took a day job. The boss at the Acme Bertram Tool Company was particularly understanding. I worked in the Acme Bertram shipping department for a couple of months, and when I had to quit because I had bookings, he was sympathetic. "I understand how it is, Dave," he said. "I know what you're going through." I could come back any time, he said. I was astounded by his generosity and understanding.

I also hung around the CBC television building, observing everything I could about the programs beings produced. I had run-ins with the security person every other day. We were both disadvantaged. I had no permission to be there. He had no sense of humour. A perfect balance. I got to know some of the dancers on "The Big Revue," and told them I wanted to audition. I also told the young and not-yet-famous studio director, Norman Jewison. Finally, one day, during rehearsal break, I got my chance. They liked what I did and hired me for the show. In my debut performance, I sang (sang?)

My television audition, 1952

"Ugly Woman" with singer Patsy O'Day, while the dancers did a calypso ballet (calypso ballet?). My main routine was a topical parody of an American senator. It was the early 1950s, and Joe McCarthy was starring in his own TV show.

> *They're calling us Reds. They say our party is turning Pink. Why? Because our leader has a cousin who had a friend whose grandmother was once married to the brother-in-law of a man who was a member of the Council of Boy Scouts of America in 1929 when they held their international jamboree in Moscow!!! Moscow!!! Why? I'll tell you why! Because the Republicans, who were in power at the time, refused to allow them to rent a hall in their own country!!*
>
> *I wouldn't say anything about the Republican Party unless I could say something good. And believe me, this is really good.*

They want to change the name of Boulder Dam. They want to call it Hoover Dam! They weren't satisfied having a vacuum named after him . . . they want to rename a dam!!! They want us to forget about Boulder. Sam Boulder. And the courageous work he did in the . . . [looking desperately through his notes] *. . . in the field of . . .* [looking at his script] *. . . Graft. Graft? Don't talk to me about graft. There isn't a man in this country who knows more about graft than I do!!! Yes, my friends, in our party we have the answers. So, when you go to the polls, elect a man in whom we can all have confidence. It's time to put a confidence man in the White House.*

You had to be there.

"All that talk about cameras being nerve-wracking," I wrote to my parents the day after, "is ridiculous." Norman Jewison had stood with his face flush beside the camera, beaming at me and egging me on throughout my entire performance. He was so positive and enthusiastic about what I was doing that I was completely comfortable about it all. Producer Don Hudson worked out a schedule where I became a regular on the show. I was on my way.

Adjusting to life in Toronto wasn't easy. There was so much to learn. In British Columbia it was common practice when leaving a beer parlour to ask the bartender for a carton of beer to take home with you. I did that in Toronto. Bad move. The bartender looked off my starboard ear and continued about the business of rinsing glasses. A few minutes later, I reminded him of my request. Again, he looked past my face. A few more minutes, and I was getting irritated. I asked again. "When do I get my beer to take out?" Finally, he looked me in the eye. "Are you a cop or what?" "I'm a what," I said, and left the bar in a state of total befuddlement.

Then someone explained to me that you cannot casually buy beer in Ontario. It has to be a deliberate, well-planned act. First, you have to have a car, so you can drive to one of the inconveniently located

Brewers Retail outlets. I assumed that the outlets were owned by the government, but they weren't – they were owned by the brewers. I walked six blocks, to the nearest one, and bought a twelve-pack. Then, I had to get it home. As I was walking back to Suffolk Street, a police cruiser swerved over to the curb beside me. The window came down and the police officer stuck his head out. "Do you mind telling us where you got hold of that carton of beer?" he asked. "Brewers Retail," I said, helpfully. "Really?" "Really. Is there another way to get hold of it?" "Never mind the smart talk." "Smart?" Realizing I was a hopeless case, he gave up. "You take that beer home as fast as you can, mister," he said. The Toronto attitude to nature's perfect nectar was hard to fathom.

A few weeks later, I was sitting in a downtown tavern with a guitar player whom I had asked to write some chords for me for a calypso song. He didn't have his guitar with him, so I very discreetly and very softly began humming the tune, as he prepared to make some notes on a piece of paper. Within seconds, a waiter was at my elbow. "Knock it off, eh!" he said. "What's the problem?" I asked. With a snarl, he replied, "You know damn well there's no hummin' in here." The guitar player explained why. The waiter was afraid that if anyone was heard humming, the management would have to pay an entertainment tax. I learned then the difference between stupidity and genius: only genius has limits.

Mavor Moore, then the chief television producer for the CBC, saw my on-camera audition for "The Big Revue" and liked it. That was lucky for me. As well as being a CBC executive, Mavor was then, with his mother, Dora Mavor Moore, a pivotal force in the Toronto theatrical community. Their New Play Society, founded in 1946, had brought new life and energy to the Toronto theatre scene. Courtesy of the New Play Society, Toronto audiences got to see not only new work from European and Americans playwrights, but also new Canadian plays by, among others, Lister Sinclair, John Coulter, Harry Boyle, Andrew Allan, and Morley Callaghan.

It was the failure of one new Canadian play to materialize that led to the creation of the New Play Society's smash hit revue, *Spring Thaw*. In 1948, Mavor had contracted Hugh Kemp to adapt Hugh

MacLennan's *Two Solitudes* for the theatre. It was due to open on April Fool's Day, 1948, and with opening day fast approaching, there was no play in sight. In a panic, a group of New Play Society actors, with Mavor as director, put together all the revue material they either had or could quickly concoct. They opened under the original title *Spring Thaw*, and audiences ate it up. At that time, revues were just beginning to take off as a popular form of entertainment. By the end of the 1950s, there would be many theatres and dinner theatres in Toronto and Montreal presenting revues. *Spring Thaw* was one of the first and most successful. It became an annual event, running from 1948 to 1973, the longest-running show of its kind in Canada.

Mavor thought I would be just right for *Spring Thaw*. After seeing my CBC audition, he immediately called his mother, Dora, and told her I should be in the 1953 production. A few days later, I got a phone call from Dora and went to meet her in person. I arrived at the New Play Society office on Yonge Street to be greeted by the great lady herself. Dora had a warm, engaging personality and an easy, welcoming smile, but I could sense instantly that within this woman was great determination. Dora, for whom the theatre awards are named, was at that time well on her way to becoming a legend. She had brought a wealth of experience to the Toronto theatre scene, starting her career as an actress, performing in prestigious theatres like the Old Vic in London. Later, she became a teacher, and eventually a producer. Dora, I discovered, was the heart, soul, and driving force of the New Play Society. I sensed she had a special appreciation for people who were keen to learn, and I quickly realized that she had much to teach.

Dora was not a woman who easily took no for an answer. Her phone rang while I was in her office. It was a worried bank manager. Dora's handling of him was quite remarkable – she demonstrated a deep understanding of psychology as well as nerves of steel. If the bank manager could not say no to her, neither could I. Not, of course, that I would have wanted to. When she asked me at that first meeting if I would be interested in appearing in the sixth *Spring Thaw*, I was delighted to say yes.

Unlike previous *Spring Thaw* productions, *Spring Thaw '53* was built around a specific star, Anna Russell. Anna was another Canadian theatrical legend. Classically trained at the Royal College of Music in London, she actually spent five years on the concert circuit as a soprano, before finding her calling as a humorist. This began in Toronto, in 1948, when at a benefit she did her first comedy sketch. She never looked back – her spoofs of Wagner would make her an international star. Most of Anna's comedy was based on parodies of operas, virtuosos, and any other musical efforts that could be lampooned. She was very funny, and I was looking forward to working with her.

Mavor Moore, whose CBC job was taking up all of his time, was unavailable to direct this year, so Dora Mavor Moore scoured the country, looking for a suitable revue director, and came up empty-handed. She then contacted an association of theatrical directors in the United States, giving them her requirements. An agreement was reached – the association would provide a director experienced in presenting satirical revues.

On the first day of rehearsals, the cast were all gathered eagerly awaiting the arrival of our director. There was a feeble knock on the door of the rehearsal hall, and in walked our man – a tired, dishevelled old geezer well into his dotage. We soon found out that he was completely unaware of anything that had happened in the theatre in the past twenty years.

As we proceeded, he revealed his philosophy of comedy. "Comedy," he told us, "is rhythm." He found a big stick, and started banging it on a table in rhythmic beat, while we tried to perform our sketches. This presented a problem, not just because the noise was somewhat distracting, but also because his rhythms varied according to the amount of alcohol circulating through his veins. It soon became obvious that the performers were going to have to work very hard to try to rescue the show, rhythmically or otherwise. The imported director was a staggering disaster.

When Mavor Moore found out about the impending debacle, he managed to arrange enough time away from the CBC to step in, and, in four very long days, he did a remarkable salvage job. We opened in May, in the theatre of the Royal Ontario Museum, with a surprisingly successful show – no thanks to the American theatrical director. Lots of thanks to Anna Russell and Mavor Moore. The alcoholic is still anonymous.

I never did see Anna's routines from the front of the house, but from the wings I caught glimpses of her piece on the history of the bagpipes. In her comic lecture, she placed the various parts of the instrument on the table as she spoke, seemingly unaware that, from the audience's point of view, the loosely assembled bagpipe parts looked exactly like king-size genitalia. The audience screamed with delight each and every night. Marie Chevrier I had seen and heard in rehearsal. She sang folk songs unaccompanied, and they almost stopped the show. Singers Jacqueline Smith, Victor White, and Andrew MacMillan, actors Jean Pouliot, Peter Mews, and Pegi Brown, comedians Alfie Scopp and Libby Morris, and actor/singers Neil Vipond, Bill Copeland, and Sheila Craig completed the cast. For my part, I accepted every sketch I was offered and gave each one my best effort. My first *Spring Thaw* was great fun, but when the show's seven-week run was completed, I was back doing the rounds, looking for work.

I had pinned my hopes on a TV show I had been writing since January, a half-hour comedy featuring – who else – me. I took the idea to agent Norman Harris, and he presented it to the CBC. After much discussion, we had finally got to record an audition in April. I was hoping we would get an instant yes, and that this would carry me

*With Bill Copeland and Peggi
Brown, in* Spring Thaw, *1953*

through the rest of the year. Boy, was I green. We did the audition and then heard . . . nothing. So instead of bursting into the brave new world of television as a full-fledged star, I answered a "help wanted" ad. I applied for a job at a resort in Muskoka: the Gateway.

The Gateway was a hotel with a difference. Located on the shores of Lake Muskoka at Gravenhurst, it had started life as a resort hotel in the early part of the century. The competition among the Muskoka hotels was fierce, and it had survived less than ten years as a hotel before being converted into a TB sanitorium. During the Second World War, it had been used as a prisoner-of-war camp for German army officers. Now, with perfect irony, it had become a Jewish resort hotel. The reason that such a place was needed was that, in the anti-Semitic atmosphere of Ontario in those days, Jews were not welcome at non-Jewish hotels. The Gateway was promoted as a kosher-style hotel. It was heavy on style, and light on kosher.

I went for an interview with the hotel manager, Berko Devor, and he seemed to like me. How could he know that I had a huge advantage over him – I was ready to work cheap. He asked me if I would consider being the "sports director." "I know nothing about sports," I said. "Good," he said, "that's exactly what we're looking for." He told me the "social director" was a young comedian from New York. I asked if I would have the opportunity to perform comedy in the hotel stage shows. "Why not?" he said. Which is Jewish for "of course."

The next thing I knew we were in Berko's car, headed for the hotel, way ahead of the opening date for the season. Berko was managing the hotel for a group of twelve owners – two were in the womenswear business, one was a hot-dog manufacturer, two were chicken wholesalers, and, although I don't know what the others did, I do know the resort was a sideline for them all.

When we arrived at the hotel, I settled into the staff quarters, wooden buildings that had been added to the original property to house the German prisoners-of-war. On my first walk around the grounds, I noticed, even though this was 1953, that there were still strips of barbed wire here and there. I found some wire cutters and took some pleasure in getting rid of it. It gave me even greater pleasure to take down, with chainsaw and sledge hammer, the last remaining lookout tower.

The past, however, was not all so easily erased. Once the guests arrived, I would notice a very attractive young woman with her tattooed death-camp number clearly visible on her arm. It was the first such number I had seen. I saw many more over the next few months, but hers was the first, and the reality was shocking.

I set to work, taking down storm windows, helping fix up the tennis courts, cleaning the baseball diamond, and soon the hotel was ready for the guests. I'm not sure I was. What did a "sports director" do, anyway? It turned out my job was to get people playing sports, something they were extremely reluctant to do. They just wanted to sit around in the sun. But that wasn't good enough for the management. I was supposed to make the guests *active*. I offered them tennis tournaments, horseshoe-throwing tournaments, and baseball games. I'd get on the PA system every morning and try to coax them out, making a joke of it. I got one fellow out playing baseball, and when running to first base, both his legs seized up. A really serious charley horse in each leg. He was on crutches for the rest of his stay. I felt terrible.

When Howie Krantz, the social director from New York, arrived, I liked him immediately. With his husky voice, Bronx accent, and New York energy, he brought an infectious enthusiasm to the job. Howie was very young – younger than me, and still a student – but

The Gateway Hotel and grounds

With Howie Krantz,
at the Gateway Hotel

he knew his business. He organized two floor-shows a week, never using the same material twice, always careful to tailor his material to his audience. "There's one thing I have to say to the owners of this place, [*extra loud*] get those German officers out of my room! They're really annoying." Where Howie got all his comedy material from, I don't know. But he brought a lot of it with him – Jewish-oriented sketches, hysterically funny and a joy to perform in. I had to learn a lot of Jewish expressions, which, coming from the mouth of a Gentile, made people laugh even more.

The dining room of the Gateway Hotel

In my own monologues, I took an approach that couldn't miss: I was a Gentile innocently trying to understand Jewish culture. In fact, the reality was not far off the mark, because this was my first immersion in Jewish social life. Friday evenings at the Gateway were a revelation to me. Everybody dressed for dinner, candles illuminated the tables, and the orchestra played haunting *schtetl* tunes throughout the meal. That summer of '53, we were also lucky to have a young New Yorker staying as a guest at the hotel, Mort Freeman. Mort had an extraordinary singing and speaking voice, and on rainy days he gathered us all together in the theatre and kept us spellbound as he read to us from the stories of Sholom Aleichem, some of which became *Fiddler on the Roof*. Later that summer, Mort had to go to Vancouver, and paid a visit to my mother. My mother asked if I was behaving myself. "Oh yes," Mort said. "He's a very good Jew. If it was a Catholic hotel, I think he would be a good Catholic, too."

Toward the end of the season, Howie Krantz had to leave to register for U.S. army service, so I took over as social director for a couple of weeks. But all too soon the summer was over. It had been a wonderful summer. I felt totally at home at the Gateway; I never felt more at home anywhere. I met a lot of wonderful people, quite a number of whom were Holocaust survivors. Many became fans, and still turn up at my shows in Toronto. Howie Krantz, who went on to be a lawyer in New York City, became a lifelong friend.

I would do two more summers at the Gateway, but none really equalled that first season. We had a new social director the next year, from New York like Howie. However, I always felt that he was a bit of a fraud. For one thing, he had no talent, no feeling for working the audience, and none of the verbal style of a Jewish comedian. I saw him more than once searching through old jokebooks looking for Jewish humour. His wife, who came with him, certainly wasn't Jewish, but had a great voice. He seemed to be happy getting by on her talent. Socially, they were a very charming couple. My last year, 1955, the social director was a slick nightclub comedian, who was loaded with clichés and putdowns of Canada.

The era of the Gateway would end a few years later, when Pierre Berton wrote a series of columns in the *Toronto Star* that exposed the anti-Semitism that existed at the other Muskoka resorts.

Gradually, as the barriers broke down, the need for a place like the Gateway would vanish. Years later, when I was driving through Gravenhurst, I decided to try to find the Gateway again. I went down all the side roads, until eventually I came across the site of the old hotel. There it was, in ruins, trees growing up through the tennis courts that I used to mop up after the rain. As I walked around, memories came flooding back – of listening to the survivors and learning from them, of Howie and all the laughter we shared, of all those generous people who had been so kind and encouraging to a young comedian. It was so sad to see something that had been quite wonderful reduced to nothing. I got back into my car and didn't linger.

Back in Toronto after my first season in Muskoka, to keep the money coming in I worked on stage crews for the London Festival Ballet and the Old Vic, who were touring from England. I saw the Festival Ballet production of *Petrouchka* from the stage. The scenes were so short, I was literally on stage with the dancers, behind one flat after another, holding them up, because there was no time to anchor them. I also saw Stanley Holloway and Robert Helpman in the Old Vic production of *A Midsummer Night's Dream*. Then, at the end of September 1953, I got what I believed was my big break. A convention at the Royal York Hotel. I invited all the booking agents in town to the event, where I was to be master of ceremonies. Finally, I thought, I had a booking where I could really show them all what I could do. They all came – every single one of those I invited showed up. I was thrilled.

As the evening unfolded my excitement turned to concern. First, the cocktail reception lasted almost two hours. Then the dinner dragged on, with a long hiatus between each course. With the other performers, I waited patiently backstage. We sat through the speech of the outgoing chairman. "As I look back over the past year, it's clear that, had it not been for the incredible team effort, we wouldn't have had these twelve months . . ." he sputtered. Then he started to thank everyone, every single last member of the company, it seemed. Some of them even had to stand up and acknowledge the applause. Then he thanked the spouses, the organizing committee for the evening, and his own wife, before introducing the incoming chairman. All the while he was sipping his Baby Duck, and getting more and more inebriated. I started to look at the clock. It was already past nine-thirty, and the evening was supposed to be finished by ten.

Then it was the turn of the incoming chairman, who came on bursting with excitement. He could hardly contain himself. "I guess this is it," he said. "This is really something. Isn't it? No, I mean it. Look at this. Here I am. I mean really. You all know what I'm talking about." Actually, they didn't know what he was talking about, but it was clear that he was going to continue to talk anyway. For a long time. To say my heart sank is a cliché, but I'll say it anyway. My heart sank. I could picture all the agents checking their watches, desperate to leave.

When the incoming chairman was done, there was another pro-tracted introduction, and on came the guest speaker, John Fisher, who as referred to as "Mr. Canada." John managed to speak for over an hour, on the scintillating topic of the status of Canada's NATO troops in Germany. I had nothing against Canada's NATO troops in Germany (I later went overseas to entertain them), but John Fisher could have picked a more dynamic topic, or given his chosen topic the ten minutes it deserved. I'm positive that the only reason he kept going for an hour was because he was hoping that something inter-esting might occur to him during that time. Unfortunately, it didn't. When they get around to revising our laws, I sat thinking, "boring the pants off an audience" should be made a criminal offence.

At this point, the gloom backstage was palpable. This audience was lost. By the time I was being introduced, mistakenly, as Barry Bradford, a stampede to the washroom was taking place unlike any human stampede I had ever seen. It topped "95-cent day" at Woodwards. Many of those who had stampeded never returned to the corral. I had spent hours preparing a strong, topical warm-up routine, and I misguidedly launched into it. Today, I would know better. I'd say "hello," and introduce the first performer.

The way it was, when our show finally got underway, the first per-former was on too long, the second performer was on too long, the third performer stayed on too long, then it was my turn to be on too long. It was past midnight when we finished. The evening had been a complete and utter fiasco.

It was a terrible setback. All those agents, whom I had invited
with such enthusiasm, had seen it. Those who didn't see it, heard
about it. When they thought of me now, they thought of disaster.
Bookings were almost non-existent. It took me a long, long time to
recover. I went into an awful depression. It is such a soul-destroying
experience to be in a no-win situation, and to have absolutely no
choice but to go on with it. I didn't sleep that night, or the next, or
the next. Anxiety started to creep in. That event, which was supposed to be the launching pad for greater things, would turn the
next year, 1954, into the worst of my working life. If you ever visit
the Concert Hall of the Royal York Hotel in Toronto, take note
of the carpet on the stage, that peculiar shade of red. It's my blood.

I was in agent Norman Harris's office one day in early December
1953, when I overheard a magician say that he'd been approached to
do some Christmas shows for the United Nations forces in Korea,
but he didn't want to be away from home at Christmas. Here was an
opportunity for a desperate unemployed comedian. I asked if it
would be rude of me to ask who had asked him to go. "Rude?" he
said. "Nothing wrong with rude. Her name is Celia Long, and she's
with Ronald's Advertising. They're organizing the tour for the
Department of National Defence. Tell her Ted Rust sent you. I hope
you get the tour." I phoned Celia Long, and she asked me to come
in and audition the following morning at 8:30 a.m. "Anyone who can
stand up and make us laugh this early in the morning gets my vote,"
Celia said, after I had done my bit.

By 9:30 a.m. I had signed my contract with the Department of
National Defence and was on my way to getting a series of inoculations. My passport was rushed to Ottawa for an emergency
updating, I was outfitted with a complete military wardrobe and
given a second series of inoculations in various parts of my
anatomy. Then, feeling as comfortable as an introverted porcupine,
I arrived in Montreal to join the rest of the troop, whom I met in
agent Frenchie Jarraud's office. Frenchie, so-called because he was
from France, was a great agent, very respectful of talent, which I
have to say is not true of all agents. Curly Reid, the guitar player on
the tour, who was sitting there when I walked in, looked at me,

puzzled. "You don't look Indian," he said. "Well, no, I'm not." "We were told there was an Indian comedian coming," he said. He was clearly disappointed. "Too bad," he added. "I was looking forward to the novelty."

There were six of us in the show: Curly, Pierrette Doré, a singer from Quebec City, Reid McLeod, a piano player who did popular songs with a jazz feel, Rick and Jean Garcia – "The Amazing Garcias" – who had a mentalist act, and myself. Rick and Jean really fascinated me. She'd be on stage, blindfolded, and he'd go out into the crowd and ask her questions about objects given to him by members of the audience. "I've got something in my hand," he'd say. "What is it?" Everything he asked her, she got right. Yet he hardly said anything to her that could convey a hint. I watched again, and again, trying to figure out the code, but I never could. Although I desperately wanted to know how they did it, I couldn't ask. You don't ask a magician how he does his tricks.

From Montreal, we all set out for Vancouver, where we performed at the Shaughnessy Military Hospital, before heading off to Tokyo and then on to Seoul. In Korea, truce negotiations between the United Nations on one side and the North Koreans and Chinese on the other had been going on since July 1951.

An armistice had been signed in July 1953, but by the time we were there, in December, although the war was supposedly over, UN troops were still in position all along the border between North and South Korea. All transportation after dark was done without lights. Military manoeuvres were a daily affair. To the north, on the other side of no man's land, the Chinese and North Korean troops were carrying out their manoeuvres, too. More than once, we woke to the sound of tanks rolling by our tent and quietly wondered whether this was an exercise or the real thing. At the Canadian base, a three-hour drive south of Panmunjom, we were allocated two tiny tents, from which we could make our way to the various detachments we were to entertain. Close by was the Maple Leaf Centre, which the Canadian Commander, Brigadier General Jean Victoire Allard, had set up as a recreation centre for the troops. The centre included an auditorium in a huge Quonset hut that could seat seven hundred.

(Left) Our advertising for the Marunouchi Hotel

(Below) With Reid McLeod and Pierrette Doré, en route to Japan, Christmas 1953

As I was the show's master of ceremonies, I went to check out the auditorium. Sitting on a rough plywood stage in the frigidly cold building was a shiny new Yamaha piano, which had just arrived from Japan that day. And there, at the piano, was Brigadier General Jean Victoire Allard. He was playing, masterfully, that same Chopin étude I had been so moved by in the service club in Calcutta. Brigadier General Allard was, among other things, the highest-ranking piano player in all of Korea – as well as being the most admired commanding officer I ever encountered. His troops loved him, they positively beamed when they saw him walking around the base. On that trip to Korea I learned quickly where troop morale came from. It was always the commanding officer. You saw troops who were immaculate – well shaved, their hair groomed, their uniforms clean, and their spirits high. Then you saw their commanding officer, and you knew right away why they were like that.

We performed for all the troops – Americans, Brits, Turks, Australians, New Zealanders, and, of course, Canadians. As audiences, they were all terrific, although I must say I think the Brits were the most receptive. I did one sketch where I was being vamped by Pierrette Doré. I played a character who was so stunned by her I couldn't remember my own name. Members of the audience started shouting out names that I might have had, trying to be helpful. They were right there, really involved.

When all our performances were over, we had enough time on the way back to Tokyo to visit Hiroshima. Not all of us chose to go, but I did. I wanted to see it with my own eyes. The thing that hit me the hardest was not the destruction – I knew about that, I had seen pictures of that. It was how much had been rebuilt in such a very short space of time, although they had not rebuilt ground zero, the exact spot where the nuclear bomb exploded. It will remain forever as it was after the bomb fell.

We were in Hiroshima for just one day, then it was on to Tokyo, where Rick Garcia had managed to get us booked into the Marinouchi Hotel for a week's run. That, it turned out, was a

At Hiroshima

mistake. Or rather, it was a mistake for me. Rick had not stopped to think that nobody would understand us. That didn't matter so much for Curly, on guitar, for Pierrette's songs, or even for Rick and Jean doing their amazing mental-telepathy act. For me, as a comedian whose stock in trade is words, it was pathetic, but I ploughed through it as best I could, delighted to be in Tokyo and to have the opportunity to see the city. I headed first for Frank Lloyd Wright's masterpiece, the 1922 Imperial Hotel, since then the victim of the wrecker's ball I'm sorry to say, and wandered all over it.

We spent a total of thirteen wonderful days in Tokyo, highlighted by visits to the Kabuki Theatre, as well as to the Takaratsuka, an all-female troupe, and the Nichigeki Music Hall. All six of us in our Canadian troupe took in the show at the Nichigeki, a very large, attractive vaudeville theatre. The following afternoon, we gave a performance of our own show for UN troops at the Ernie Pyle Theatre. Mother Nature decided that halfway through my part of the program was the perfect time to hold an earthquake. As the building rumbled, the audience gasped, stood up, waited for a minute, then sat down again. It was not the first time an audience had been ready to leave in the middle of my show.

Before we left Tokyo, we were asked if we would do a show for patients at the UN military hospital, and of course we said yes. They put all the beds together in a group, in the hospital's largest ward, and rolled in a piano. Reid got going, with Curly on guitar, and I started with my intro, followed by my first spot in the show. There was no reaction. Nothing. I was looking out at all the GIs in their blue UN pyjamas, and there was no reaction. Curly, Pierrette, Reid, Rick, and Jean all went over well. Then it was my turn again. Again, nothing. The fact that I was a white Canadian and they were all black Americans couldn't have anything to do with it. I had entertained white and black GIs at the U.S. base with no problem. I worked harder and harder. The perspiration was pouring down my face. I couldn't believe the lack of response, the waves of indifference coming at me. Not a giggle. All I could think was "this can't be happening." But it was. It really was.

As I became more and more frantic, with perspiration now literally cascading down my body, some of the soldier-patients in the nearest beds began to chuckle. *Finally*, I thought. *At last it's coming alive.* At the end of the show, as I staggered out into the corridor, relieved it was over, the Red Cross woman who had set up the engagement came up to me, and asked cheerfully, "How did you enjoy performing for the Ethiopians?"

I got back to winter in Toronto to find everything topsy-turvy. Norman Harris, in whose office I had heard about the Korea trip, was no longer an agent. The American Guild of Variety Artists, my union, was no longer my union. "The Big Revue" producer, who had hired me for the show, was no longer a producer. Mavor Moore was resigning from the CBC. *If it gets any worse*, I thought, *I'll be going back to Korea as a private.*

Chapter 4

GETTING READY FOR HUNGER

I loved working with Mavor Moore, the Renaissance man of Canadian theatre. Mavor was not only a producer, director, actor, writer, composer, and lyricist – he also understood lighting, staging, and costuming, and, as an added bonus, he had a pleasant temperament. Intelligent and generous, he was a natural teacher. All you had to do was listen to him, watch him. There was no ego, no arrogance, just a great respect for talent.

When I returned to *Spring Thaw* for a second season in February 1954, it proved to be one of the few bright spots of that year. I asked Mavor if I might do a solo piece, and he readily agreed. I had made the foray into lampooning politicians with my impression on television of the American Senator, but it seemed silly for me to be doing an American, when there was so much political action going on in Canada. So I made my next political characterization Canadian. I took elements from three different people. The intonation came from E. C. Manning, Preston Manning's father, at that time premier of Alberta. He was also a working evangelist with a weekly broadcast called "Back to the Bible Hour." The fiery quality I stole from Billy Graham. The way I moved came from another American TV evangelist, Bishop Fulton Sheen. Watching him, I learned what to do on television: say your set-up line with great passion, staring into the camera, and keep staring at the camera as you silently pace the floor. Then stop pacing, turn your body directly to the camera, drop

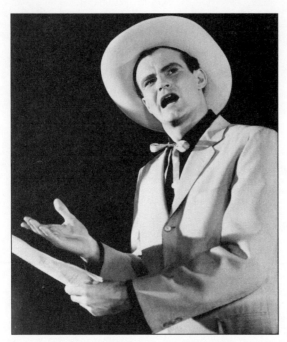

*The Member for Kicking
Horse Pass, 1956*

your voice, and deliver your punchline. Little did the bishop know
how much he had helped a young agnostic.

I put a first political monologue together and showed it to Mavor.
"What you've got here is fine," he said. "But this character needs a
name. He's a member of Parliament, he's obviously from the West.
Why not call him the Member for Kicking Horse Pass?" And that's
how the Member for Kicking Horse Pass, an audience favourite to
this day, was born.

*As a man deeply involved in and committed to the political life
of this country, I found myself some years ago becoming frustrated with the Canadian political process. I asked myself why.
Why was I frustrated with our political parties? The answer was
obvious: there were only four to choose from. It saddened me
that the members of four political parties in existence could
never look at issues logically, the way I saw them. Apparently
Canada needed a fifth party.*

And so, necessity became the mother of convention, and the New Apathetic Party was born. The party adopted the name "Apathetic" in order to appeal to the average Canadian. And now, finally, after years of determined effort, we are beginning to see the light at the end of our long tunnel. Apathy is on the march!

I have been asked on occasion by some non-believers in our cause what qualifies me to be the leader of a political party. I humbly refer these doubters to the historical and unfailing good judgement, and, if I may say so, wisdom, of my constituents.

When I received the nomination at the founding convention of our party in Kicking Horse Pass, it was a landslide. I was their national dream come true. The conventioneers were perceptive enough to see that I was Mackenzie King, Louis Riel, and Bobby Hull all rolled into one . . . with a dash of Genghis Khan thrown in.

What, you may ask, is my background? My grandfather was the first French-speaking Jehovah's Witness. In the Second World War, my father was presumed missing in Camp Borden. He was the first Canadian soldier to have a drink named after him, the Zombie. My mother, a self-taught trucker, was the first woman to be recognized by the Teamsters. However, she eventually gave all that up to become a celibate nun and to work with a lay priest amongst the Westmount Rhodesians. My cousin was the first Canadian actor to win the Order of Canada medal for best supporting actor in an American film. And because my family owned a distillery, we held a position of moral leadership that made the Eaton family look like hillbillies.

Still, I could not take my acceptance for granted. I did everything expected of a one-hundred-percent Canadian. I sold my company to an American. I bought a Volkswagen. I bought Indian paintings and Eskimo carvings. I even did a bit of chiselling on my own. I experienced the great silence of Sunday in Edmonton and the greater silence of Dominion Day in Trois Rivières.

I knew that to reach Ottawa as a representative of my party would mean relentless campaigning throughout the riding, and I did just that – day in, and day out, astride my Shetland pony, spreading my charisma behind me.

My first priority was to heal the ethnic wounds of the past. Doing that took considerable ingenuity. I gave a dinner for the Orange Order, the Knights of Columbus, the Sons of Freedom Doukhobours, and the Canadian Legion. Chief Dan George was the guest of honour, Rabbi Feinberg accepted my invitation to hand out the funny hats, and W. A. C. Bennett flew in to cook the sukiyaki.

During my after-dinner speech, I spoke about my vision of a Just Society, and saw toughened old veterans of two world wars break down and cry. When I spoke about participatory democracy, an old white-haired woman wearing a rosary swore she saw a halo forming around my head. I tried to deny it, but it was too late. I had the Catholic vote wrapped up.

I spoke briefly in Italian, Ukrainian, and Chinese, and held the Jewish members of the audience spellbound while I praised the reforestation of Israel in Hebrew. Then with a couple of references to "Occupied Arab Lands," I was able to win over the anti-Zionists in the crowd.

After the speech came the dancing, with music provided by the Oscar Peterson Trio. By midnight, the people of Kicking Horse Pass were ready to lynch anyone who stood against me. And so I went to Ottawa . . .

Spring Thaw '54 was way ahead of '53, thanks to Mavor being personally involved from day one. There were only nine of us in the cast, and as I had at least eight parts, most of my energy was invested in changing costumes. However, once the show closed, there wasn't a lot of other work. I did a few conventions and banquets but the Royal York disaster had really taken its toll. I was back at the Gateway through the summer, and in the fall, as it had been so slow in Toronto, I thought I would try my luck in Montreal. I did the round of agents, and then, as I had heard that there were some Ikedas living in Montreal, I decided to try to track down my old Vancouver friend, Walter. It turned out to be as easy as picking up the phone book. Within the hour, I was on his doorstep – after a thirteen-year hiatus, reunited with a childhood friend. "Let's have something we would have had back in Vancouver," he said. So we ate as if we were kids. Toast and jam. It was great to see him in such good health, with his wife, Shirley, and their two boys, but what he had to tell me about what had happened in those thirteen years was not so great.

After Pearl Harbor, they had been given forty-eight hours to move out of their homes, and into the livestock building on Hastings Street. Walter was fourteen at the time, and was allowed to leave the building during the day, to pack up possessions from the family home to be put into storage. Their house was then confiscated and Walter's elder brother Tommy was shipped east to a work camp. Walter was put on a swamping crew. His job was to gather up the luggage of the people who were being shipped east, and take it to the train station. With the rest of the family, he was then sent to a camp near Slocan, in the interior, to spend a winter of forty-degree-below temperatures under canvas. Then, because his older sister had moved east – away from the coast – before the war, Walter was allowed to follow her. He was given fifty dollars by the government, and set out on the train. His mother, for reasons best known to the Canadian government, was not allowed to accompany him. In Montreal, Walter got a job as an apprentice machinist, and soon became part of the war effort. This was not the only irony in Walter's story. All through the war years, his father was stranded in Japan; he had been there on business when the war started. In Japan, Walter's father, a Canadian, was considered an enemy alien. He, too, was interned. By the Japanese authorities.

I told Walter my story, and we reminisced a bit before he confessed that he had been a bit apprehensive about seeing me. He was no longer as religious as he had been when we were young, and as he remembered me as such a religious zealot, he wasn't sure what he should say. He needn't have worried. I was no longer even attending church.

Work in Montreal proved as scarce as it was in Toronto. I did one week-long engagement, at the Radio Hotel in Rouyn, which I got to by bus. A bus driven by a man who seemed to be steering by compass over prehistoric trails. It hadn't occurred to the agent who booked me for the Radio Hotel that I was a unilingual English-speaking comedian, and that this was a mostly unilingual French-speaking audience. I got a few chuckles here and there, but it was tough. The experience was not made easier by one of the customers deciding he wanted to be part of my act. I was doing a calypso number when a slightly drunk man emerged from the audience, with a tray loaded with upright beer bottles balanced carefully on top of his head. He made his way up onto the stage, balancing the tray of bottles, and danced slowly around me while I was performing the calypso. He was obviously captivated by the music, but it was hard to have two totally different things going on at the same time. On the other hand, he saved my show. He certainly got more applause than I did.

With the Rouyn engagement over, I decided to head back to Toronto. I stayed first at the apartment of a waitress from the Gateway Hotel, who offered to put me up if things were difficult, but as soon as I had the money and Simone had an empty room, I moved back into 18 Suffolk Street. I ended a tough year by going back to Quebec, to a job as a comedian-social director at a ski resort in Ste. Agathe des Monts. The guests of the resort spent all day every day skiing out on the hills in the cold Laurentian air. Then they came back into the main lodge, had dinner, and sat in comfortably upholstered chairs in a warm, inviting room near a glowing fireplace. The challenge for me was to perform loud enough to cover the snoring. One night, I was successful.

In show business, things can turn around on a dime. It shouldn't have surprised me that suddenly, in 1955, for no apparent reason, I was busy. There was my third venture with *Spring Thaw*, "The Wayne and Shuster Show," *Fine Frenzy*, a revue written and directed by Don Harron, and the CNE grandstand show. Oh yes, and I also did "The Ed Sullivan Show." You could say it was a turning point. From the bottom, I went straight to the top.

It was a big year for *Spring Thaw*, which moved to the old Avenue Theatre, a converted movie house on Eglinton West. This time, I did more than just perform in the show; I wrote four or five numbers, with Owen Duffy and Jack Fulton. I had met Jack through our mutual friend Owen. "You know," Owen said, "with your sense of humour, there's someone I'd like you to meet." So we headed along Bloor Street to the Chez Paree, to meet the Monsignor, a.k.a. Jack Fulton. (He was dubbed Monsignor after Bishop Fulton Sheen.)

The Chez Paree, on Bloor Street near Avenue Road, was a restaurant, but it had the feeling of a lounge. It was a great gathering place – journalists, actors, musicians, and opera singers rubbed shoulders with businessmen of all kinds, enjoying the jazz played by the excellent musicians. The Chez Paree was known as a very tolerant place, customers who at other venues might be known as drunks at the Chez Paree were accepted as eccentrics. The Monsignor held court there. It wasn't his "office" – that was in the Elliott House Hotel beverage room – but he did spend a lot of time at the Chez Paree. Jack never actually had a job. His mother, a nurse, had been very careful with her money, and somehow Jack managed without a visible income. There was also a rumour, which he vociferously denied, that he was writing speeches for someone in the provincial government. That was the only hint that he might have gainful employment. Jack was a witty, clever, and original thinker, and I could see instantly why Owen wanted me to meet him. Owen was no slouch himself. He wanted to be a writer, although he did have to take a paying job from time to time. Once, he worked for Eaton's. "They don't know what they're doing here," he said, the day after he started. Eaton's was a venerable company that had been in business for about a hundred years, and in Owen's mind, they didn't know what they were doing. Owen, it seems, was ahead of his time.

Jack and Owen had good satirical ideas, and in no time, as a team, we had written a production number to open *Spring Thaw*, a parody of a fashion show for the middle of the production, the monologue for the Member for Kicking Horse Pass, and a parody of the Academy Awards as the finale. When we presented the material to Mavor Moore we were surprised that he accepted it all. Journalists Pierre Berton and Frank Tumpane, composer Godfrey Ridout, and comedians Wayne and Shuster also contributed sketches to the show. Raymond Jessel (who later became famous for writing the "Loveboat" theme) and Marion Grudeff wrote some great music and clever lyrics, and when singer Robert Goulet joined the cast, I could see this was shaping up to be a sensational season. In 1955, Robert's career was just taking off. He had appeared in Mavor's production *Sunshine Town*, to great acclaim, was regularly on Canadian TV, and was about to make his Broadway debut. Robert was five years from his really big triumph, as Sir Lancelot in the 1960 production of *Camelot*, but you could see he was on his way. What impressed me most working with him was his professionalism – he was always willing, no matter how late it was, to keep on rehearsing until he felt we had got it right.

Spring Thaw '55 turned out to be the most exciting stage show I had ever been involved in, in spite of the fact that we were working in a converted movie theatre, and our "dressing room" was an extremely narrow passage behind a black cloth at the back of the stage. You couldn't talk while changing – the audience would have heard every word – and you had to find your way out to the parking lot if you wanted to use the washroom, which was in a trailer.

That year the show went on the longest pre-Toronto tour ever, playing cities and towns all over Ontario. In Ottawa, the Speaker of the House of Commons took the cast through the Parliament Buildings. MP Ellen Fairclough took us all to lunch, and then introduced me to the real member for Kicking Horse Pass, the member for Edmonton West. In May, we opened in Toronto, to excellent reviews, although *Toronto Star* theatre critic Nathan Cohen did suggest the Member for Kicking Horse Pass should be put out to pasture. The show ran on and on, and once the preproduction costs were paid, Mavor gave the cast a pay increase every few weeks.

After the show closed in June, I did a final season at the Gateway, leaving early to take part in the Grandstand Show at the Canadian National Exhibition. I was billed as "Canada's top comedian" (news to me) and felt some pressure in living up to the billing. For the show I developed a strong, topical monologue for the Member. I entered in character, wearing a white western suit and white Stetson hat, driving a Mercury convertible very close to the first row of people in the grandstand and just missing a security officer. He yelled at me. I yelled back at him, "I'm the Member of Parliament for Kicking Horse Pass! I'm looking for Highway 2! Get me a map and I'll get out of here!" While he got the map, I took over the audience. At the dress rehearsal, the response from the large, invited audience was everything I had hoped for.

The next afternoon, however, I received a phone call from the producer, Jack Arthur. "We've had a meeting and the feeling is your piece is too controversial," he announced. "My assistant says you have a safer monologue in the same character. We want you to do that tonight." I didn't think he was serious, but he listed his objections, which seemed endless. He didn't like references to a couple of scandals (for instance, one at the military base at Petawawa where it turned out they had horses on the payroll). He didn't like references to a ridiculous nuclear-bomb shelter sitting outside Toronto City Hall, and he also didn't like references to popular broadcaster Kate Aitken's cooking show, which I had referred to as "dangerously subversive." "Kate might be upset," he said. I pleaded with him. "After all these weeks of preparation and after a dress-rehearsal ovation, you want me to memorize and perform a totally different, bland monologue in front of twenty-five thousand people five hours from now?" I asked, not quite believing what I was hearing. "That's right," he said. "It's too late," I said. "My mind's made up," he replied. "You have to switch."

I was in a state of shock. Opening night! Every move I'd rehearsed, every line I'd written and memorized, everything was to be jettisoned. I went to the CNE grounds immediately, with the old, bland script, and began rehearsing it. As I did, the producer's assistant saw me, and with what passes for a smile in show business, said "Don't overtrain, now, Dave." Little did he know how much I wanted to kill him.

Opening night came and went. I was beside myself with frustration, knowing how it could have been. I did a second night of the bland routine, then suddenly I had an idea. I went to the producer with my costume packed in my suitcase. "This is goodbye, Jack," I said. There was a sudden look of panic. "Goodbye? What does that mean? We can't do the show without you. There's a major set and costume change happening while you are on." "Exactly, Jack," I said. "But I'm not doing what I was hired to do, so I'm not doing the show. You want a comedian to do out-of-date material, hire someone else." I walked out of his office, and kept walking toward the exit gate. I could hear him running after me. I kept on walking. As I stopped to go through the gate, Jack grabbed me, and spun me around. "Okay," he said. "Do your new monologue."

That first night back with the new monologue wasn't the joy that it should have been, but at least I was doing material that I cared about and believed in. The next night, I was back in the groove. I was in such a euphoric state that when I came off, it took me fifteen minutes to stop hyperventilating. Twenty-five thousand people laughing themselves silly. It was like that every night from then on. On the final night, not only was the Grandstand packed, but extra rows of chairs were added at ground level. The sound of that crowd when I hit the punchline and drove off into the night the final time I could never forget. I've never heard anything like it since. The whole audience was screaming, whistling, and pounding the bleachers with their feet. It was deafening. As Shakespeare would say, "such sweet thunder."

From the CNE, I went directly into rehearsals for a new revue, again at the Avenue Theatre, called *Fine Frenzy*. The cast included Don Harron, Eric House, Barbara Franklin, Bill Cole, Peter Mews, Araby Lockhart, Jane Mallet, all of them veterans of Canadian show business – and me. Don Harron had not only written most of the material for the show, but between acts, in his dressing room, he was busy writing the book for the musical version of *Anne of Green Gables*, a stage production that is still being produced all over the world.

Don and I had become professionals at roughly the same time, but he was always ahead of me. Back then, before coming to specialize in comedy, he also played leading-man roles. While I was still doing *Spring Thaw* tours, Don was already under contract to Paramount Pictures. When I was touring England with another review, Don was already playing in the West End in *Mary, Mary* with Maggie Smith. He had also played at Stratford, Ontario. My early comedy experience, performing at banquets and conventions, which eventually led me to doing what I'm doing today (banquets and conventions), was something Don didn't take up until much later. I was very glad when he moved into the convention business with his fantasy friends, Charlie Farquharson and Valerie Rosedale. When we had conflicting schedules, we could substitute for each other. *Fine Frenzy* was the beginning of a friendship that has lasted for almost fifty years.

The content of the numbers we did is very hazy in my memory – the whole cast did a parody of *Oklahoma!* entitled *Manitoba!* which included a parody of the song "Pennies from Heaven": "Every time it rains, it rains dust storms from Moose Jaw." Don did a disc jockey who lost all his records, and had to sing all the songs himself, a strong Charlie Farquharson piece, and a monologue as a clergyman, delivering a very funny sermon, which left me with my strongest memory of the run.

It was a warm night. Don and I were outside the stage door, in our costumes, waiting to start the show, when a gang of young boys arrived on the scene, and started making a horrendous racket. Don went up to them, in his clerical garb. "Are you lads from my parish?" he asked, in his best sanctimonious manner. The boys were caught off guard. "No," they said. "Then," said Don, "fuck off." It was as if a thunderbolt had hit them. They vanished in an instant.

It was during the run of *Fine Frenzy* that I got an unexpected phone call from New York. Would I do "The Ed Sullivan Show"? Ed Sullivan had hosted the CNE grandstand show, and had decided he wanted me. Doing "The Ed Sullivan Show" was considered by most folks to be the biggest break one could get in show business. Most folks. Not all folks. When I phoned home to let my mother know I would be appearing on "Ed Sullivan" the following Sunday, there was a pause at the other end of the line. Then a demure, almost wounded, response. "Must you work on the Sabbath?" she said.

I felt I must. I flew down to New York, and on that memorable Sunday afternoon at three o'clock I was sitting ready for a run-through at what is now called the Ed Sullivan Theatre. After I had waited an hour, Ed Sullivan left the stage to scamper to the washroom, breezing by me. "Don't go away, Davie," he said. "I'll get to you soon, just as soon as I'm finished editing Smith and Dale."

I could hardly believe what I was hearing. Smith and Dale were in the absolute top echelon of inspired comics. They had been together since 1900, and had spent years in big-time vaudeville, playing alongside stars from Lillian Russell to Al Jolson. Their routines were filled with malapropisms and word play. Audiences loved them. Sample patter:

DALE: Pardon me. Is this the Ethiopian National Bank?

SMITH: Yes. I'm the President.

DALE: Are you Ethiopian?

SMITH: If this was the Eagle Pants Company, would I have to be an eagle?

DALE: With your beak you could be.

Their speed of delivery was incredible, part of what made them so funny. Ed Sullivan, a former sports writer, was presuming to *edit* these geniuses. This did not look promising.

Finishing with Smith and Dale, Ed turned his attention to the internationally famous D'Oyly Carte Opera Company, which performed Gilbert and Sullivan. No doubt *The Mikado* was in need of an edit or two. "Don't go away, Davie," he said, again, as he passed by on another washroom break. "I'm going to be right with you, once I've figured out how to get those Mikado costumes through the scenery without causing a major catastrophe."

That done, Ed Sullivan faced an even bigger challenge: trying to get Nat King Cole's wife to sing on key. This lovely woman was married to one of my heroes, but she was not known as a singer, either before or after her "Ed Sullivan" debut. It was now twenty-five minutes to eight. The show went live to air at eight. "Okay, Davie," said Ed finally. "I'm ready for you. I want you to do exactly what I saw you do up in Canada." I reminded him that, when he saw me in

Canada, I had made an entrance driving down a stadium track in an open convertible, and then got into an argument with a police officer. I told him I had prepared a different start to my piece. He insisted on hearing it. When I got to a bit about Korea, he interrupted. "You can't mention Korea," he said. "We have troops there." I wanted to say "So do we" but there wasn't time. He called for a cue-card printer and we went upstairs to the theatre office.

I ran through the whole routine for him. He was amazed that I had altered references from what he had heard at the CNE. I explained that I'd changed Canadian names because the American audience would not respond – they'd have no idea what I was talking about. "You're just like a boxer who's a great success on the road," he said. "Then, when we bring him to New York, he changes his style, and he's defeated." "I have no intention of changing my style," I said. "I just want to change some words, so I can be understood."

There I was, in Ed Sullivan's office at 7:45, the clock ticking, going through my routine again, stopping and starting as Ed told the cue-card man what changes he wanted printed on the cards – cards that in a few minutes I would be reading in front of millions of television viewers. At five minutes to eight, we had to quit the editing, which was a good thing. I was confused and ready to climb walls.

As I made my way in total panic to the stage wing where I was to await my entrance cue, the most amazing calmness suddenly came over me. To this day, I don't understand where that calmness came from. It may have been from knowing that, as I walked into the valley of death, my mother would *not* be watching. As it happened, once I started with the audience, I knew I had to go back to doing the piece the way I planned to do it in the first place, and no matter what, avoid looking at the cue cards. That's what I did. An appearance that should have been a dazzling moment of glory turned out to be a traumatizing ordeal. I was learning quickly that, in the career I had chosen, nothing was ever going to be easy.

Despite the last-minute drama, my "Ed Sullivan Show" appearance was a success. Ed Sullivan seemed pleased with what I had done and I received favourable reviews in the New York newspapers – a minor miracle, given the circumstances. Back in Toronto, friends watching the show were more nervous watching it than I was doing it, but they were all proud to see a Canadian fly down to New York, walk out there, and razz the American public successfully. For my part, I was glad to get back on the plane, and come home again. I later learned from other comedians that my experience with Mr. Ed was all too typical. Ed Sullivan was no creative genius. He was a like-able, decent, charming man. A short man, with a tall budget.

Working with Johnny Wayne and Frank Shuster was a different matter entirely. We had got to know each other over the years I'd been in Toronto. I was a frequent visitor to their radio-show per-formances and vividly remember my very first visit. While doing a warm-up routine for the audience, Johnny put on a Second World War gas mask. Lumbering around the stage, with the mask's long, accordionlike breathing tube hanging, Johnny looked exactly like a lost elephant. It was hilarious. After the broadcast, I went backstage to say hello and was surprised to find police officers all over the place. The show had received a bomb threat. I asked Frank why anyone would want to bomb a comedy show. He said, "Everybody doesn't have the same taste."

Johnny and Frank waited to make the move to TV, and when they finally did make it, with their own show in 1955, they were far ahead of everyone else. Their show had wit and intelligence, it was glam-orous and exciting; they had great sets and costumes, and Johnny and Frank always looked terrific, in their tuxes, doing their patter. One day, sitting in the CBC cafeteria, we were chatting about the show. I was complimenting them on it. If ever they needed anyone to do a bit part, I said, I'd love to do it. They looked at each other, and at me. "We never thought that anyone as established as you would be interested in doing bit parts on someone else's show," they said, almost in unison. Wrong. Dead wrong. My thinking was, if a show is this good, be part of it if you can.

From that moment on, they asked over and over again. I never said "No." One of the funniest moments for me on that show came during a dress rehearsal of a Superman sketch. (Frank's cousin Joe was Superman's creator.) Johnny was playing Superman, and went into a phone booth to do the quick change from Clark Kent to Superman. In the process, his glasses slipped down his leotard into his crotch. Unable to get them out fast enough, he had to walk out of the booth with the outline of his glasses clearly visible inside his leotards. "Does it have to see, too?" Frank asked. They were both so quick on the uptake – it was part of the joy of working with them.

All my roles were small, but I was eager to do the best I possibly could. During another show, when I came back to the dressing room for a quick change, Johnny was sitting there, at the mirror. He turned and said to me, "Now, that's the way to do a part." It was his tone of voice, as if I had done something special. It made me very happy.

I found Frank and Johnny a pleasure to be with and a pleasure to work with. They were cultured, educated men, with a remarkable awareness and understanding of the world. I had met quite a number of other comedians by then, and they were a cut above all the others. Their comedy was literate, and much of it was timeless. Audiences watch Wayne and Shuster sketches today, and still laugh as they did when they first ran back in the 1950s and 1960s. "Rinse the Blood Off My Toga," in which the assassination of Julius Caesar is played as a hard-boiled detective story, and the Shakespearean baseball sketch are particular audience favourites. My own favourite was "The Picture of Dorian Wayne," their version of an Oscar Wilde story, in which Dorian makes a pact with the devil, lives as he pleases, and never gets old. In the Wayne and Shuster version Dorian is a compulsive overeater who never grows fat.

Frank and Johnny were surprisingly relaxed through the rehearsal period, when things are usually difficult. It was only when they got into the studio that Johnny, a complex man, who had a lot of

With Johnny Wayne and
Frank Shuster

free-floating anger in him, would get upset. He would be very abusive
to Frank – never to anyone else, just to Frank. One day, after watching this, I asked Frank why he put up with it. "I'll tell you why," he
said. One day, Johnny had been particularly hard on him. "Surely,
you're not going to do it that way, are you, Frank?" he said. This was
asked, in sarcastic tone, in front of the entire cast. Frank looked at
him. "I don't have to be here, you know," he replied. "I could be in
Palm Springs playing golf. I don't need this. I really don't." It was the
first time Frank hit back at Johnny. Johnny stared at him in disbelief.
He turned white, then ran from the studio, into the dressing room,
sat down, and burst into tears. He couldn't stop crying.

That, Frank said, was why he just did his job. He refused after that
to let any of Johnny's remarks get to him. Whenever Frank spoke to
me of Johnny, it was always with the greatest respect. It was never
Johnny, it was always "my partner." In his way, Frank was a giant. He
saw that Johnny needed that outlet and he was willing to absorb the
anger. With most people, the team would have broken up years ago.

Of all the things I did, *Wayne and Shuster* was the thing that
seemed to impress my father most. I never really talked to him or to
my mother about my career because, deep down, I felt they were not
interested in what I did and might not approve. Yet my father could
surprise me. I went back to Vancouver on a visit, shortly after doing
a Wayne and Shuster show. As I was riding up in the elevator with
him, in the building where he had his office, one of his fellow salesmen asked me how things were going in Toronto. "He's working with
Wayne and Shuster," my father blurted out, beaming with pride. We
had listened to Wayne and Shuster on radio together when I was just
starting out, and they had seemed a world away. Now, unbelievably,
I was working with them.

After returning to Canada following my second Christmas tour of
UN military bases in South Korea, I was asked to be a part of a
different Christmas entertainment. Sheila Billing, a former Miss
Toronto who had been on the Korea trip, guitar player Greg Curtis,
and I were invited to do a voluntary Christmas performance at the
Home for Incurable Children on Bloor Street in Toronto (as I mentioned before, they were blunter about names then). Nobody's

presentation could be less suited to an audience of children than mine. Nevertheless, I figured that, by focusing on some funny musical material and being as visual as possible, I could get by. If we had been paid, I would not have agreed to do it. I had by this time done a good number of shows in hospitals, but always for adults. I was completely unprepared for this visit to these children. The word "incurable" hadn't sunk in.

After the performance, as we made our way among the beds, meeting the children, I was overcome with admiration for the women who were caring for them. But I felt ashamed that the emotional impact on me was more than I could handle. I said goodbye to the last child, walked to the stairs, ran down to street level and out into the cool night air. I sat there, on the steps, with my head down between my knees, trying not to pass out. Breaking down and sobbing uncontrollably would have helped, but I was determined it wouldn't happen – not there, anyway. Sheila, meanwhile, had gone among the children in their beds, giving a genuine caring smile to each one, and presenting to the most unfortunate child, a small boy with extreme encephalitis, the bouquet she had been given earlier in the evening. She was still there, spreading joy, while I sat overwhelmed on the steps outside, trying to get the blood back into my head.

These Christmas shows were all moving in their way. But there was always a lot of commercial sentimentality about Christmas that I didn't care for. I finally decided I had to do something about it, and concocted a Christmas piece, a parody of Dylan Thomas's *A Child's Christmas in Wales*.

A Child's Christmas in Hogtown

One Christmas was so much like another in my early years. I can never remember if it snowed for nine weeks when I was eleven, or snowed for eleven weeks when I was nine. Anyway, who cares?

This Christmas I'm tellin' you about, I was twelve and it snowed for six bloody months. I remember bein' awakened that

Christmas mornin' by a terrible racket coming from Mom's bedroom. She was having a fight with her new boyfriend, Tyrone Gabortnik.

It was lucky for him I woke up when I did. Mom would have killed him.

I couldn't believe the load of stuff I got that Christmas. A set of handcuffs from my grandpa, a book on infectious diseases from Mom, a roll of film from an aunt who thought I had a camera.

What a Christmas. We were supposed to chip in and get Grandpa a hearing aid. But it was too much money. So instead, we stopped talkin' to him.

I just started countin' my Christmas presents when the local priest came in makin' his regular Christmas visit. He came and sat next to me in the livin' room.

The next thing I know, there's a commotion goin' on in the kitchen. I heard Mom telling Tyrone, "You do those dishes! There's no way I'm gonna leave that priest in there alone with my twelve-year-old son!"

The priest must have heard it too. He took his hand off my knee.

At that point, my buddy Arnie arrived.

He came over to ask me if I would go around with him on Boxing Day, and do the "Dying Mother" sob story door to door, and sell off all our Christmas presents. The year before, we made enough money to buy eight cases of beer. We hid the beer till New Year's Day, when all the stores were closed, and we doubled our money.

While I was talkin' to Arnie, the doorbell kept ringin'. It was two smilin' Jehovah's Witnesses. "Come in," says Arnie. "We're all perverts here, and horny as hell." They took off so fast, we only hit them with one of our snowballs. But it was a real hard one. Not much snow. Mostly ice.

We were just about to shut the door when we noticed a beaten-up old geezer staggerin' through the blizzard, holdin' a half-empty bottle of rye. He was so hung over and had such a swollen eye, I recognized him right away. It was my biological dad, out on parole. He looked me in the eye, almost. And passed out.

When he came to, Bio-Dad offered a dollar to anyone who would go outside into the snow and find his teeth.

That's when Tyrone insisted we had to play charades. We made up two teams. Mom, Tyrone, and Bio-Dad on one team. Arnie and me on the other. Someone on the other team had to act out a movie title. Dad said, "I can handle that!" With that, he put on his hat and coat and walked out the door and into the howling blizzard.

We never saw him again. Too bad in a way. We eventually figured out the movie title, Gone with the Wind. *For once in his life, Dad could have been a winner.*

What a Christmas.

Conventions, banquets, and television appearances were flying by, and soon it was time to prepare for another *Spring Thaw*. The show had always run with one female understudy and one male understudy, it was all the budget could run to. This year, Robert Goulet was leaving partway through the run to honour another commitment. Before leaving on a business trip to England, Mavor Moore had arranged for an understudy, Bill Yule, to take over all of Robert's roles. Then, the night after Bill Yule took over from Robert, cast member Andy Macmillan's father died. Andy left the show immediately, to go to his father's funeral in Montreal. After a scramble, Dora Mavor Moore found someone to replace Andy. An opera singer who had never done a revue, knew nothing about comedy, and had never heard of *Spring Thaw*.

He spent the day with the cast, trying desperately to remember where to move, how to speak, and what to sing. We groped our way through the evening performance, only to learn that the father of

The cast of Spring Thaw, *1956. Back row, left to right: Andy MacMillan, Dave Broadfoot, Barbara Hamilton, Robert Goulet, Diana Laumer, Paul Kligman, Sheila Billing. Front row, left to right: Peter Mews, Margo McKinnon*

another member of the cast, Paul Kligman, had died. Paul left the next morning for Winnipeg. After a frantic search, Dora found another opera singer to replace Paul. Paul was a comedian. The opera singer wasn't. He had no idea how to deliver comedy, and there was no time for him to memorize anything. He went on stage with the scripts in his hands, as we gently pushed him from one position to another, hoping for the best.

The next morning, we received a panicky phone call informing us that another cast member, Peter Mews, had come down with a virulent case of laryngitis. He had no voice whatsoever, and would be unable to perform for at least two or three days. I immediately went to Dora, and asked if we could please give customers their money back and close the show for a few days. Dora would have none of it. I don't know where she found them, but another opera singer showed up to replace Peter. The opera singer didn't know the show, had never seen a revue, didn't know how to talk, and had no sense of humour. Dora was batting a thousand on the opera-singer front.

There I was, the only original male member of the cast, with four replacements (three opera singers and a dancer), only one of whom had the remotest idea of what should be happening on stage. The week was the most catastrophic theatrical experience I have ever lived through, an utter humiliation. I know the show is supposed to go on, but this was now hardly the show we were supposed to be going on with. I felt this was very unfair to the audience, who had paid good money to see a show that had a wonderful image. We'd had great reviews, but what they saw that week had nothing to do with what they had bought tickets for. It was a disaster every night, for a whole week. At one point, when I ran off stage between numbers, I looked in the mirror and the crimson blush of mortification was showing right through the Max Factor.

Not knowing the workings of Dora Mavor Moore's mind, it took a long time to figure out why all the replacements were opera singers. I came to the conclusion that all the actors Dora called sensed what they would be getting themselves into and firmly refused to have any part of it. The opera singers were either naive or desperately hungry. Let's say "hungry." When the terror-filled week was over, the indomitable Dora issued one of her classic comments on professionalism. "The only time an actor leaves a theatre for a funeral, Dave," she said, "is when it's for his own." If only that were true.

I still can't figure out how we managed to get all the performers, musicians, and instruments into just two cars and one station wagon, but we did. That's how the Mart Kenney Show made its way across Canada in September 1956. The car I was in was dedicated to the bass fiddle. There was just about enough room left for the humans, three of us – the saxophone player, the vocalist, and me. We took the northern route across Ontario, through Haileybury, Cobalt, and Iroquois Falls, and then headed on to play places like Dryden, Moose Jaw, and, memorably, Melville, Saskatchewan, where the man who had booked us took one look and said, "You didn't bring your piano?" "We did," I said, "It was a Yamaha. One of its tires went flat and we had to abandon it." After much scurrying around, a piano was produced from the local school auditorium, and the show went on.

Poster for the 1956 extended tour of Western Canada, accomplished with just three automobiles and one laundry truck

Mart Kenney and his Western Gentlemen are a legend in Canadian show business, and wherever we appeared people viewed him as a personal friend. He was very down-to-earth, no airs and graces, and very relaxed on stage. You could not dislike him. There was nothing about him to dislike. He had toured the country from one end to the other for years, and had built up a great deal of admiration and respect in his audiences, particularly the ex-servicemen and women he had entertained in the Second World War.

I learned many things from Mart. For instance, never be distracted by making unnecessary stops en route to your destination. No matter what, get to your destination. *Then* get distracted. I asked Mart about the semi-drunk people who came up to him night after night, looked him defiantly in the eye, and said things like: "You don't remember me, do you? We danced to your orchestra on our honeymoon." Mart was always infinitely patient and courteous. He taught me never to use that type of greeting to anyone, to never say,

"You don't remember me" or "You may not remember me, but . . ." or "I know you won't remember me." Never put a person on the defensive, he said. Just put your hand out, look them in the eye, and say your name. I've been doing that ever since.

On the tour, I got to see places I had not seen before, and learn more about the country. It's funny the small things you remember, like eating in a Banff restaurant, and one of the band ordering steak. The waiter asked him how he wanted it done. "I'd like it well done," the musician replied. The waiter stared at him in stunned disbelief. "Mister," he said, "you've never *tasted* steak."

Waterton Lakes at Glacier National Park, on the B.C.–Alberta–Montana border was the standout. We spent a precious day off in Waterton and were invited to a barbecue in the home of a local Mart Kenney fan. Our host had caught well over the legal limit of rainbow trout. "How many?" someone asked him. "Thirty-five," said our host just as the local Mountie walked through the door. Without missing a beat, he continued: ". . . years ago, I was out catching fish and having no luck . . ." A masterpiece of ad libbing, coupled with exquisite timing. I love exquisite timing.

I had read a short piece by humorist Eric Nicol in a published collection of his Vancouver *Province* newspaper columns. Entitled *Nicol of the Mounted*, it was written as an adventurous detective story, with the Mountie trying to track down a dangerous Wench of the North. As soon as I read it, I contacted Eric Nicol in Vancouver and asked how he would feel about me turning it into a performance piece. Eric agreed and I was soon sending him embarrassingly small royalty cheques. Embarrassment, at that point, was all I could afford.

That was the birth of Sergeant Renfrew, a character I would first perform in the 1957 revue, *Clap Hands*, produced by John Gray and Araby Lockhart. Little did I know that, forty years later, that character would have gone from Sergeant down to Corporal, then from Corporal back up to Sergeant, those three stripes presented to me personally, at Mountie HQ in Ottawa, by the then Chief Commissioner Robert Simmons. Then came the promotion of Renfrew's dog, Cuddles, from Constable to Corporal. Another Renfrew promotion, from Sergeant to Staff-Sergeant, came from Commissioner Norman

An early performance of
Sergeant Renfrew, Club
Kingsway, Toronto, 1957

Inkster. Next came the presentation of the Long Service Award, again
from Commissioner Inkster. And then, in 1996, under Commissioner
Philip Murray, Renfrew would make it to Sergeant-Major. All ranks
honorary, of course. Today, an entire wall of my office is covered with
plaques, awards, and trophies from the Royal Canadian Mounted
Police – no small thanks to Eric Nicol. The premise was everything.

The Fay Ding Wao *[pronounced Wow!]* Case

I'm Corporal Renfrew.
The story you are about to hear was taken from Mountie files
and until now has not been missed.
I was sitting in my lonely log cabin on the fourteenth floor of
Mountie headquarters with my invincible canine assistant,

Cuddles, when suddenly the Chief was on the intercom. Unfortunately, it could not take his weight.

"Renfrew," *he said*, "a beautiful Chinese industrial spy by the name of Fay Ding Wao has kidnapped the Minister of Culture and threatened to have her way with him unless he reveals the secret formula that allows Canadians to party all night and still function the next morning.

"The Minister had no choice. He had to turn over the secret formula. He couldn't face the alternative. He has always considered his body to be a temple. In fact, some call it a cathedral. I'd call it a chapel. Well, at the very least, a Christian Science reading room."

"I get it, Chief," *I replied*. "If Fay Ding Wao gets away with that formula, it could jeopardize the whole future of our Canadian way of life."

"Exactly, Renfrew. Once Fay Ding Wao got her hands on that formula, she let the Minister go. Then she hijacked a helicopter, then bus-jacked a Greyhound, then cab-jacked a taxi. And finally, black-jacked a lumberjack. She is now believed to be hiding out somewhere due north of us."

I handed the Chief a map. "All right, Chief," *I said*, "show me her position."

The Chief misunderstood.

When I regained consciousness, I harnessed up my snow-mobile, grabbed all my Chinese equipment, my chopsticks, a bag of Minute Rice, my ping-pong bats . . . and balls, and headed north.

The incredible Cuddles found a hidden trail. We followed the trail till we came to a fork. We stopped. Picked up the fork. It was a cheap plastic fork from a take-out restaurant.

I knew I was on her tail. Her trail!

We kept pushing on through the bush till Cuddles led me to an abandoned theatre that some opportunist had just converted into a barn.

I flung the door open, and there she was. Fay Ding Wao. The most inscrutable woman I have ever seen. Picture the eyes of Tammy Faye Baker. The hair of Margaret Thatcher. The body of Mao Tse Tung. In no way was she scrutable.

I demanded the secret formula. She pretended she didn't understand. I began to frisk her. She really didn't understand. She pressed her lips against mine. All my years of Mountie training flashed before me. She had the kind of lips a Mountie dreams of . . . One on the top, one on the bottom.

Suddenly, from out of her incredible hairdo, she snatched the secret formula, shoved it in her mouth, and ate it! Then she pressed herself against me again.

My hopes were crushed.

So were my ping-pong balls.

The evidence was gone. I needed a confession. I told her there was a price on her head. She told me there was a discount for men in uniform. I became so frustrated, I was feeding Alpo to my snowmobile and trying to kick-start my dog.

But at least that secret formula is still secret. Canada's culture has not been compromised.

As for Fay Ding Wao, she's still being held for questioning. Every chance I get. A Mountie always get his . . . man.

In late 1957, I was offered a contract to become the social director of a new resort hotel being built by a group of Canadians in Ocho Rios, Jamaica. Among other things, the owners wanted me to produce the hotel's nightly entertainment. It was my first opportunity to act as a producer, and as I had never been to Jamaica, I thought it would be an interesting adventure. I set off with high hopes.

You got to the Arawak Hotel, on the other side of the island from Kingston, along a long road that took you through a magnificent cathedral-like grove of trees. Ocho Rios, now a large tourist destination, was then only just beginning to develop. It turned out to be a very tough job, as I was responsible for everything in the hotel's world of entertainment – daytime activities, social activities, nighttime entertainment – the whole thing. I was working all day every day, and all night, too. I produced and appeared in two stage shows a week. All the other performers were native Caribbeans, except for a husband-and-wife dance team I suspected were hiding out from the U.S. police. The band, a group of top-notch musicians, was from Kingston. The show dancers, with their choreographer Mike Quashie, were from Trinidad.

The hotel's opening night was also the night of our first big show. We had rehearsed everything to within an inch of its life, and it went off well. The show over, and the hotel guests well into their own

*On the beach at the
Arawak Hotel, Ocho Rios,
Jamaica, 1957*

dancing mode, I walked over to the hotel lounge to take a break. Some plantation owners beckoned me over. "We want you to know how terribly much we enjoyed your very funny pieces," the woman said to me in a very tony British accent. "You were absolutely delightful." Then her husband chimed in. "We call those other parts of the show nigger stuff." I looked at him in stunned silence, then turned and walked out into the warm Caribbean night, feeling as if someone had just shoved a knife into me. It was 1957, Jamaica was not yet independent from Britain, and there were still many British plantation owners living on the island. This was their attitude. The hotel management turned out to be not much better.

After the two-a-week stage shows had been rolling along for a while, one of the dancers came to me. He explained that they earned very little for what they did, and that while they were not asking for more, they would like something they were accustomed to on show nights: a bottle of rum to share among them. "Could you ask the hotel manager if this is possible?" he said. "No, I can't," I replied, "but I can arrange a meeting for you with the manager, and when you make your request, I'll be there backing you up." The next morning, we met with the manager, a white, native-born Jamaican. When he heard the request, he acted as if some monumental, earth-shattering event was taking place. "Oh, I don't think so," he said. "I don't think there is any possible way we can arrange a thing like that, is there, Mr. Broadfoot?" I looked him in the eye. "Why not?" I asked. The manager stared at me in disbelief, then turned and walked away.

The next night, and every performance night thereafter, there was a bottle of rum in the dancers' dressing room. But my rapport with the management had come to an end. The manager noticed that what little free time I had, I spent with the waiters and other hotel staff, nearly all of whom were black. Apparently, he found this quite upsetting.

I was called into the owner's office one day. "Dave," he said, "our feeling is, if you stay here, eventually our workers will go on strike. So it's up to you. You can either leave or be fired." It was Grade Nine all over again. My contract was for a year. I had only been there five months, but I immediately fired myself. The next morning, during breakfast, I let one of the waiters know I would be leaving in a couple of days. Within minutes, wherever I looked, I could see people sobbing. I was incredibly touched. I hurried off to my cabana, to be alone and collect my thoughts. The chambermaid, who was making up my room, would not look at me. When she finally did, she burst into tears. I felt terrible. What was there I could say? "I'm leaving," I said, "but I'll be back." It was a lie. A white lie.

I flew from Jamaica to New York, and found a cheap hotel on West 45th Street just off Times Square, one block from where my merchant navy "tenosynivitus" hotel had been. I had decided to go to New York, rather than return to Canada, because I wanted to find out whether I could produce the kind of material that would keep Americans laughing for an hour at a time, the way I could Canadians. I was aware that not knowing the local concerns, I would be facing a sizable disadvantage. All I was sure of was that I spoke a similar language. Even though I had asked myself where professionalism ends and masochism begins, I still wanted to put myself to the test. The first challenge was the depressing but necessary process of visiting booking agents and auditioning for them. With my green card in hand, I headed over to the Brill Building, which at that time was crawling with agents, and started knocking on doors.

I went into one office and introduced myself. "Broadfoot, Broadfoot," the guy mused. "The name doesn't work. How about, just off the top of my head, Dannie Dixon?" No talk of work, just change the name. There is no adequate way to describe the mortifying experience of doing comedy for a hard-nosed booking agent in an empty office, with a telephone that somehow knows how to ring during your punchlines. I found a lot of the agents, to put it mildly, to be second-class human beings.

"What do ya do, kid? What do ya do?" one demanded as I sat down.

"Well, I'm a comedian."

"Do you sing?"

"No."

"Well, do ya dance, what do ya do? Juggling?"

"No."

"You don't do juggling, you don't sing, you don't dance. What do ya do? What kind of novelty do you have?"

"Well," I struggled to tell him, "I'm a verbal comedian. I talk."

He looked at me as if this was a new concept, one he couldn't quite understand.

"What do ya mean, ya talk?"

"I'm a talking comedian."

"Well, give me some of your talk. Let's hear your talk."

So, in the empty room, with the agent sitting at his desk, I launched into a routine. Just as I came to the first punchline, the phone rang. Naturally, he picked it up.

"What do ya mean the costumes aren't there? What do ya mean she hasn't got her costumes? We shipped them. Was she at the stage door? She said she was gonna wait at the stage door!"

He hung the phone up, angry.

"Okay, kid, go ahead," he said.

I launched in again, and the phone rang again.

"She can't pull that stuff. I told her it was three shows a night. She knew damn well it was three shows a night."

Down the phone went again.

It was the worst ordeal possible, trying to imagine an audience out there laughing, and you were looking at this poker-faced individual who understood the word "commission" and that's all he understood. Those New York agents could be pretty scary people. Mind you, I was meeting the bottom level, but I didn't know anyone, so what else could I do? One performance on "The Ed Sullivan Show" had not made Dave Broadfoot a household name.

I did a few minutes of comedy in one office, when the agent cut me short. "I can't do anything for you, kid," he said. They call you kid, even if you are fifty years old. "I tell you, they have this place downtown, where they have auditions on a regular basis. You wanna go down and try it?"

He didn't volunteer the address, so I asked.

"Number One Fifth Avenue," he said.

I went down there and auditioned, a total stranger, and they hired me. Howie Krantz, from Gateway days, now a successful New York lawyer, drew up a contract for me, and I opened the following Tuesday. The next morning, I had a phone call at my hotel. It was the agent who had reluctantly divulged the Number One address. "Where's my commission, kid?" was all he wanted to know.

Number One Fifth Avenue was a small, elegant nightclub with a relaxed ambience, and a reputation for taking a chance on new performers. Comedians Ted Zeigler, Harvey Korman, and Phyllis Diller were all just getting started then, and they all played there. The music was supplied by two concert grands facing each other and played by two terrific piano players.

Generally, it was a good place to perform, but I also remember it for giving me one of the most challenging nights of my career. I had launched into a Renfrew routine, which I was trying out on an American audience for the first time, when it became clear that I would not be the only performer that evening.

"It was the schooner Hesperus, that sailed the wintry sea," a woman's voice boomed out. I looked out into the audience and saw a woman sitting with two men, obviously feeling the effects of their hospitality. I pressed on. "My assignment was to track down a dangerous Wench of the North . . ." Not to be outdone, the woman kept up her recitation. "The skipper had taken his daughter, to bear him company." She knew the words, which was unfortunate, as this was a long poem. We both kept going, in competition with each other.

There was no malice in the woman, she was just having the time of her life. But the audience was hearing an odd mix of lines.

ME:	*I had to question Michelle's sister . . .*
CUSTOMER:	*to bear him company . . .*
ME:	*I knew she had a French name . . .*
CUSTOMER:	*Hesperus! . . .*
ME:	*She was twenty-one . . .*
CUSTOMER:	*her bosom white as hawthorn buds . . .*
ME:	*I forgot the question.*
CUSTOMER:	*I can weather the toughest gale!*
ME:	*I was using the German sled. The dogs were in the rear . . .*
CUSTOMER:	*through the whistling sleet and snow . . .*
ME:	*and mush!*

It was all I could do not to disintegrate into hysterical laughter. The trouble with having a heckler when you are doing a character routine is that you can't drop out of character. It's one of the real difficulties with doing characterizations in a nightclub. If you are doing stand-up, as yourself, you can stop and go to work on the heckler and put them out of action, which I have done many times. But in the context of doing a character and telling a story, you can't do it. You have to go on to the bitter end, which I did. And so did she. The closing line of "The Wreck of the Hesperus" was also the punchline for my performance. "God save us all from a death like this." When we were finished, we both got a round of applause.

My engagement at Number One Fifth Avenue ran for several weeks, and during that time I got to know the singer on the bill with me, who introduced me to two businessmen I had seen in the audience many times. They seemed to be her backers. They were very friendly, and invited me to their suite in midtown Manhattan. When we entered their very luxurious apartment, I couldn't help noticing there were several very, very attractive young women already there. They responded to every whim of the two businessmen. A few days later, the singer told me her two friends really liked me. "That's nice," I said. "You don't understand," she replied, "they really like you. They want to talk to you about your future." I met with her backer friends, and sure enough, they told me I could make it big in show business with their help. I was flattered that these two businessmen would be willing to invest in my future, but to my eyes, they both had criminal written all over them. I figured I'd be better off starving. I don't mind starving, I do mind Mafia.

I was saved from offending these two refugees from the pages of Damon Runyon by a perfect bit of timing. In early 1958, a telegram arrived from Bernie Rothman in Montreal, a VTWCMABM, Very Talented Writer Composer Much Admired By Me. He invited me to appear in a new stage revue he had conceived, *Off Limits*. Written by the hottest young English-language comedy writers in the country, John Aylesworth, Frank Peppiatt, Sol Ilson, Bernie Rothman, and Allan Mannings, the revue was to be directed by one of my favourite people in show business, Norman Jewison. I said yes without hesitation, and left New York to spend one of the most enjoyable summers

(Above) In Off Limits, *with Jack*
Creley, Montreal, 1958
(Right) *Bragging about my wrist TV,*
with Sammy Sales lugging the antenna

of my life at the Mountain Playhouse, a small theatre on the top of Mount Royal. To put the icing on the cake, it was my one opportunity to work with a wonderful Toronto comedian, Sammy Sales. Sammy specialized in character comedy, and was not unlike the silent screen star Harry Langdon. We did a sketch together about "wrist TV": I wore a tiny television set on my wrist, and Sammy followed laboriously behind holding its huge TV antenna.

My "free" afternoons were spent working with writer Ron Clarke on a TV sitcom about a window cleaner who had an interesting perspective on other people's lives. It was a good premise, with endless possibilities, but we were not able to sell it. When *Off Limits* closed, at the end of the summer, I set off to Toronto, to conduct auditions for a new revue. I did not know it, but my life was about to change direction.

Chapter 5

PARTNERS IN TIMING

We first met in an empty banquet room in the King Edward Hotel in Toronto. Jean Templeton had come to audition for a cabaret revue I had agreed to produce with Montrealer Jack Greenwald. She was blond, beautiful, bright – and also, it turned out, a terrific comedienne.

What Jean did not know, as she got ready to perform her audition pieces, was that I was getting desperate about this show. It was all Jack's idea – although you could hardly call it an idea, as all he had was a title, *Poise 'n' Ivy*, and a location, Café André, in Montreal. Jack wanted a revue to replace his enormously successful cabaret revue *Up Tempo*, which had had a long run and was about to close. I had liked the idea of doing a revue at Café André, one of the few good English-language cabaret rooms in Montreal, and began planning for it right away. It was only when I began calling around that I discovered that none of the performers I had in mind was available. That was when I learned that there is something harder than doing auditions – supervising auditions.

Of all the people who auditioned that day at the King Edward, Jean was the standout. She was unassuming, eager, and very well prepared. She first did a characterization of an overconfident Anglo-Saxon dowager. A moment later, she had transformed herself into a precocious four-year-old child. Her ability to switch voices and physical mannerisms in a nanosecond was uncanny. I was bowled over by the voices, and by the authority and accuracy of her characterizations, and had that sense of awe that comes when one is in the presence of genuine talent. When I discovered that she had written all her audition pieces herself, I was more than impressed. I was smitten. The remarkable combination of beauty, intelligence, and talent was quite overwhelming to all who were present. Namely me. Naturally, I hired her.

I never did discover the reason Jack Greenwald decided to call the show *Poise 'n' Ivy*. It made no sense to me. We had no poise and the only Ivy I knew was a Billie Holiday impersonator, who wasn't in the show. We had just started read-throughs, and things were beginning to take shape, when Jack called from Montreal. He announced that *Up Tempo* wasn't going to close after all. My heart sank. "There's no problem," Jack said. "I'll run both shows simultaneously." He had hired the Montreal Studio Playhouse for us. With that news, my heart sank even lower. Everything was planned for the intimate and casual environment of cabaret, not the more formal atmosphere of the theatre. My instinct was to pay everyone the union rate for having signed contracts and cancel the whole thing. Jack insisted that we should go ahead.

Although worried, I was still determined to give it my best effort, so we made our way to Montreal and began rehearsals. I knew we had some strong solo pieces, but as we went along rehearsing, my anxiety kept building. Building to such a point that, when the opening-night performance was over, I went into my dressing room, locked the door, and completely disintegrated. It made no sense, but I could not stop crying. That disintegration is one of the five greatest embarrassments of my life. As for the show itself – all right, six greatest embarrassments.

The one good thing about *Poise 'n' Ivy* was meeting Jean. What began as a working relationship quickly became a romance, the first really serious romance of my life. I had had other girlfriends, but it was soon clear to me that Jean was different. She was full of ideas, curious, creative, with a great sense of adventure, particularly adventure of the mind. Jean took delight in discussing almost anything. But she balanced her brightness with great humanity and warmth, accepting people right off, uncritically, for what she found in them.

She was very basic in that regard. She really liked people, and once she became your friend, she was extremely loyal.

It always seemed to me that Jean was formed in reaction to her parents. Irwin and Mae Robb were decent and well-educated people, but they were typically conventional North Torontonians. They had none of Jean's brightness or her free spirit. I think they must have wondered sometimes whether they had a changeling child, because Jean was so unlike them in every way. Irwin was an English teacher and known on the street where they lived as "a scholar," while Mae had a reputation for being delicate. Keeping up appearances mattered to her. Jean could not have cared less. One day, after an argument, her mother locked her in her room. Jean climbed out of the window, down the drainpipe, and at the age of seventeen walked out of her parents' lives. She never went back home to live, although she eventually re-established a very good relationship with both her mother and father. When I met her, she had already been married once, to Hugh Templeton, who was not in show business. That marriage had not lasted long, and was over by the time I met her, but Jean's career as a comedienne was just getting started. She had produced a show that ran at the Royal Ontario Museum theatre, *Now We Are Six* (no relation to the book by A. A. Milne), which was a commercial failure but had shown that she was a talented writer. She had also been to acting school, and had very effectively portrayed a motorcycle moll in *The Bloody Brood*, a very low-budget Canadian movie, produced and directed by Julian Roffman.

Soon, we were never apart. When *Poise 'n' Ivy* closed in 1958, and I was invited to take part in the Vancouver International Festival, in a revue called *Jubilee*, I did not hesitate to recommend Jean, and we were both hired on as members of a very large cast. Together we headed out to Vancouver, rented rooms in a very pleasant home where English Bay turns into False Creek, and set to work, writing and rehearsing.

Our attitudes toward comedy were very similar; the things that made Jean laugh made me laugh, and we would test ideas out on each other. One night I went to Jean's room to discuss a sketch idea. Jean had already gone to bed, so I ended lying on top of the other half of the double bed, only to have the whole bed crash down

*With Paul Kligman and
Corinne Conley in* Jubilee,
1959 stage production

onto the floor and its huge headboard topple down on me. Early the next morning, we were evicted – either for immorality or for breaking the furniture, perhaps for both. Fellow cast members quickly found us another place to stay.

Rehearsing *Jubilee* became an uncomfortable experience. For some reason, all through rehearsals, the director, Brian Macdonald, who previously had enormous success with the McGill University satirical revue *My Fur Lady*, made life extremely difficult for Jean. I felt so lucky to be involved with someone so gifted and attractive that it was a shock to see the way Brian treated her. He would give Jean a sketch to perform, then, when she had memorized it and rehearsed it, take her out of it and give it to somebody else. He continued this perverse treatment throughout the entire rehearsal period and on into the run of the revue. I had never experienced anything like this from a director before. It wasn't direction. It was sadism. I half-suspected that he was trying to teach me a lesson: don't solicit work for your partner. Many people would have quit, but Jean stuck it out, even though it was really hard on her. All her solos were taken away, and she was left to perform only small roles as part of the company. Under the circumstances, she did extremely well.

Months later, when we were back in Toronto, Jean and I ran into Brian Macdonald in a restaurant on Bloor Street. He was sitting at a table near the door and we could not avoid speaking to him. The conversation was brief and awkward. Brian suddenly looked straight at Jean and said, "You really suffered in that show, didn't you?" He looked almost pleased. "That was what I wanted," he added. "I wanted you to suffer for everything you might achieve." Today, miraculously, Brian Macdonald is still alive. And highly regarded at that.

During the *Jubilee* run, my feelings for Jean were growing by leaps and bounds. I had a hunch she might be feeling the same way, so I decided to take her home to meet my mother. I hadn't said anything to Jean, but I knew I wanted to marry her. One Saturday, after rehearsal, we returned to our lodgings on West Pender Street to change before heading off for the big visit. Jean went to her room, and fifteen minutes later there was a knock on my door. I opened it, and there stood Jean – lovely, very attractive, tanned, blonde, vivacious – wearing an unbelievably skimpy (at least two sizes too small) bright scarlet dress. Her breasts, squeezed into the dress, were desperately trying to force their way out, and were on the brink of success. All that occurred to me was, What will my mother think?

Maybe my sensitivity to appropriate attire had been affected by years spent in the clothing business. Maybe I was just too Baptist. Jean, standing there, beaming, was unaware of her provocative appearance. To my eye, her apparel would have been appropriate for a very different kind of young woman, perhaps on her way to pose for a swimsuit calendar or audition for a *Playboy* centrefold. Maybe an audition for a receptionist in a small-town house of ill repute. It seemed to me to be not exactly the right look for an audition as possible daughter-in-law of a dedicated, orthodox, fundamentalist Baptist.

"What's wrong?" Jean asked, sensing my stupefaction. At that moment, I wished I could disappear into another dimension for an hour or two. "My mother has colour allergies," I muttered. "Extremely bright red is a problem for her."

"What's the real problem?" Jean asked.

"I just want things to go . . . I want her to see the real you," I managed to get out. Silently, Jean gave me a look of subdued fury. She turned, contemptuously, and headed back to her room. Five minutes later she reappeared, ready for North Vancouver, wearing an expression that was at one and the same time insulted, wounded, and cowed – but not wearing the flaming red sex-bomb dress. My mother loved Jean the instant they met, and was quick to compliment her on her lovely beige suit.

We had only known each other a couple of months when I asked her to marry me but she said yes without hesitation. We decided to hold the wedding at Bloor Street United Church, at Bloor and Huron in Toronto, and met with the cleric, who, in the manner of the day, tried to give us what he thought was sound marital advice. I was six years older than Jean, he said, stating the obvious. He then chose to point out that, when I was losing my virility, Jean would be at her sexual peak. We would have to deal with this, he said. He had

With Jean Templeton

no suggestions on how, but he did have other advice. "Keep your priorities straight," he said to me. "Don't spend your money on other things when your wife needs a new foundation garment." Why, I thought – as I sat there with Jean in his tiny office trying not to laugh – is this cleric giving me advice about corsets?

The wedding took place in the fall of 1959. Only Jean's parents, Jack Fulton, and another friend, Louise Glennie, attended as guests. The reception was at the Park Plaza Hotel, and when it was over, Jean and I went straight back to work. We moved into a small apartment in the heart of the city, at Church and Wellesley, and settled into a life of undomesticity. All our time was spent focused on our writing. One day, as we were talking about cleaning the apartment, Jean went to a cupboard and produced a vacuum cleaner. She set it on the floor near the bedroom door. Then she had an idea for a sketch. Five days later, the vacuum was still sitting there, unmoved and unused.

Jean's writing was very exciting to me, because it was not derivative. Whatever she wrote was totally original. She would have a blasé couple, meeting for the first time at a dance party in a beautiful underground bunker, oblivious to the fact that nuclear bombs were falling in the Third World War; or a sketch in which a big amoeba tries to establish a romantic relationship with a small amoeba; or Pyramus and Thisbe, with the Berlin Wall dividing them. They were always slightly oddball ideas, with a real freshness to them.

We would write our own individual material, and also write as a team. This proved challenging, exhilarating, and exhausting. Whichever one of us came up with the concept or premise for a sketch would write out the first draft, making it as funny as possible. Then the other one would go through it and try to make it funnier. It worked well. The only time things got a bit off-track was when I brought in my old friend from Montreal, Bernie Rothman, to join us in our writing efforts. I soon noticed a high level of discomfort between Bernie and Jean. I have no idea what the problem was. All I do know is that they were both smokers, and by the end of the writing session, even though the apartment windows were open, I had trouble finding either of them in the thick clouds of smoke. As I checked the street to be sure that no fire trucks had been called by a well-meaning neighbour, it was clear to me that this writing trio was not going to work. I had thought that the more people there were involved in the creation of comedy, the funnier the comedy would be. This time it didn't turn out that way, and the writing was going to have to be done by just the two of us, Jean and me.

[House hunting – *Dave* as a real estate salesman, *Jean* as a prospective buyer]

DAVE: *Seven bedrooms. Isn't this great?*

JEAN: *Oh, yes, but we only have one little boy. He'll be three in June.*

DAVE: *Ah, yes. But I'm sure you'll be adding to your family.*

JEAN: *No. I like this cupboard, though. George told me to check the cupboards.*

DAVE: *Mrs. Freebly, that's your living area. The cupboards are in the Togetherness area.*

JEAN: *Togetherness area?*

DAVE: *Yes. That's the spot where you line up together in front of the bathroom door.*

JEAN: *But George wants a split level.*

DAVE: *You'll love this supermatic kitchen. It does all the housework for you.*

JEAN: *But what would I do with my husband?*

DAVE: *I'm sure we could work something out.*

JEAN: *Say, do I hear running water?*

DAVE: *That's the trout stream.*

JEAN: *Oh, George would love that. A trout stream in the backyard.*

DAVE: *Actually, it's in the basement.*

JEAN: *In the basement? A trout stream?*

DAVE: *That's what the builder called it the last time it happened. Isn't it a gem of a home?* [A loud sound of cracking wood] *Mrs. Freebly . . . did you say split level, Mrs. Freebly? Let me take you on another tour of this house.*

Publicity shot with Jean, long before the hernia

The switch from solo writing and performing was a big step. Jean was pleased to join me, but I think she always retained a feeling that we were not equal, which was not my feeling at all. One day, she made a drawing and handed it to me. "This is you and me," she said. She had drawn a great giant, standing there holding the hand of a little girl. We were now spending all our life together: discussing ideas, writing them, rehearsing them, performing them, going home, trying to sleep, and starting all over again the next day. At the beginning, I had no idea how tough it was going to be, being married to your on-stage partner.

As a comedy duo, we were in demand, doing three sketches a week on a CBC network radio show, "Tempo." Then, as we slugged away at our radio spots, we were asked to audition for something for which I had no ability whatsoever: a television show for children, "Junior Round-up," which was later renamed "Razzle Dazzle." When I saw the line-up of other performers asked to audition, I thought we had as much chance as two kosher caterers in the Vatican. But to our amazement, we got the job. I later asked the producer why he chose us. "You two were the only ones who didn't talk down to the children," he said. We were the show's hosts, appearing with puppeteers John and Linda Keogh. Jean and I only did the show for one

season – before it had acquired its "Razzle Dazzle" name and reputation as required viewing for school-age children.

I was still working on solo pieces. Sometime during 1959, I was
driving home with the car radio on. A sportscaster was interviewing the then-young hockey star Gordie Howe, in his pre-articulate
days. As soon as I got home, I rushed in and wrote down everything
I could remember from the interview. Within hours, a character by
the name of Big Bobby Clobber was born.

This is the first Bobby Clobber piece ever performed.

ANNOUNCER: *Hi there, sports fans. We're happy to have with us here tonight, in front of the TV camera, a star of the hockey playoffs, Big Bobby Clobber. The big fella's gonna give us a preview of the next season in hockey as he sees it. Big Bobby.*

Dave as BIG BOBBY: *We, first off, I want to say, we want to say thanks you for . . . we . . . I want to say thanks for you . . . to . . . you . . . givin' us . . . me . . . this oppor . . . chance to . . . what you're givin' us . . . me.*

I think it's pretty certain what's gonna happen in the comin' year . . . There will be a decision on it pretty soon. I'm pretty sure there will be . . . Maybe. As on the other hand as far as us personally is concerned, we, I figure it's gonna take the best part of the season. [Smiles] Course I'm only guessin' on that, as we say. [Serious] By that, I mean I got nothin' against the team personally. They all play . . . hockey. As far as the rumours about the coach . . .

That was just a lot of dirty . . . There's nothin' to it at all. He was fired for something he done long before all that stuff got started. We couldn't prove it was our money.

ANNOUNCER: *Which team is gonna be the toughest to beat, Bobby?*

BIG BOBBY: *Which team is gonna be the toughest to beat Bobby? Well, they're all pretty tough. And some of them are pretty tough to beat. And some of them are dirty.*

ANNOUNCER: *Which do you see as the problem team?*

BIG BOBBY: *I'm gonna be honest with you. I don't understand the question.*

ANNOUNCER: *Let me put it to you another way.*

BIG BOBBY: *Okay.*

ANNOUNCER: *Which team is going to give you the most trouble?*

BIG BOBBY: *Oh. My own?*

ANNOUNCER: *So how would you sum up?*

BIG BOBBY: *So how would I sum up? I have to answer your question with a reply. I'd have to say it looks like an interestin' . . . interestin' . . . IN TER EST ING season. There's gonna be a lot of new blood out there on the ice. But most of all it looks like it could be a kind of wait and see season . . . like we haven't seen.*

ANNOUNCER: *Well, thanks a whole lot, Bobby, for that very revealing preview of the season in hockey as you see it . . .*

BIG BOBBY: *Before.*

ANNOUNCER: *Hmmmm?*

BIG BOBBY: *Like we haven't seen* before . . . *I should have said.* [Smiling. Pleased with himself.]

ANNOUNCER: *We're sure sorry you won't be playing next season, but we do want to wish you lots of luck in your new career as a member of Parliament.*

Late in 1959, John Bassett, owner of *The Toronto Telegram*, called Jean and me to a meeting. He was sponsoring a tour, organized by the Department of National Defence, to entertain the UN peacekeepers stationed in the Middle East in the aftermath of the Suez crisis. I was eager and willing to go. I believe that if soldiers are prepared to risk their lives in trying to keep the peace, then we as performers have an equal responsibility to back them up.

We were to travel to Gaza, Rafah, Sharm el Sheik, and Cairo. At the time, that particular UN peacekeeping force consisted of Brazilians, Indians, Danes, Yugoslavs, Norwegians, Swedes, and Canadians. With that mix of languages, we had to develop some purely physical comedy. Singer/dancer Sheila Billing, the former Miss Toronto, who had been on the Korean tour with me, joined us, along with Igors Gavin. Sheila and Igors, who was a talented guitar player-actor-singer, took care of most of the musical content of the show. Jean and I handled most of the comedy.

The Gaza Strip was manned by peacekeepers, but a state of war still existed at that time between Israel and the United Arab Republic, the temporary union of Egypt and Syria. We were reminded of this when we saw all vehicles in the Gaza were running without lights. Only hours before we arrived, a night train had hit a truck carrying newly arrived Indian troops. The Swedish army had flown in an entire portable hospital, with a fully equipped operating room – they were performing surgery there just hours after the accident occurred. It was a reminder that the troops we were to about to entertain were risking their lives.

The poster for our tour of the Middle East. No expense was spared in its production.

The conducting officer for our tour turned out to be a civilian, a former YMCA basketball instructor from California. After noticing his great concern about our troupe getting to see the Great Pyramid, and his less-than-great-concern about us getting to entertain the Yugoslav peacekeepers, I came to the conclusion that at one of his basketball games at the YMCA he had landed on his head, and this was the only other work he could do.

At Rafah, we sang and danced and pranced our way through our first show, an hour-and-a-half presentation. After Rafah, it was on to Sharm el Sheik on the Gulf of Aqaba, Cairo, and a godforsaken spot, a so-called oasis in the middle of the Sinai desert, manned by some very lonely Yugoslavs. We did one unscheduled performance for the Yugoslavs, for those who had somehow missed the scheduled show. By the time we arrived at their base, the troops had been sitting waiting in the open air for over two hours. It was very cold and damp, and so dark, a row of Jeeps was formed in a semi-circle behind the audience with all their lights focused on us. That broke the lighting regulations, but it was the best lighting we had on the whole tour. Halfway through that show, I had just put on an outrageous costume backstage. It covered me completely. No eyeholes. Standing backstage, I missed my footing and went hurtling down a long wooden staircase. Nobody noticed. When nobody sees an accident like that, a comedian can't help thinking "what a waste." After the performance, we were invited to the Yugoslav army officers' mess. The commanding officer was handsome, and remarkably young. Jean asked him how it was that someone so young could be in command of so many troops. "In my country," he said, "we had a civil war. I was on the winning side."

Back in Toronto, Jean and I settled into a routine that included radio shows three times a week, our children's television show, "Junior Round-up," every day, and banquets and conventions in the evenings. We found ourselves on a working treadmill that never seemed to stop. I had gone from being a hungry performer to getting more work than I could handle. The hard part was learning to say no; I found it very difficult to turn down work. From the time I'd left school, I'd never turned down a job. Always, in the back of my mind, all through my life, was the fact that my father had had it all, blew it, and never recovered. Growing up in the Depression years, like many other people, I never got over that insecurity. *How can I turn down a paying job?* I'd think. Looking back, this was one of the busiest times of my life, partly because I hadn't yet learned my limits.

Cramming in everything that came along led to some interesting moments. Our tapings for "Junior Round-up" took us out of town with a camera crew, to places like White Pine Lake, where there was a summer camp for children. We taped a tour of the camp, and when it came time for Jean and me to enter the kitchen, the show producer suggested that we needed a surprise. "Something unexpected," he said.

"Dave could be looking at one of my pies," the chef volunteered. "I could suddenly grab it and hit him in the face with it."

"Sounds good," said the producer.

I wasn't against the idea. It wouldn't be the first time I had taken a pie in the face. Unfortunately, the chef was not skilled in the art of pie throwing. The pie that hit me in the face came with a heavy porcelain plate attached to it. When we were done, and I was washing the blood off my face, I heard the chef complain that the last time he had done this trick, the guy's nose hardly bled at all.

While we were doing out-of-town tapings, we were also performing nightly back in the city in *Spring Thaw*. At first, I wasn't aware of how much tension our work schedule was creating, but then I began to notice that each time we arrived at Jean's parents' home for dinner, I felt a great sense of relief at being away from all our obligations. Stressed from overwork, I was also beginning to realize that nothing in my life to that point had prepared me for a long-term intimate relationship with a beautiful and talented

With Jean (right), and other members of the Spring Thaw *cast, 1961*

woman. In my family, you did not talk about your feelings. So, although I was tense, nervous, and almost at breaking point, I was completely incapable of discussing any of this with Jean. Emotionally, I was extremely immature.

One thing I did talk to Jean about was my difficulty in admitting that I no longer believed in God. It is hard to communicate to those who haven't grown up in religious homes exactly what this means to those of us who have. First off, I had a huge reluctance to face the fact. It is such a big thing to walk away from religion when it has been instilled in you from birth, from the time you were able to hold a picture of the baby Jesus. When your whole family has deliberately centred their lives around the church, as mine had, it is even harder. My three sisters had all become missionaries. My father constantly read aloud from the Bible. My mother worked at the church every day. Now, I was rejecting the idea of God, turning my back on the Church, saying, in effect, that I thought they were all wrong. I did not want to talk about this to anyone, and I particularly did not want to tell my mother. It felt like an enormous betrayal of her and all she believed in. She had a gentle view of religion, and I knew she would be hurt. My father would also feel wounded. So losing God came at the price of really hurting the people I loved. But I couldn't see the point of a fundamentalist religion that promised glory and comfort in a future life, about which we knew nothing, in return for rejecting so much of the joy in this one.

My early conditioning was so extreme that it was a long, long time before I had the courage to say the words "I don't believe" to anyone. Fear was a big part of it – fear of changing anything because of the massive amount of guilt I was carrying about switching brands. Now, there are organizations like Born Again Anonymous, to help people like me. Then, there was nothing. I tried to explain to Jean I was brought up with the belief that the worst crime you could commit was to turn your back on God and reject Jesus as your personal saviour. She looked at me very seriously. "No, Dave," she said, "there's a worse crime than that."

"What is it?" I asked.

She looked me in the eye and, with absolutely no expression in her normally very expressive voice, said, "Being boring." It was funny, and exactly what I needed to hear, but it seemed to be getting harder to hang onto the joy and laughter we had started with.

Much of the joy and laughter we did have came during late-night visits to the Chez Paree on Bloor Street. We'd finish at the theatre at around eleven and head off to the restaurant to join whoever showed up that evening. It was all very casual, a mixed group of people, many of them regulars. Owen Duffy and Jack Fulton could be relied upon. There was also George Carter, who sold pharmaceuticals, Bert Newman, who was in the clothing business, Nore Flynn and Harold Nelson, who worked for CBC News, and Alistair McCrimmon (I never did figure out what Alistair did). Peggy Forrester, the hostess, was a big part of it all. She'd lock the door at 2:00 a.m., which was only a signal for the jokes, the wine, and the jazz to continue. Among the regular customers there were a few opera singers who were not averse to presenting an impromptu concert at two in the morning.

Jean loved the Chez Paree as much as I did, and entered into the spirit of the place. One night, she hadn't removed her false eyelashes after a *Spring Thaw* performance. Across the room she saw an actor we knew. Jean removed the eyelashes, and put them carefully into an envelope with an unsigned note that read "Why not take all of me?" She then asked the waiter to deliver the envelope to the actor, who was sitting on the other side of the room. As she watched, he opened the envelope, looked at the eyelashes and the invitation, and blushed the deepest crimson any human had ever achieved, then began desperately staring at each person in the room, trying, without success, to determine who had sent him such a generous invitation. He never found out what had happened, and Jean, who knew him well, never told.

In retrospect, the patrons of the Chez Paree were a remarkably well-behaved lot. I think it was partly because of Peggy Forrester, who was a very special hostess, partly because of the excellent musicians who always played very tasty jazz, and partly because of the consistently reliable spare ribs. One night, however, a customer caused an uproar when, for no apparent reason, he began violently punching a person who was standing near his table. While Peggy called the police, one of the opera-singer regulars, Allan Crowfoot, who weighed in at three hundred and seventy pounds, came to the rescue. He quietly got up from our table, walked over to the raving troublemaker, and, without saying a word, took hold of both the raver's wrists, forced him to the floor, and sat on him. The raving troublemaker became so quiet that, when the police closed the handcuffs on him, it was the loudest sound in the room.

In 1961, an agent friend, Sylvia Train, called to tell us about a room above the popular Italian restaurant, Old Angelo's, that she felt could easily be made into a dinner theatre if we were interested. John Belli, the owner of Old Angelo's, was willing to modify the room to please us, if we were interested in doing a satirical show there. We were very interested.

DAVE BROADFOOT
and
JEAN TEMPLETON

Promotion piece, 1961

John Belli started on the modifications, while Jean and I set about writing and rehearsing our show. Officially it was called *Well Rehearsed Ad Libs*, but everyone called it *Dave and Jean at Old Angelo's*. We wrote all the material ourselves, and our accompanist, a brilliant young musician named Ben McPeek, who later went on to run his own recording studio, wrote all the music. The show ran and ran and ran.

Among Jean's solo items were a satire on women's magazines ("Did you know that Jackie Kennedy's husband is president of the United States?"), and a sketch in which she picketed the audience ("Mackenzie King is alive in South America"). We did several sketches together – a couple in an overcrowded fallout shelter equipped with Muzak; a sketch about a young boy and girl, set in the future, when sex has become a triviality, but the boy is terrified when the girl insists on having a conversation with him (as it turned out, not far off the mark). We also introduced into that show a game you could play to embarrass people, which we called the elevator game. You manoeuvre the person you want to get even with onto a crowded elevator, but don't get on yourself. Then, just as the doors are closing, you call out any of the following, loudly:

I don't say it's wrong, Jerry. I just think it's unusual to evict your own mother.

It's been great to see you again. Glad we could raise your bail.

You look so different. I wish I could afford to have mine fixed.

If you don't give it up soon, Stanley, you'll go blind.

I don't know what to suggest. I've never had lice.

No trouble. You give my lawyer a call. He's handled plenty of paternity suits.

The show also included a solo piece, which I worked long and hard developing. The character was an Aboriginal "public-relations" man. Today, this would be considered cultural appropriation, speaking in someone else's voice, and it is a technique that is, at the moment, much frowned upon. I have used appropriation countless times in my career, but always, I hope, with respect, affection, and above all, accuracy. I have no trouble doing dialect: I've always been proud of my accuracy, and I really believe that people always know whose side I'm on. I can tell instantly if a person impersonating a minority doesn't like the minority. The curious thing is whenever I have "appropriated" the voice of a person from, say, New Delhi, it's always the former residents of New Delhi who are the first to arrive at my dressing room with congratulations and a request for an autograph. "Never leave us out of your comedy," one Indian businessman who had chosen to settle in Canada once said to me. "You make us feel part of the family."

The tribal public-relations man was an early foray into this now-controversial territory. Growing up, as I did, not far from a reserve, and having two sisters from the reserve as childhood friends, I never had the feeling of "them" and "us" that so many people seem to have. My father's attitude was more typical of those times, and it caused me a great deal of distress. He thought God had given the land to the British and, when I asked him who gave it to the indigenous people, he dismissed them. "They are not important," he said. "When God gave this land to us, there were hardly any of them here." For good measure, he added that there were hardly any of them left, and that they would eventually disappear. Even as a child, I found it hard to accept the idea that the whole gift-receiving operation was masterminded not by Wolfe, Pitt, and George the Second, but by the Father, Son, and Holy Ghost.

As the revelations of injustices toward native peoples mounted, I wondered how a comedian could comment on the situation. I had done one-liners on the subject, but wanted to do something more substantial. In 1961, I became aware of a small group of native people who were holding regular meetings at the Toronto YMCA. I asked if I could attend one of their meetings. They agreed. The first thing that struck me was that these people, huddled together in the heart of Toronto, were aliens in their own land. I listened carefully to their discussions, and later made notes. From there, I went to a CBC radio producer who I knew had done a documentary series on native people. With his permission, I listened to hours and hours of recorded interviews with native people from all walks of life, and again I took notes.

I gathered my research, developed a character, and decided to introduce him in our Old Angelo's show. Music played softly in an indigenous rhythm, as I made my way to centre stage in an authentic beaded and fringed buckskin coat, wearing a leather headband and carrying an authentic tribal peace pipe. I introduced myself as the tribe's public-relations officer, and in the gentle manner and cadence that I had heard in so many of the radio interviews, I proceeded to enunciate the current problems of my people, gradually filling the pipe with tobacco as I talked.

In Canada, an Indian like me has two choices. He can live on a reservation and accept the government bounty, or he can renounce the reservation and give up the bounty . . . and I'll never forgive my father for leaving. It's pretty nice to have four dollars a year . . . comin' in regularly.

The last time I went back to visit my people, we had a very important meeting. We sat around, smoking like hell, and finally decided the tribe could not go on any longer without a public relations man. We had a hard time finding someone with the right amount of overconfidence . . . [quietly] but here I am.

The first thing I have to set straight is why we're called Indians. Many years ago, Columbus sailed across the ocean looking for India. He couldn't find it . . . so that's why we are called Indians. If he'd been looking for China, we'd be called Communists.

We notice how many Canadian people complain about the immigration laws. They say the government is not careful enough who it lets in. We made the same mistake when we owned the country. It was an easy mistake to make. You gave us things we'd never seen before . . . whiskey, guns, measles, the Bible . . . We still haven't figured out how the Bible works. It's hard enough to understand the whiskey. If I have too much of it, I'm called a drunken Indian. If you have too much of it, you're called an alcoholic anonymous. I guess we kind of got even with the tobacco.

We know a lot of you non-Indians are sorry for us, but we liked it better in the old days when you were scared of us. The white men were never scared of our women though. That's how we learned the golden rule. Do unto others and then . . . zzzzzzzzt . . . take off.

You white people think you survived in this country because you are superior. [Shakes his head.] *You survived because we had a sense of humour. We've never condemned you. We tried to help you. And it isn't easy. We teach you how to hunt, how to fish, how to look after yourselves in the woods, but the minute we leave you on your own, you go right back to your old ways again. You won't give up your bulldozers. We want to help you, but as we say on the reserve . . . How . . .*

[Indicates that peace pipe is broken, and can't be smoked after all. The same native rhythm comes in as at opening. Sings]

> *This land was my land*
> *And now it's your land*
> *This land they stole*
> *For you, from me.*

The tribal public-relations man had a life after Old Angelo's. I did it at the Black Swan coffee house in Stratford one evening and a friend, a member of the Blood tribe from Alberta, told me that Duke Redbird, an Aboriginal performer and comedian, had arrived too late to catch the show. She pleaded with me to do the monologue again after the show for Duke. To please her, I went through it for a fascinated Duke Redbird, and thought nothing more of it.

Five years later, I would be interviewing the native singer and film-maker, Alanis Obomsawin, in a television pilot show. I did a few lines from the tribal public-relations officer monologue to see if she thought they accurately reflected a native point of view. "They certainly do," she said. "Those are the words of Duke Redbird." Alanis said that Duke Redbird had been performing those lines at pow-wow after pow-wow, all over the country. She could not believe that I had written them. A year after that, I caught a TV show in which Duke Redbird was performing the monologue. He had added lines of his own, but I was most impressed with how well he had remembered mine. I wrote to the producer of the TV show, describing the painstaking hours of research I had put in to write the monologue, and that, without attribution, it amounted to outright theft. On the other hand, I added, I couldn't help feeling a certain joy that finally a native person was stealing from a white man.

During our run at Old Angelo's, Jean and I had booked a table one night for the woman who was cooking and cleaning for us, since we had no time to do it ourselves. From backstage, I caught a glimpse of her with her two friends, standing at the back of the room. A few minutes later, Jean peeked out, and noticed they were still standing at the back of the room. Fifteen minutes later, we checked again. They were still there. The room was now full. We had booked the best table in the room for them, and other people had now been given that table. Finally, I saw that our friends were being seated where they had been kept standing for so long. At the back of the room.

The show was about to start, so I ran downstairs to the main floor, out to the front of the building, up the front stairs, found the maître d', and grabbed him. "What the hell is going on?" I asked. "You didn't tell me your friends were black," he said. I could hardly believe what I was hearing. In a rage, I went backstage. Jean had already sensed what had happened and was dissolved in tears. It was showtime. Jean didn't want to go on, and neither did I. I took about ten deep breaths, and put my arms around her. "Here's what has to happen," I said. "We have no choice. We have to go on. But at inter-mission, I'll go and give the boss our notice. Then we'll do the second half of the show, and that will be the end of it. We'll be gone." We both rose to the occasion. Nobody but our friends and the maître d' knew there was a problem.

At intermission, I went to the owner and gave notice – not just that we were leaving, but that we were leaving that night. The owner, a man I liked, was dumbfounded. He asked what could pos-sibly have happened to bring this about. When I told him, he was stunned. "Good God, I can't afford that," he said. "The Brotherhood of Railway Porters holds their banquets here!" By the end of the intermission, the maître d' had been fired. We retracted our resig-nations, and went on with the show for many months. At the end of that particular performance we sat with our friends and tried to explain what had happened. The humiliation was partly smoothed by knowing that the maître d' was gone for good.

The critical acclaim for that little Old Angelo's show was quite remarkable. Every performance was played to a packed house. Much later I learned that critic Nathan Cohen, a man who was known to fearlessly speak his mind, had said to a mutual friend that he should do everything he could to make sure we never split up. The combi-nation of Jean's writing and my timing, he said, was unbeatable.

So many good things were happening. We had worked so hard, Jean and I, and we were on a roll with everything seeming to go right. And yet, emotionally, I had turned into a zombie. I didn't realize it then, but Old Angelo's, combined with our radio and television commitments, gave me a work schedule that was beyond my endurance. Jean handled the pressure far better than I did. But then, I'm a worrier by nature. People would ask me, What are you going to do between now and showtime? "I'm going up to my dressing room," I'd reply, "and I'm going to worry." It comes from taking your commitments very, very seriously – which I always have, and always will. I never want to give a performance that is three-quarters of what it should be. Every time I go on stage, I say to myself: This is going to be the best performance I've ever done. And whatever it takes to do it, I do it. If I have to lock myself in a room, and rehearse, and rehearse, and rehearse, I do it. If you have that kind of attitude, and you become overcommitted, life becomes almost unbearable.

At the peak of the workload, when it was no longer possible to ever feel rested, Jean and I had a call asking us to do a benefit performance at 8:00 a.m. on the same day we had a radio taping, a TV taping, and an Old Angelo's show. I believe in doing benefits whenever possible, but in this instance, I felt we just had to beg off. Taking on anything extra at that point would have been catastrophic, and I told the caller so. Two days later, he called again, asking us to reconsider. Again, reluctantly, I turned him down. The next week, the caller tried again – you have to give him credit for being persistent. "Dave," he asked, "what's the problem? Is it the fact that there is no fee involved? If that's the problem maybe we can work something out." I explained that this had nothing to do with it. We believed in benefits, but we were both mentally and physically exhausted. Taking on anything extra would have meant more writing and rehearsing. "We are trying to maintain our sanity and our marriage," I told him. "Please, enough calls already." The next day, he called again. "You win," I said. "We'll report at seven for the sound check." It was the last benefit, and one of the last performances, that Jean and I ever did together.

Overloaded with work, depressed and unhappy, I simply had nothing left to give to Jean, whom I cared about more than anything else. A huge state of tension had built up between us, to the point that, one day, I found myself pushing her around. I was shocked. It was *me* doing this. It was so out of character, I knew I could not take a chance with it. I had to go. I moved out, and into a small apartment hotel near Old Angelo's. When I told Jack Fulton, he could not believe it. "What have you done?" he asked. What should have been a time of great triumph wasn't. To this day, it is hard to talk about, hard for me to understand what happened. I went to see a psychologist, and later made regular visits to a psychiatrist. Both said that the problems I was having in my marriage had nothing to do with my wife, and they were right. My relationships with others were nearly always superficial, or at least not really close. And detachment sure doesn't work in a marriage.

Jean moved on. Alexander Cohen, the Broadway producer, had caught our show in Toronto, and saw in Jean the same qualities he had seen in Elaine May, the brilliant American comedienne. He asked Jean if she would be willing to go to New York to be on standby for a role in an upcoming production. I thought it was a novel idea to bring someone in, without something very concrete for them to do. But if you want to work in another country, you have to go there and make it happen. "It's up to you, Dave," Jean said. "If you don't want me to go, I won't. Just tell me, do you want me to go or do you want me to stay?" It was the toughest question I had ever been asked. I was numb. I could not respond.

In the end, she decided to go to New York. I took her to the airport. I can still see her standing there, me still feeling absolutely paralyzed and wishing I could have responded to her. "It's up to you," she said, one last time. "I won't take this flight if you don't want me to." My response was, "If it's going to help your career, go." And I don't think that that's what she wanted to hear. As I watched that plane take off, I knew that was the end. If I had been in a normal frame of mind, I would have said, No, don't go. But I was so strung out, I was like an automaton. I had no feeling. We didn't see each other again for ten years. By then, we had divorced, and had both remarried.

Chapter 6

WHEN I REGAINED CONSCIOUSNESS

It was back to working alone, and the usual round of one-nighters, banquets, and conventions. My routine was interrupted one day in 1962 when director John Gray called. He, with his wife, actress Araby Lockhart, had produced the revue *Clap Hands*. They had made arrangements to tour England with the show and wanted me to be part of it. I was excited about the prospect, until Jack told me he was planning to hire Peter Mews. Peter was a good all-round performer and one of the mainstays of *Spring Thaw*, but I had been through some trying experiences with him. These mainly related to his drinking. I thanked John for the offer but said I would not be available. He was so upset by my rejection, and so determined not to take no for an answer, that I levelled with him, and told him the real reason I had said no: namely Peter and his drinking. "Trust me, Dave," he said, "it won't be a problem. I won't let it be a problem." With that promise, I agreed to sign on.

Reservations about Peter aside, I was pleased to be touring England with a Canadian satirical revue. The show had enjoyed a successful run at the Hart House Theatre in Toronto, and it deserved a wider audience. I sublet the small apartment I had rented, put my belongings in storage, and sailed across the Atlantic on the ss *Carinthia*, bound for Southampton. In London, I joined the other cast members – Araby Lockhart, Corinne Conley, Jack Creley, Eric House, and a supposedly reformed Peter Mews. I found lodgings in

Corinne Conley, Jack Creley, Peter Mews, Eric House, me, and Araby Lockhart in Clap Hands, *London, England, 1963*

Paddington, and had a few days to get acclimatized before plunging into rehearsals. It was an exciting time to be in the city – the Beatles were just beginning their rise to world domination, the famous haircut was imitated everywhere, and Carnaby Street had started its rule as the fashion centre of the universe.

Settling into rehearsals, we worked very hard, because we all felt so much was at stake. Satire was at the height of its popularity in England at that time, not only in the theatre and in clubs, but also on television, where David Frost was about to become host of the irreverent late-night show, "That Was the Week That Was." We felt we had to prove that Canadian satire was as good as the local variety, but it was a tricky thing trying to figure out which pieces would be a hit with the English audience and which pieces might miss. Sometimes the comedy one assumes will travel well doesn't. As we began out-of-town tryouts in Wolverhampton, moving on to Oxford, Cambridge, Bournemouth, Torquay, and Brighton, what travelled and what didn't became apparent.

I quickly realized that my Mountie character, Sergeant Renfrew, would have to go. It hadn't occurred to me until it died on stage at Wolverhampton that, for Canadians, a Mountie is a daily fact of life. He may be telling you where to park your car at the airport, or to reduce speed on the highway, or that you are in the country illegally, or that he has to arrest you because of what he has found in your suit-case. Doesn't matter – you know what he does. In Britain, a Mountie was just a glamorous image in red serge on a tourist postcard. The character of Renfrew and his dog, Cuddles, left the Wolverhampton audience mystified. This was not the way it was supposed to be – only Renfrew should be mystified, not his audience.

There was another sketch that did not work, but it took me a little time to figure out why. I had been told about this piece by a friend, who had seen Robert Nielson, of the ice-cream family, perform it at a convention. I had gone to see Nielson about acquiring it, and he had agreed that I could have the piece for a small fee. It was an endless series of non sequiturs, and I had performed it in a show in Canada to huge success. In England, this huge success was greeted with massive indifference, which puzzled me because I thought it was really funny. When I asked around, I found out that it was familiarity that bred contempt. Peter Sellers performed an almost identical piece – so similar, in fact, that this was no accident. I was shocked. I dropped it instantly.

Other sketches were gradually removed or rewritten. Each night, after the performance, I went from the theatre back to my lodgings, wrote till two or three in the morning, then brought what I had written to the daytime rehearsal so we could have it ready for the next show. It was beyond a compulsion, this writing, rewriting, and fixing. I saw things I thought could be better, and set to work. We hired two young English writers, Piers Stephens and William Webster, and they helped a lot. Tuned into the English awareness, they made some splendid contributions that fitted smoothly into the show: among them, a sketch about Canadian parents trying to enrol their son in an English public school, which played on the different British and Canadian attitudes to class, and a parody of James Bond, in which I had the pleasure of playing James Bond.

By the time we got to our last out-of-town tryout at Brighton, anxiety and overwork had got to me. I never learn. I found myself sinking into the worst despondency I had ever experienced. There is no explaining this: things were going well, the show was getting better, I was working hard to make it better, and yet, despite this, I felt such a failure. I was drowning in my own inadequacy, both professional and personal. The break-up with Jean was still preying on my mind.

One night, after we had finished the show at the Royal Theatre, some of the others had gone to a nearby restaurant to eat. Corinne Conley was there with her husband. She looked up at me as I stood by the table. "Aren't you going to sit down?" she asked.

"No," I said. "I think I'm going to do some walking."

She stared at me, with a questioning look. "Do you think you should?" she asked. It was as if she sensed that something was wrong. I left the others at their meal and went out into the cold November night, down to the beach, and started to walk out in the direction of the water. When I reached the water, I didn't stop. I kept walking, and walking, and walking, further and further out into the water, which was getting deeper and deeper. "Hang on," something inside me said, "hang on. This despair will fade away. Just hang on." I did hang on. turned back to the shore. And it did fade away. Once it was over, it was over for good. I never felt that low again. Ever.

The next day, a Sunday, was a travel day, and we took the train to London. On the train, I pulled some paper out of my briefcase and began writing a monologue. I knew something was happening,

---

The Member for Kicking Horse Pass, November 1962

As a Canadian member of Parliament, I feel it my duty to say something about the future of the Commonwealth. This is a matter that behooves each one of us, as we've never been behooved before. First, let me say that Canada is the most modern country in the world today. We have no flag, no national anthem, no national policy, and we're broke. So there is no possible way Britain can hurt us. Except emotionally. Canadians become alarmed when they hear about changes like these highrise buildings that are going up in London. Do you know that now, from the grounds of Buckingham Palace, you can look right into the rooms of the new highrise hotels!! A shocking loss of privacy for hotel guests.

We liked this country the way it was. Unique. For years, this was the only country that people from all over the world could come to as long as they'd been conquered first. The population explosion has changed all that. I see now that the Church of England has even approved the sterilization of certain types of people. Imbeciles, psychopaths, and Baptists, I believe it is. So far, they haven't mentioned any names.

But what is happening to the Commonwealth? Back in Canada, the alarmists says the only thing that's holding the people of the Commonwealth together is Schweppes. They say Canada is going to be taken over by Americans. Americans? That's silly. They already own us. First we got American cars. Then we got American unions. Then came the ultimate weapon. Reader's Digest. *Now, you can't tell us apart. I was in Latin America recently. People were shouting at me "Yankee go home! Yankee go home!" Of course, once they understood I was from Canada, they showered me with . . . hand grenades.*

We do try to co-operate with the Americans in our defence policy. Our policy basically is this: "We must do something about defence even if it's wrong." The amazing thing is we have so many dictators on our side. Chiang Kai-shek, Franco, Salazar, de Gaulle, Beeching, and others like them. We'll all know more about de Gaulle when his memoirs are published. They're coming out soon in English, entitled Me the People.

There wouldn't be all this anxiety about defence if there was a little bit more understanding in the world. All America and Russia are trying to do right now is hang on to their friends. By force, if necessary! The Americans still want to invade Cuba, but only in the interests of freedom and democracy and the United Fruit Company. America and Russia are really working together now. They've just made an agreement to land on the moon simultaneously. So help me. America and Russia are going to share the moon. Like Berlin. They'll have to wait for the bricks.

Some of the congressmen in the U.S. want to push on to Mars. They say the moon is obsolete. More redundancy. Can you imagine those American pioneers on Mars. White children going to school with green children. They'll need a strong army out there.

While we're on the subject of children, a report has just been issued showing the basic difference between Russian and American children. Apparently, it's this: In Russia, if a boy in school is told his teacher is forty, he'll automatically say, "I must respect her. With age comes wisdom." In America, when a boy is told his teacher is forty, he'll automatically say, "Cool. What is she around the waist?" Well, they're both on the right track.

In Canada, we're not concerned about our educational system. We're not trying to get men into space. We're trying to get our prime minister back on the ground. He keeps telling us that business is looking up. Of course it is. When it's lying on its back there is nowhere else to look. Living in an economy with our prime minister is like being on a ship with Christopher Columbus. He's not sure where we're going. He won't know where he is when he gets there. And he's doing it all on borrowed money. That's why, when he was in England recently, he tried to persuade some of the top British businessmen to invest in Canada. Men like E. P. Taylor, Garfield Weston, Roy Thomson, Lord Beaverbrook.

But I wouldn't let our prime minister, or anyone else, discourage you from eventually becoming part of Europe, because, if all Europeans can get together, in one market, you'll never be enemies again. Let's face it, when you have de Gaulle for a friend, you don't need enemies!

because I could feel the rising sense of exhilaration. Three days later, on November 15, 1962, when we opened our London run at the Lyric, Hammersmith, I performed the monologue I had written in a fever on the train. It literally stopped the show. It was the only time I had ever had to take bows in the middle of a revue. When the applause finally calmed down, Eric House, who was waiting to start the next sketch, watched me walk off, then turned to the audience. "Damn funny, these Australians," he said. That, too, got an enormous laugh.

Our reviews were good – "a lively good-natured team that is using its intelligence," *Punch* noted, and the *Evening Standard* said we would surely end up in the West End, which we did. All the hard work was paying off – the show was a success, business was brisk, and there was hardly a night when there wasn't a British celebrity or movie star in the audience. Noel Coward was the only one I actually met – he put his arm around me and said with a smile, "I love your Australian accent."

Unfortunately, another production had a commitment with the Lyric, Hammersmith, for a Christmas pantomime, so we had to get out, but our impresario Norman Fielding was able to book us into a small new theatre, near Leicester Square, the Prince Charles. There would be a two-week hiatus before we opened, which gave us time to prepare ourselves physically and psychologically for the big opening night in the heart of the West End. Switching houses is a very difficult challenge. It's a huge risk, even with a successful show, even at the best of times. But we were prepared and ready.

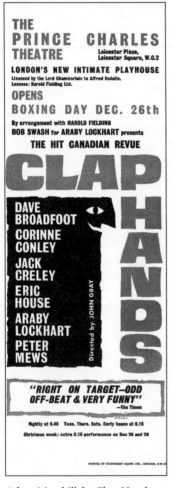

Advertising bill for Clap Hands

Our big night came. Showtime was getting close. Tension was building. Why? Because there was no sign of Peter Mews. The curtain went up. We fumbled and stumbled our way through the opening number as best we could with one cast member missing. Near the end of the number, Peter came staggering through the stage door, looking like a cadaver. He had spent the two-week hiatus making his bid to enter the *Guinness Book of World Records* as the world's greatest consumer of alcohol in one fortnight.

Peter was rushed from the stage door to his dressing room and put into a military uniform. The next number he was in was a military parody in which four people had to stand in ramrod-stiff positions. Peter started the number looking like a khaki-covered Leaning Tower of Pisa. As he slowly became conscious that the other bodies on stage seemed to be standing at a different angle to his, he began to straighten up, but he couldn't hold the stance. Going past vertical, his body continued on, so the Tower of Pisa ended up leaning again in the opposite direction. From then on, the number consisted of three military officers, and a human pendulum. The audience was mesmerized by the slow movement of this swinging body – not exactly the reaction one hopes for while doing a brilliant comic parody of the military. After a while, even the audience realized that mesmerizing was not what they had paid for.

We struggled all night with the challenge of trying to minimize the disaster brought on by Peter's drunken stupor. In the midst of all this rescue work, I went backstage for a quick costume change and saw the producer sitting there, holding his head in his hands. "Dave tried to warn me," I heard him moaning. "He tried to warn me. Why didn't I listen?" After this fiasco, two understudies, Roberta Maxwell and Douglas Chamberlain, were hired to avoid it ever happening again.

We survived the disaster of that opening night, but barely. Because of the shaky start, the show was not the success it had been at the Lyric. I also had to survive a really disastrous personal mistake in judgement. While we were touring, I had written a letter to a friend in Canada, Dave Caplan, in which I unburdened myself of all the anxiety and frustration I was experiencing with the show, or at least thought I was. I suggested that, if the show was a success, it would not be because of the producers but because of all the extra work that the members of the cast were putting in.

One day, shortly after we had opened, Corinne came to me in the dressing room. "Dave Caplan," she said. "Is he your friend?"

"Yes," I said, wondering why she was asking.

"Are you sure?" she asked. It turned out that Dave, who was a free-lancer for the *Toronto Star*, had given my complaining letter to Nathan Cohen, the paper's legendary theatre critic, and Nathan Cohen had published it verbatim in his column. Naively, I was astonished that something like this could happen, that someone would publish a private letter. Maybe I shouldn't have written the letter, but I was just off-loading frustration to a friend. I never expected to see it in the press. I was embarrassed and hurt, and could never bring myself to talk to John Gray or Araby Lockhart about what had happened. Araby and John are still very nice to me to this day, which is to their credit. I determined, after this incident, to keep my frustrations to myself.

On Sunday nights, when we were not working, I was able to indulge my passion for jazz and get to regular concerts given by the John Dankworth band at a club on Oxford Street. One evening was devoted entirely to Duke Ellington tunes, and as Ellington was playing near London that night, Dankworth had invited the Ellington musicians to join him, if they could make it after their show. As the band got down to the last few numbers, I noticed John Dankworth constantly glancing toward the entrance. No luck. The band was playing the final tune, "Take the A Train," when Cat Anderson, the renowned Ellington trumpet player, walked in, clutching his trumpet case. The band repeated the final chorus of "A Train," Cat Anderson whipped his horn out of its case, and as there was nowhere to stand on stage, he grabbed the lid of the grand piano, and let it down. He then jumped up and sat on it, put his horn to his lips, and blew a riff. The band blew back. Then the process reversed. It went back and forth, building in excitement. No rehearsal, just pure improvisation at its exciting, magical best. To see a black musician thousands of miles from home walk in and have this kind of communication, this kind of rapport, with a bunch of white Englishmen, what could top it?

When *Clap Hands* closed, I received an invitation to appear at one of London's better nightclubs, the Blue Angel, near Berkeley Square. The Blue Angel experience was fun, working on the same bill as Graham Chapman who, with John Cleese and others, went on to create "Monty Python's Flying Circus." When this engagement was over, a telegram arrived from Canada, inviting me to head up a special revue as part of the 1963 Vancouver International Festival. I had enjoyed performing in England, but I was homesick, and couldn't wait to get back to Canada.

The review was entitled *The Best of Spring Thaw*, and it ran at the Queen Elizabeth Playhouse. It was the first time *Spring Thaw* had played outside Ontario. The cast was made up entirely of Vancouver performers, with the exception of dancer/actress Marilyn Stuart, who was from Toronto. Mavor Moore had come out to Vancouver to rehearse the show, but once it opened he headed back to Toronto, leaving me in charge. The show turned out to be the hit of the Festival – every performance was sold out, and people were being turned away. It was at this point the general manager of the Festival, Gordon Hilker, asked to meet me. It led to one of those ironic moments that seem to increase as you get older.

He came to the meeting with his wife, who I had the vague feeling I had met before. Gordon Hilker was anxious to keep the show going after the Festival, and to move it from the Playhouse into the much larger Queen Elizabeth Theatre. There was clearly money to be made. I sensed a certain amount of fawning over me, hoping that I would try to get a "yes" from Mavor, and from the other cast members. As the meeting progressed, it came to me where I had met Mrs. Hilker. She had been in the Theatre Under the Stars production of *Roberta*, from which I had been fired many years ago. Then I remembered a rumour that had circulated at the time: the reason I was *not* in *Roberta* was because she *was* – and she had wanted to work with James Johnston, not with me. I realized now that I had no interest in reminding them that I was the guy they had spurned at Theatre Under the Stars. It was too long ago. Nobody cared. Not even me. We agreed to move the show to the huge Queen Elizabeth Theatre, and there it again sold out. The Hilker fawning continued, and I wallowed in it.

*Proof that I once shared billing
with Jane Russell*

When *Best* eventually closed, it was still summer, the weather
was gorgeous, and I had no particular reason to leave Vancouver.
So I stayed. I appeared at the Cave Supper Club a couple of times,
once, memorably, with Jane Russell. People don't believe me
when I say that Jane Russell, who is mainly thought of as an actress,
did the best version of "Mack the Knife" I ever witnessed. Nothing
at all like the upbeat, jump tempo versions that make the words
irrelevant. Jane focused totally on the words, and used dramatic
lighting to highlight her body and her slinking, slithery manner.
As she made her way through the lyrics, the whole atmosphere
became ominous, and you got the sense of what Mack the Knife
really was, a ruthless killer. Bertolt Brecht and Kurt Weill would
have been delighted.

In addition to the Cave, I also performed that summer at a
flourishing coffee house on Seymour Street, the Inquisition. This
turned into an extended run, and then I moved to another coffee
house, the Secret, in Victoria. The coffee house circuit in the 1960s
played host to an incredible roster of talent. Folk singers, poets, jazz
groups, comedians, more folk singers, blues singers, one-act plays,
sketch comedy, sometimes even a painter, and still more folk singers.
Among my contemporaries on the circuit were singers Joni Mitchell,
Ian and Sylvia Tyson, John Lee Hooker, Gordon Lightfoot, Ed
McCurdy, Buffy Sainte-Marie, Sonny Terry and Brownie McGhee,
Malka and Joso, and comedians Larry Zolf (yes, that Larry Zolf, who
later became a CBC stalwart and well-known columnist), David
Steinberg, and Bill Cosby. Some were then established stars, but most
were just getting started. You might walk in on an evening when poets
and musicians and painters were all performing simultaneously.
An evening like that is now called a mixed-media event – then it

was called a happening. The coffee houses that focused mainly on folk music held evenings in which great numbers of folk singers performed one after the other in a veritable non-stop marathon of music. That kind of evening was a hootenanny.

I spent a great deal of time in coffee houses during the 1960s. They were thriving all over the country. There was a large number in Toronto, five on Avenue Road alone, and at least five in Yorkville. Some of the names I recall: the Penny Farthing, the Village Corner, the First Floor Club, the Concerto, the Purple Onion, the Fifth Peg, the House of Hambourg, and the most dynamic of all, the Bohemian Embassy on St. Nicholas Street. Under the proprietorship of actor/comedian Don Cullen, the Embassy presented a full range of entertainments, from happenings to hootenannys to jazz sessions to several versions of an original satirical production called *The Village Revue*. The cost of producing the first *Village Revue* was six dollars and seventy-five cents. These were not elaborate productions. Outside Toronto, there were coffee houses such as the Depression in Calgary, the Inquisition in Vancouver, the Louis Riel in Saskatoon, the Black Swan in Stratford, and le Hibou in Ottawa. In Quebec, the coffee houses were called "une boite à chansons," and they served liquor, which was definitely not the case anywhere else.

I played all of the above – and more besides, with names I've now forgotten. I followed Bill Cosby into the Fifth Peg. One of my favourites was the House of Hambourg in Toronto, named for its creator and owner, Clem Hambourg. Clem was a retired member of a string quartet, who had toured internationally, playing concert halls all over the world. Everyone who met Clem liked him, and the jazz musicians who played at his club loved him. What a treat it was to hear this elderly, white-haired man introducing them. "The music these cats make is so cool, I know you're all going to dig it." Clem ran the house and booked the talent, which was normally jazz, although when I appeared there the audience seemed to have no trouble accepting a comedian. Clem's charming and hard-working wife ran the kitchen, producing delicious smoked-meat sandwiches and coffee. Coffee-house food was basic fare – soft drinks, light food, and, of course, coffee.

Another favourite venue of mine was the Black Swan in Stratford. I did more than one summer there, which was fortunate, because summers can sometimes be a major problem for a performer if you don't have a commitment for the whole season. The occasional one-nighter is not enough to keep you sharp and it is always a challenge to go onstage and be sharp for an audience when there have been no audiences lately to keep you that way. I was thinking about this on a sunny June day, when I received a phone call from a young man by the name of Harry Finlay, asking me if I would like to do July and August at the Black Swan. By then I knew better than to say "yes" immediately to an offer. There was much to consider. I took at least ten seconds to make up my mind.

Arriving in Stratford, I found the Black Swan was run by Harry and his partner, Bev Adam, who worked very hard with help from their friends to keep the place going. None of these friends seemed to be paid. They did the carpentry, wiring, plumbing, cooking, serving, whatever needed to be done, all for their accommodation, as none of them was from Stratford. Harry provided my accommodation, too, but he also paid me. Not much – the fees in coffee houses were of necessity modest – but fair. Everyone who performed there was paid the same amount, a system now called "most favoured nation," one of those useful expressions that makes no sense.

The biggest audience each night was the one that arrived just a few minutes after the final curtain at the nearby theatres of the Stratford Festival. Every night, at that time, the place suddenly became packed with tourists, celebrities, politicians, a very upbeat audience. Like all the other coffee houses, there was nothing elaborate about the Black Swan. Basically, it consisted of a large room filled with wooden chairs, a small raised dais for the performers, and a few stage lights. Harry saw to it that his coffee house ran smoothly, as did most of the other coffee houses.

There was one exception: the Purple Onion in Yorkville. It got my vote as the worst run. I tried not to notice how filthy the dressing room was. I was making my way to the stage on my opening night when I suddenly realized I couldn't walk properly. I took my shoes off to discover cigarette butts from the dressing-room floor stuck to the bottom of my socks. When I did get on stage at the Onion, the butts on my socks were nothing compared to what was waiting in the audience. Even though there was no liquor licence, a middle-aged alcoholic had entered the room already drunk. His shouts during my performance were extremely loud and completely incoherent – each time I came to a punchline, what the audience heard instead was "yazzawoozwazza wawawa." I had no choice but to cut my act short. "Let that be a lesson to all of us," I said as I left the stage, determined not to show my true humiliation. "Never drink on an empty head."

In retrospect, the heckler may not have been drunk. He may have been insane. Or maybe he had gone in there assuming that a coffee house was a place you go to sober up. It was the one and only time I was ever heckled in such a place. Nightclubs were a different story. In nightclubs, your show could be more of a competition than a performance. You'd be signed to do a forty-minute show two or three times a night. Out of that 120 minutes, you might do thirty minutes of comedy. The rest of the time would be spent coping with drunken hecklers.

The pattern is always the same: a drunk in the audience becomes convinced that God has chosen him to put the comedian to the test, to determine whether the comedian is professional enough to withstand an onslaught of inane heckling. Once the heckler gets into your rhythm, it's all downhill.

With very few exceptions, the nightclub managers were always on the side of the hecklers. I could never understand that, until one day, after I had been mercilessly heckled by the same person every night for five days, I asked the nightclub owner why it wasn't possible for a waiter or manager to go over to the heckler and quietly strangle him. "Dave," the owner said, which was exciting in itself, an owner who knew my name. "Dave," he said again, "follow me." He took me into his office and pulled out the bar bills paid by the drunken heckler that week. Until that moment, I hadn't really understood how much people are willing to invest in getting drunk. I suddenly realized that, without obnoxious alcoholics, the nightclub simply couldn't afford comedians like me.

All you can do is realize that being heckled comes with the territory. As you go on stage, remember that you will be heckled, and try

to be ready when it happens. It's always a challenge, but because
hecklers are nearly always drunk when they are performing, there is
not much a sober comic can't get away with. Some responses to try:
*The cost of a brain operation is quite reasonable now. You're far too
nice a person to be going around without one.* Or you could try: *Why
not act like a gentleman? Or don't you do impersonations?* Or, if that
fails, how about *I have to admit, you've got some great lines. If you
were a professional, you could cover them with makeup.* Or, to a
heckler who was determined to interrupt a Member for Kicking
Horse Pass monologue, *Did you ever think of teaming up with a ventriloquist? It's in the paper today. A ventriloquist paid eighteen thousand dollars for a dummy. We're getting you for nothing. That doesn't
seem fair. You need an agent! Don't sit there handling yourself. Get an
agent! A travel agent! I'll help you pack!* As my mother was always
reminding me about death, it is important to be ready.

With the success of *The Best of Spring Thaw* at the Vancouver
International Festival in 1963, Mavor Moore decided that it was
finally time for a national tour. The first *Spring Thaw* cross-Canada
tour started in January 1964. The cast – headlined by Barbara
Hamilton and myself, along with actor Peter Mews, singers Jack
Duffy, Bill Cole, and Liane Marshall, dancers Dean Regan, Diane
Nyland, and Marilyn Stuart and understudies Tink Robinson and
Shirley Millner – assembled in Vancouver for rehearsals in early
January. We opened later that month in Victoria, with a revue that
was an amalgam of the show's best numbers over the past sixteen
years. Critics and audiences were both enthusiastic. After three days
in Victoria, performers, musicians, technicians, and instruments
were stuffed into a large bus; scenery, props, and lighting equipment were loaded into a large truck, and we were on our way. Eight
months, forty-four stops, and some four thousand miles later, the
first national tour of *Spring Thaw* ended in Charlottetown, P.E.I.,
where we were part of the first Charlottetown Festival.

    One of the first stops was Nelson. Following our performance, a
reception was given in our honour, a reception that produced an
awesome moment for me. I was told that the person pouring the tea
was "Frankie." Frankie was the legendary survivor of the Frank slide,

(Above left) playbill for The Best of Spring Thaw; *(above right) with Barbara Hamilton in* The Best of Spring Thaw, *1965 – Barbara as a Moisiev dancer, me as Sol Hurok; (below) Peter Mews, Jack Duffy, Barbara Hamilton, and me, in* Spring Thaw

an event that almost destroyed the town of Frank in 1903. She was a baby at the time, and had been found, miraculously alive on the railway tracks, by a railway engineer. Poems and songs had been written about Frankie, one of which, "The Ballad of Frankie Slide," had been very effectively presented in an earlier *Spring Thaw* by Robert Goulet. And now, here this legend was, in the flesh, being Mother with a teapot.

I was discreetly asked by the hostess of the reception not to mention the landslide. Frankie had said everything she had to say about it, long ago. I obliged the hostess. My conversation with Frankie was fairly limited. "Tea?" she asked. "Why not?" I answered, thrilled to be spoken to by a person from the pages of history.

The only outright disaster of the tour occurred when we arrived in Melville, Saskatchewan, where we discovered that the presenter had made a mistake in the advertising. He had listed the performances as being 6:00 p.m. and 8:00 p.m., instead of 6:00 p.m. and 9:00 p.m. Customers were arriving at 7:00 p.m. for a performance that didn't begin until 9:00 – this in the depths of a Saskatchewan winter. Through the dressing-room window, we could see them lined up out in the freezing February air, enjoying a wind-chill factor that had just said goodbye to the thermometer.

As I was in charge of the show, I asked each performer if he or she would be willing to shave some time off our meal break, so we could start the second show before 9:00 p.m. Everyone said yes, as long as the union steward was agreeable. I went to see the steward, Bill Cole. "Bill," I said, "the presenter made a mistake in our starting times. Can we shave a little time off our break?"

"Absolutely not," he shot back.

I tried again. "Those folks out there are paying our salaries, Bill. They are the reason we are here."

"We have a contract," he said. "It stipulates there will be a one-hour meal break between performances."

This was hard going. "I know that, Bill. We both belong to the same union. Are you saying that, even though our customers have frozen faces, there can be no compromise, that logic can never take precedence over rules?"

"Right," Bill said. And that was it.

I did speak to Bill again, but I never forgave him. The Bill Coles of this world will never bow to logic or compassion because they are in possession of *rules*. There is a word to describe them, but it is not used in polite company. I have one question for them: if you don't care about the audience, why the hell are you in the audience business?

In Toronto, we played at the Royal Alex for over a month, and impressed Ed Mirvish by filling the theatre every night. To him, we were living proof that a Canadian production could make money. In Montreal, we played at La Comédie-Canadienne, on Ste. Catherine Street (now Théâtre du Nouveau Monde). I had visited the theatre as a merchant seaman when it was known as the Gaiety, and had seen some exciting vaudeville shows there, including one with the legendary exotic dancer Lili St. Cyr. Over the years, the building had been transformed into an important centre of French-language theatre. At the time of our visit, the great man of Quebec theatre, Gratien Gélinas, was the proprietor. He had booked an Anglo revue into a French-language theatre, which prompted one Westmounter

Mavor Moore staging "Quebec Secedes," a hilarious sketch set in Westmount. Left to right: Diane Nyland, me, Marilyn Stuart, Dean Regan, and Mavor Moore.

to say to me after the show one evening, "I think you people are playing the wrong theatre." He was wrong. We weren't. It was packed every night, and we never received a bigger welcome anywhere on the tour. The run in that house was fabulous, and I think the physical set-up was part of it. As soon as I walked on stage on opening night, the theatre became my favourite house in the whole country. It had the most open, yet intimate, feeling imaginable. The proscenium was long gone, so you were not standing in the middle of a picture frame. It was completely open. The box seats were sitting on an extension of the stage. The main-floor audience was only slightly below eye level, the first balcony was very slightly above eye level, and you could look up to the second balcony without tipping your head. It felt as if you were standing in the audience. Performing a monologue to standing-room-only crowds in that theatre was a heady experience. On opening night, after we had taken at least ten bows and were about to make our final exit, someone in the balcony was so carried away, he shouted out, "Now let's hear it for the drummer!" There was yet another tumultuous cheer.

After that, Mavor Moore came on stage and spoke *en français*. More ecstatic cheering. Mavor thanked the audience for its warm reception of this first performance of *Spring Thaw* in Montreal. He then especially thanked Gratien Gélinas for letting us use the theatre. He told the audience he considered Gratien to be the father of Canadian revue, and said how strongly he had been influenced by seeing the revues Gratien presented in the late thirties and forties, *Les Fridolinades*. When Mavor was done, Gratien himself walked on stage and the roar of the crowd was thunderous. It was a moving and all-too-rare occasion to see these giants of English-language and French-language theatre on stage together. I was happy to witness it. I had such admiration for Gratien Gélinas. He was always writing, always developing things. I said to him once that I thought it was the greatest thing in the world to be able to write the way he did. "Oh, you will, too, one day," he said, "you will." He was wrong. I've never been able to do long form. My writing talent is limited to monologues and sketches.

At the Charlottetown Festival *Spring Thaw* played in repertory with *Laugh With Leacock*, and the Festival's great musical success,

With Eric House in
Laugh with Leacock,
Charlottetown Festival, 1965

Anne of Green Gables. Many of the *Spring Thaw* cast also played in *Anne* – Barbara Hamilton, Peter Mews, Bill Cole, Jack Duffy, Dean Regan, Diane Nyland, Marilyn Stuart, and Liane Marshall all did double duty. I also appeared in two shows. I was in *Laugh With Leacock.* Actor John Drainie assembled the Leacock material for this production and worked with Mavor Moore on the direction. Our set was the backside of the Green Gables set. Everyone in the cast had a variety of roles – I played a lighthouse keeper, a German officer, a golfer, and a bank manager in the story that Leacock is most famous for, "My Financial Career." It was the only time I ever had the opportunity to work with the great John Drainie, who many of us considered the best actor in English-speaking Canada. He played the part of Stephen Leacock and was utterly convincing. Working with him was beyond a pleasure, it was a privilege.

The official opening of the Confederation Memorial Centre took place on October 7, 1964. It was a "command performance," whatever that may mean. (I think it means Lorne Greene is going to show up in a set of tails and be the master of ceremonies. Anyway, he did, and he was.) I was one of those "commanded" to appear before Queen Elizabeth II and Prince Philip. As the day of the show approached, there were countless rumours flying around about a possible attempt on her life by the Front de Libération du Québec (FLQ). I had never seen so much security. There were Mounties everywhere, mainly in plainclothes. They were on the roof of the Confederation Centre, on the street around the centre, in the lobby, backstage, up in the fly gallery, in the audience, and in the dressing rooms.

I had to consider what I would perform for the show. Mavor, who was producing, had asked me to do the Mountie character, Renfrew, because he felt it would be a representative piece of Canadiana and non-controversial. I had other ideas. I wanted to appear as myself and do a monologue that would be not only Canadian but topical and relevant. As it happened, the day before the event, a Toronto reporter had found the escaped Seafarers' International Union thug, Hal Banks, on a dock in Brooklyn, New York. Hal Banks was a favourite *bête noire* of mine from my merchant-navy days, and I was determined to work him into the show. Given the tension and anxiety in the air, I felt it wrong to play it safe and do humour that was inconsequential. Mavor listened as I laid out what I had in mind for my solo, then looked at me for a moment. "Do it!" he said. How can you not love a man like that?

When I got on stage, I slowly looked up into the fly gallery, then off into the right wing, then the left wing. Then, slowly turning to the front and looking at the audience, as if in complete bewilderment, I asked, in an absolutely innocent way, "What are all these Mounties doing here? Hal Banks has been found. He's in Brooklyn!" There was a silent moment as the audience took in what I had said, followed by a explosion of laughter. The tension, which a moment earlier you could have cut with a knife, completely evaporated. After that, I could do no wrong. By intermission, Prince Philip was using my material. Quotes from the monologue appeared in newspapers

Forcing a confession from a monarch. Her Majesty tells me she prefers the balcony to a box seat.

all over the world. Even some Canadian newspapers carried them.

When the show was over, the Queen was most appreciative. "Where do you get your ideas?" she asked. Since I wasn't sure, I changed the subject, and asked her how she liked sitting in the front row of the balcony, rather than in the traditional box seat. "Why do you ask?" she said.

"I sat in a box seat once," I replied, "and all I saw was half a show and a lot of stagehands."

"I see what you mean," she said. "Where do you get your ideas?"

Then it was Prince Philip's turn. "Where are you from?" was his inevitable question. The response of North Vancouver didn't seem to ring any bells. He did say I reminded him very much of his friend, a yachting man from the Isle of Wight. Unfortunately, I couldn't use that in my brochure: "'Broadfoot reminds me of my friend, a yachting man from the Isle of Wight' – HRH Prince Philip." It doesn't work.

Standing next to me in the receiving line was Anna Russell, with whom I had not appeared since *Spring Thaw '53*. She had sung a song for the Queen that included many strange animal noises. "I can do those strange noises, too," the Queen said to her, "but not when I'm wearing my tiara." Later, Her Majesty told Prime Minister Pearson that I was her favourite. I was so satirical, she said. I wouldn't lie about a thing like that. You can look it up. It's in Lester Pearson's *Memoirs*, Part 2.

Confederation Centre, Charlottetown, Command Performance

[Dave]

What are all these Mounties doing here? Hal Banks has been found! He's in Brooklyn.

It's all very well for Judge Norris to call Hal Banks a hoodlum, a thug, a gangster, an Al Capone, an egocentric, and a Hitler . . . but no union leader is PERFECT. *Hal may have hurt shipping a little, but look what he's done for bicycle-chain manufacturers.*

Trusteeship of unions is one of the things to be discussed at the founding convention of the New Apathetic Party. This new party has been named Apathetic to appeal to the average Canadian. Already you can feel the groundswell. Apathy is sweeping the country.

As you know, we have four national political parties at present. We have Liberal, which is like Conservative without experience. We have Conservative, which is like Liberal without warheads. We have NDP, *which is like Labour without doctors. And we have Social Credit, which is like Conservative without the inconvenience of democracy.*

In the new party we have taken a strong stand on DIVORCE. *We want to make it so difficult to obtain a divorce that no one will consider marriage. This will abolish desertion.*

In the area of crime, we want to bring back public hangings. We believe capital punishment is a deterrent, and we want to deter as many as possible by holding public hangings on Friday nights in shopping malls. We believe crime can be controlled by the federal government. Just as it now controls the CNR. We want to make sure crime does not pay.

On biculturalism, we believe our French-speaking citizens must stop thinking of themselves as second-class citizens, and realize that all Canadians are second-class citizens. We believe the future course of Confederation must be to this goal: a weak federal government and ten strong, autonomous provinces, loosely connected by fear.

We accept as inevitable the God Complexes of our provincial premiers. How can a premier own his own Hydro Power without getting a sense of . . . "Let there be light."

In Foreign Affairs we demand the permanent recognition of Chiang Kai-shek as the real leader of the people of mainland China, and we demand permanent trade agreements with Mao Tse-tung, whoever she is, to insure the farm vote.

We believe in privatization and will work toward the sale of Parliament Hill to a developer.

We believe birth control to be useless unless it can be made retroactive. The attitude of the Anglican Church has been most discouraging to us. They have already approved, in principle, the sterilization of imbeciles, idiots, psychopaths, and Baptists. This takes in far too many of us.

We are opposed to any extension of Old Age Pension programs. We believe the hardships of old age should be privately owned.

With regard to unions, we will establish private trusteeships that will get corruption out of labour unions and back into management where it belongs.

In defence, we are against abandoning our naval frigate. We see nothing wrong with a sailor using that kind of language.

As far as military cutbacks are concerned, we must stop scrapping and start selling our old obsolete weapons to poor

> *unsuspecting countries. Then we will be in a position to buy*
> *new obsolete weapons.*
>
> *As for this country's ongoing identity crisis, we have strug-*
> *gled to produce a distinctive national flag. We started by includ-*
> *ing the symbols of the two founding groups. A symbol for males*
> *and a symbol for females. This gave us a pornographic flag. So*
> *we covered it with a Maple Leaf.*
>
> [Dave exits.]

Throughout the summer in Charlottetown, I continued my usual practice of spending days trying to write new material. I had collected a substantial number of new sketches and monologues, and at the end of the season I packed these, along with all my personal belongings, and headed back to Toronto, to look for work.

I arrived in the city to find an International Conference of Shriners under way. Every hotel from Port Hope to Hamilton was booked solid. After spending a few hours on the phone, calling obscure hotels to no avail, I called a writer friend, Eve Law, who was living on Avenue Road just north of Bloor, and asked if I could leave my luggage with her, until I had sorted out my accommodation problem. She said, if I was desperate, there was an attic at the top of the house in which she was staying. She could arrange for me to use that until the Shriners had left town. I thanked her, made my way to Avenue Road, and took my luggage up several flights of stairs to the attic. There was no bed, just three tired-looking mattresses. At the back of the room, there was a door leading to a fire escape that led down to the laneway behind the house. Three mattresses and a fire escape – what more could I ask?

I made my way back down the interior staircase, and walked up to Yorkville, and in no time ran into an old friend, the multi-talented Larry Zolf, who was still working the coffee-house circuit as a stand-up comedian. We got talking about various satirical ideas, and I told him about a piece I had been working on in the summer. He liked the idea. The script was in my briefcase, only half a block away, so

I decided to go and get it. I ran back to the house and upstairs to the attic.

My briefcase was nowhere to be found. I ran down and asked Eve if anyone had come in while I was out. "No," she said. "Nobody." I knew then that the fire escape was my undoing. Out on the street Larry was waiting for me, and I told him my briefcase with all my summer's work had disappeared. Larry thought for a moment, looked off into infinity, and then, for some inexplicable reason, said "Webster." "What was that?" I asked. "Webster," he replied. "I think we should check out the Webster Café."

So up the street to the Webster Café we went. Larry and I took a booth, ordered coffee, and watched the goings on. It wasn't long before a young man of about twenty came in and sat down in the booth next to ours. Larry looked at me. "There's your man," he whispered. Without a word, we both got up and, uninvited, moved into the young man's booth. He was trapped. Larry began talking about how Toronto was changing so quickly, and how careful people had to be to protect themselves from theft of property. "Just tonight," he said, "a briefcase was stolen from the attic of a house right here on Avenue Road." It was time for me to do my part. "And what is so ironic," I chimed in, "is that the briefcase contained a shaving kit of very little value, and a bunch of scripts of absolutely no value to anybody except the guy who wrote them." The young man looked at the two of us, and turned a whiter shade of pale. "Isn't that stupid," Larry went on, "that a guy would bother to steal scripts he can't use." I was dumbfounded by the young man's response. "I didn't know they were scripts," he said. With Larry firmly ensconced at the young man's side, I went to the phone to call the police. I got back to the booth in time to hear Larry tell the young man, "I would hate to be your lawyer."

By the time I had paid for the coffee, a police officer had entered the café and had our suspect in custody. The officer invited thief and victim to sit in his cruiser. Larry wished me good luck, and took off. The police officer said it was up to me whether I wanted to lay charges. The young man panicked. "Please don't give me a criminal record," he begged. The police officer gave me the young man's name, address, and phone number, and told me to think about it.

"You can lay a charge later," he said. "It doesn't have to be tonight." The shaving kit could be replaced, the scripts couldn't. "If the scripts are returned by the morning," I said, "I won't lay charges."

Early the next morning I arose from my three mattresses and, when I opened the fire-escape door, there were my scripts, neatly sitting in their folder. When it comes to intuition, Larry Zolf takes the prize.

Not long after I found a Toronto apartment and settled in, I received a letter from Jean, asking if I would be kind enough to go to court to obtain a Canadian divorce. After obtaining a quickie divorce in Mexico, Jean had married Canadian CBC-TV producer Ross McLean, in New York, which is where they were then living. However, technically and legally, in Canada she was still married to me. Because of this, Jean and Ross were reluctant to come back home.

The name of the presiding judge at the divorce hearing was Mr. Justice Léo Landreville. When I showed up in his courtroom, the ensuing dialogue went almost like a comedy sketch:

JUDGE L: Mr. Broadfoot, as I understand it, you are here seeking a
           divorce.
DAVE: That's correct, Your Honour.
JUDGE L: The person you wish to divorce is Jean Broadfoot.
DAVE: That's correct, Your Honour.
JUDGE L: Mrs. Broadfoot is not residing in Toronto?
DAVE: No, Your Honour. She's residing in New York.
JUDGE L: Mrs. Broadfoot is presently residing in New York.
DAVE: Under the name of McLean.
JUDGE L: McLean? McLean is Jean Broadfoot's maiden name?
DAVE: No, Your Honour, Jean's maiden name is Robb.
JUDGE L: Robb? R-o-b-b?
DAVE: Yes, Your Honour, but Jean is not known as Robb. She is
           known as Jean Templeton.
JUDGE L: I know your wife is an actress. Can I assume Jean Temple-
           ton is Jean Broadfoot's stage name?
DAVE: Partly, Your Honour.
JUDGE L: Partly?
DAVE: Jean McLean's first husband's name was Templeton.

JUDGE L: That's how Jean Robb became known as Jean Templeton?

DAVE: That's correct, Your Honour.

JUDGE L: But, at this time, as far as this court is concerned, Jean Templeton is legally Jean Broadfoot.

DAVE: Yes, Your Honour. That is correct.

JUDGE L: So why is she living under the name of McLean?

DAVE   While I was living in the United Kingdom, Jean was living in New York. She flew from there to Mexico and obtained a divorce in Mexico, and then got married in New York.

JUDGE L: Your wife got married? To whom?

DAVE: Her husband is Ross McLean, Your Honour.

JUDGE L: Your wife's husband is Ross McLean. *(Looking very bewildered.)* Who are you?

DAVE: I'm Jean Broadfoot. I'm sorry, I'm *Dave* Broadfoot, Jean McLean's . . . uh, Jean Templeton's northernmost husband.

JUDGE L: So, in the U.S., presently, Jean Templeton is Mrs. McLean, but if Jean Templeton were here, Mrs. McLean would be Mrs. Broadfoot.

DAVE: As far as I know, Your Honour.

JUDGE L: Mr. Broadfoot?

DAVE: Yes, Your Honour.

JUDGE L: Are you, by any chance, acquainted with Pierre Berton, the man who writes about Canadian history?

DAVE: I am, Your Honour.

JUDGE L: Do you suppose he could be persuaded to come down here and explain this to us?

DAVE: I'm willing to try, Your Honour.

Realizing what the judge had just asked me, the court reporter literally collapsed over his little typing machine. Everyone else in the courtroom had broken into what can only be described as a suppressed giggling. The way it worked out, Pierre Berton didn't need to come and explain things. Within months, I was technically a free man, Judge Landreville had taken early retirement, and Mr. and Mrs. McLean were on their way to another divorce.

Jean later married a fourth time, then, sadly, developed epilepsy. She would die tragically in 1978, from a fall down her basement stairs. She left many shining comedic moments. They are not forgotten.

During a visit to North Vancouver I made in the spring of 1965, my father looked me in the eye and quietly said, "They tell me I have cancer." After a lifetime of avoiding pork, which he believed caused the disease, this must have been quite a blow. Yet the calm way he accepted the cancer and the courageous way he dealt with it made me more proud of him than I had ever been. He was magnificent in this acceptance – no self-pity, no "Why is this happening to me?" He just went on living his life, as he always had, until the moment of his death. Every day, he went to his office, without complaint, and worked. His last day there was a Friday; he died on the Monday. He was eighty-three. I don't know that my father showed me how to live, but he certainly showed me how to die.

After the funeral, as we were coming back to the house, my mother sat beside me in the car. There was a long silence, and then she spoke in that special, gentle voice she had. "He could have been such a nice man." It was the oddest thing to say, but it said it all.

My father and mother in their eighties

There is no getting away from the fact that he was inconsiderate and neglectful of my mother. Everything was on his terms. He abused her over small things that didn't seem to matter to me – whether the kitchen stove was burning properly was a favourite beef of his. It took me a long time to realize that all his anger and abusiveness had nothing to do with the state of the stove. The hardships of the Depression had changed him. I'm sure he was frustrated about his whole life. He had started from zero, climbed to the top of his profession, and when it all fell apart – at least partly as a result of his pride – he took it out on my mother.

My father was never abusive to me the way he was to my mother, but we were never close. Perhaps, if he hadn't been so obsessed with religion, we would have had a better relationship, but his obsession with the Bible coloured everything, and created a huge divide between us. He also truly believed that the British were a lost tribe of Israel. "Do you believe this, what your dad believes, that you are really Jewish?" his friend Solly Ruben asked me one day.

"No, I don't," I replied.

"Me neither," Solly laughed back. Yet my father would go on and on about the British being Israelites, in a way I could never really understand.

He would have been thrilled if I had shown an interest in his other great obsession, cricket, but the atmosphere at cricket games always made me feel like an alien. The only time I felt close to my father was when he talked about business, which seemed the absolute opposite of the way it was for most people with their fathers. Percy Broadfoot had a way of bringing the clothing business that he loved to life, and I was always fascinated. It was a business I had come to love, too. All the businessmen he dealt with said the same thing about my father. "One thing about your dad," one of them once told me, echoing many others, "he's as straight as a die. You don't have to worry when you do a deal with him. You don't even have to write it down." Above everything else, my father was an honest man. In retrospect, I can say that I inherited two things from him and I'm quite content with them: honesty and long legs. Ironically, if you're honest, you don't need long legs.

Chapter 7

MONTREAL! THE TIME OF MY VIE!

In the summer of 1966, I was invited to be part of a bilingual revue that would run throughout Expo '67 at the Canadian Pavilion. As Johnny Wayne, Frank Shuster, and Gratien Gélinas were the producers, I accepted the invitation with enthusiasm. Things had gotten very quiet in Toronto. Club dates were slow, so I had done what I always try to do when this happens, produced my own revue, *Canada Goose*, which played at the Dell Tavern. The reviews had not been great, and although it had done well enough, the run was short. I was glad of the prospect of a long run in Montreal, and I headed off to a meeting there that summer to discuss the content of the show, and to look over the Canadian Pavilion. I also wanted to make arrangements for accommodation for the duration of the run – there were all sorts of rumours about how busy and expensive Montreal was going to be in Centennial Year. A friend suggested I get in touch with Diane Simard, who worked for Radio-Canada. She dealt with a lot of visiting entertainers in her work, and he thought she might be able to help me. I called Diane, and that conversation changed my life. She did help me. She's still helping me. I still need help.

"Come on over," she said when I called. When I arrived at her apartment off Côte-des-Neiges, she introduced herself, gave me a glass of wine and a few suggestions about accommodation. We talked for a bit. Then, as I was only in Montreal for the day, the time

With fellow actor Sean Sullivan, on the set of Winds of Choice, *1966 motion picture*

came for me to take the plane home. But all the way home, I thought about Diane. I was very taken with her.

Back in Toronto, I had to complete shooting my first movie role in *Winds of Choice*, for the Ontario government. That done, I thought, I'm going to Montreal to work next year anyway, things are slow here, why don't I move now? I went back to Montreal to see Roy Patterson, who owned the Montreal restaurant, Mother Martin's, and suggested to him that I do a one-man show in the Martin's cabaret room. Roy readily agreed, and the engagement lasted until the end of 1966. Meanwhile, I was in Montreal. I could get to know Diane.

She was, I soon found out, a very courageous person. Behind the warm, easy smile, which instantly puts everyone at ease, behind the remarkably sunny disposition, which was and is a joy to be with, is an incredible strength. Diane had polio as a child, and although it had no lasting effects, like many people who have faced down a serious illness and beaten it, she has a different perspective on life. Diane knows what really matters. I was impressed by everything about her. To me, she was and is the perfect combination of intelligence and compassion. Plus she could speak both official languages fluently, could speak some Spanish, and in her limited spare time was studying Russian. She was also not in awe of celebrity. The reason for this, I soon discovered, was that, in her work as an assistant to a television producer and later as a full-fledged producer herself, she met and worked with too many famous people, from Jacques Brel to Jack Benny, to be overwhelmed by them.

It wasn't long before I moved in with Diane, in her apartment off Côte-des-Neiges, which we shared with her two wonderful Siamese cats, Cleo and Antoine. Antoine, the affectionate one, had a bit of a limp – not surprising, as he was the survivor of a fall from a fifth-floor balcony. Cleo was adventurous. I'd put her on my shoulder, and go off to buy the groceries, and she would just sit there, calm as could be, watching it all with interest.

The sociability of that first winter in Montreal was a revelation. I knew the temperatures were lower than Toronto, and I knew there was more snow, but what I hadn't realized was the frequency of winter parties. It seemed as if there was a party in someone's home every week. I quickly realized that, with Diane to guide me, I was getting a crash course in Quebec social life, culture, and history. We would often walk through the nearby Côte-des-Neiges cemetery, which fascinated me. There is a lot of history in that cemetery. We found headstones of men who took part in the Papineau Rebellion of 1837, marked with the fact that they had "served" so many years in Bermuda, which was then a penal colony. Diane and I then went looking to see who else we could find. She was convinced that there were also men who had been sent to Australia and Tasmania, as punishment for their part in the Rebellion, and it turned out there were. I learned more about Quebec history that first winter with Diane than I had in all my previous forty-one years. I had appeared in Montreal before, and was in touch with all the Montreal agents. I had done my season at the Mountain Playhouse, had stayed with friends Reid and Jean McLeod on Tupper Street in Westmount, but I had never been in francophone Montreal to any great extent. All that now changed. My French did not improve – it never has improved in the forty-odd years I have been trying to learn the language, but obviously never trying quite hard enough. What did improve, though, was my knowledge of the culture.

Diane took me to Casa Loma, a club on Ste-Catherine Street East,

Diane, at the time we met,
1966

where we saw a teenage girl, with a phenomenal voice, a girl who in my opinion went on to become the best pop singer this country ever produced, Ginette Reno. At La Comédie-Canadienne, we saw Gilles Vigneault, whose "Mon Pays" was on the way to becoming an anthem for Quebeckers. Even then, English Canadians thought of Vigneault as a dangerous separatist. What I saw when he came on stage was love – you had the feeling of someone who loved where he lived, loved what he did, loved the people he was doing it for, and they reflected that love back to him. I have never seen anyone who had more impact on an audience. Even though I could not under-stand the words, there was no misunderstanding the emotion.

Diane also took me to see the comedy team Les Cyniques (Marc Laurendeau, André Dubois, Serge Grenier, and Marcel St.-Germain), and again, even though I could not always follow the language, I could follow the humour. They did outrageous and often sacrilegious satire. St. Joseph's Oratory, the shrine which held the heart of Quebec's popular faith healer, Brother André, became in their hands "The Miracle Mart." It was such fine satire, you could not take offence.

As I settled into life in Montreal, I began to learn a basic truth about the difference between Quebec and the Rest of Canada. In the Rest of Canada, the entertainment focus is Hollywood. In Quebec, it is Montreal. That seemed to apply to everything in entertainment – comedy, theatre, movies, dance, jazz, symphony, recordings. It was all right there, in that remarkable city, in a way that it didn't seem to be in Toronto – at least, not then. The Québécois attitude toward their performers was different. When a successful Quebec singer or comedian appears in Montreal, thousands will turn out to see them. What a Quebec star can earn in a week at Place des Arts would take their counterpart in the R.O.C. at least a year. There is also a different kind of respect – a respect that I could feel. Even I was a beneficiary. Over the years, as I became better known, there were numerous times in Montreal, when I went to a theatre box office to pick up tickets, I'd place my money on the counter, only to have it pushed back to me with the words, "Oh, no, Monsieur Broadfoot, you don't pay." That's not a custom I'm advocating – I think everybody should pay to see performers work, especially other performers. But picking up the tab is a way of showing respect.

My run at Mother Martin's was over at the end of the year. That Christmas Diane and I spent with her family in Hull. All the uncles and aunts came – the small house was full of people coming and going, and not to church. This was living proof to me of the Quiet Revolution. Quebeckers, at least the ones I knew, were no longer a people governed by the church. There might have been talk of going to midnight mass that Christmas, but no one went. I couldn't help thinking that leaving the church seemed much easier for these Catholic Quebeckers than it had been for Baptist Dave. That Christmas, we ate and drank and partied, and had a wonderful time. It all seemed so much more joyful to me than Anglo-Canadian life in North Vancouver. There probably were Anglos in North Van who had a lot of fun, but I never seemed to run into them.

There was one thing on which Diane and I did not always see eye to eye: the future of Quebec. Diane had her own point of view on this. I had my point of view, too, about the future of Canada. It was a meeting of two nationalists – she was a nationalist about Quebec, I was a Canadian nationalist. I had to learn how strongly she cared about Quebec. Even if I disagreed with her, I found the strength of her belief and her concern about her culture attractive. She was, and is, a liberated woman, one of the generation who were the Quiet Revolution. Not living in Quebec any more, we no longer talk about it a great deal. Who knows, if I had been born in Quebec, maybe I would have felt the same way.

Diane was quite surprised when I asked her to marry me. She hadn't realized how much I cared for her. "Dave Broadfoot," she said, "you're joking." But I wasn't; it wasn't something I would joke about. We were married on January 13, 1967, which if you look on your calendar you will find was a Friday, and the luckiest day of my life.

The following day, we set off on our honeymoon. I must have been extremely naive about the travel business, because I allowed a representative of Thomas Cook to convince me that there would be no possibility of finding hotel accommodation in the Caribbean at that time of year on such short notice. I know better now, but he was then able to convince me that the only hope for a getaway two weeks after New Year's Day would be on a cruise, so we joined a cruise ship, the ss *Oceanic*, in New York. The interesting thing about that was that it gave us a first-hand look at the nasties who were working the New York docks. They were alligators disguised as human dock-workers, who looked at the passengers as though we were so much vermin they were obliged to tolerate.

Once on board, we were assigned to a specific table in the dining salon. It was clear that our tablemates all knew each other. The men were pipe-fitters from New Jersey, accompanied by their semi-unattractive spouses. Two days of dining with this team, and I began having very dark thoughts. However, murder is not in my vocabulary. One of the spouses told me how proud she was of her youngest son. He had been riding the New York subway when a professional photographer, about to miss his stop, jumped up and got off the train, leaving all his equipment behind. This proud mother's son grabbed the whole lot of camera equipment, and walked off the train as if it were his own. "The subway's lost-and-found will find the owner, I'm sure," I ventured helpfully. "Why should my son give such valuable stuff to the lost-and-found?" she replied. "They'll only sell it." "What did your son do with it?" I asked. It turned out it was gathering dust under his bed. As I tried to digest the logic of this, she went on to tell me how proud she was of her older son, who was serving in Vietnam. In the course of telling me this, she unconsciously revealed she had no idea where Vietnam was. She apparently had it confused with Guatemala. I didn't know then – I'm still not sure – how to move yourself to another table in the dining room without giving offence. It seemed we were stuck for the duration of the cruise. I have recently given more thought to this very serious cruise conundrum. I have so far not revealed my solution, as it involves a great deal of lying.

Things got worse. At our destination port, Nassau, it was impossible not to feel the oppressive colonialism of the time. The first large shop we came upon didn't have a single black employee. Then, on a street corner, we bumped into a couple I had met once in Toronto. There I was with Diane, my bride of a few days, and the hometown couple wouldn't stop talking about Jean Templeton. "How is she doing?" they asked. "What went wrong between you two?" I could picture their later conversation. "Gee, for a comedian, he's not very cheerful." As I've said before, genius has its limits. Unlike stupidity.

It seemed to me that the return voyage would never come, but finally we were headed home. After two weeks at sea with our mentally challenged company, Diane and I both understood what an animal must feel like, caught in a nasty trap. The only escape would have been to hurl ourselves overboard, but that would just have encouraged the sharks.

Shortly after coming back, I began rehearsals for the Expo show, *The Katimavik Revue*. As promised, Wayne, Shuster, and Gélinas produced, Stan Daniels and Gilles Richer did a lot of the writing, and Alan Lund did the choreography. *Katimavik* was unlike any other revue, before or since, in that it had a unique and very positive concept – francophones performed in French, anglophones performed in English. A lot of the material was visual enough that unilingual visitors (in any language) could understand what was going on. Musical numbers, we all did together. There was even a ballet. Hard to believe, but I was in it. In tights.

For six months, we did two shows a day, six days a week. Five hundred people got to see each performance, and many were turned away. Critic Robert Fulford called it the "least sexy and least controversial revue in the history of the world." That's not surprising, partly because it was produced for the government, and partly because it started early enough for children to come to see it. But not being sexy or controversial didn't stop it from being a success. Marilyn Stuart, Jack Duffy, Paul Berval, Jean-Guy Moreau, Bob Ainslie, Betty Hader, and I were appearing with the two hottest comedy stars in Quebec – Dominique Michel and Denise Filiatrault, who were then enjoying a huge success on television starring in their own sitcom, "Moi et l'autre." Dominique began *The Katimavik Revue*, appearing from the back of the audience, walking to the stage, impersonating an Expo visitor. When the audience saw who she was, there were screams of delight and recognition. She then mimed an Expo visitor waiting, and waiting, and waiting in line to go into the pavilion, and trying to stay awake. Suddenly, she collapses, and pretty soon two fellows show up with a stretcher, put her on it, and take her into the pavilion. Just as they are going in, she gives the audience the V-sign. It was Johnny Wayne's idea, and the audience loved it. They'd all been through the wait themselves, many times.

In my own favourite moment of the show, I played Moses. Wearing a white robe and sandals, with long flowing hair and a beard and carrying a staff, I approached a security guard and asked the way to the Pavilion of Israel. The guard points in the right direction, and I head off. "No, no, no," the guard yells, "you can't go that way, it's all water!! You have to go around and over the bridge." I stare at the security guard, raise my staff, and point it out over the water. There is thunder and lightening. I walk straight ahead, through where the water supposedly was, and on to the Pavilion of Israel. A classic Wayne and Shuster idea. I also enjoyed performing my own creation, an illustrated slide show on Expo, in which my assistant Paul Berval dropped the slides, and reassembled them in the wrong order. As I talked about the symbol for Confederation, what flashed on the screen was an image of two double-yoked oxen struggling to plough a field together. That always got the biggest laugh of the evening.

Every day, I arrived at the Expo site on Îsle Notre-Dame to be greeted by the sound of a Trinidadian steel band echoing off the water of the man-made lake. I never got tired of it. Could there be a happier daily greeting? Although I was working every evening, Diane and I managed to visit most of the Expo pavilions, sampling all the different cultures and cuisines. We indulged in margaritas at the Mexican pavilion, queued time and again, without success, to see the National Film Board's "Labyrinth," marvelled at the many avant-garde movie techniques on display, expecially in the Czechoslovakia pavilion, where actors leaped off the screen onto the stage, then back onto the screen. We loved the spectacular military tattoo that re-enacted the whole story of Canada, including the D-Day invasion of Normandy. There were fabulous jazz concerts to see, from Dave Brubeck's quartet to Oscar Peterson's trio. Since Diane was working at the Broadcast Centre on the Expo site, we both spent most of that summer of '67 at Expo.

As *The Katimavik Revue* went rolling along, I started collecting and writing material for a new cabaret revue. I had talked to Roy Patterson, the owner of Mother Martin's, and he was willing to become a producer. I had always wanted to work with Ted Zeigler, who was best known for playing Johnny Jellybean on a children's television show originating at CFCF in Montreal. Ted was a very physical performer – a skinny man, who was able to do a lot of funny things with his rubbery body. When I asked him if he would like to work with me, it turned out he was very interested. So was a singer-actress, a graduate of the National Theatre School, Peggy Mahon. I also wanted to work with an exciting young musical director, Jerry de Villiers.

The result was *Squeeze*, a satirical stage show, which began its run at Mother Martin's early in 1968. I decided on *Squeeze* as a timely and appropriate title, and made a logo for the show in which Planet Earth was caught in a huge clamp. One half of the clamp was the U.S.S.R., the other half, the U.S.A., which was appropriate for those Cold War years. Across the Canadian part of the crushed globe was the word *Squeeze*. The revue was topical, but not too topical, as we were hoping for a long run. Canada's *deux cultures*, or as we say in English, "two floundering peoples," provided targets for the satire, as did Indian gurus, pregnancy, student power, suburbia, and then Canadian prime minister Lester Pearson.

[*Dave as* Prime Minister, Lester B. Pearson]

As your Prime Minister, I am very grateful for this opportunity to explain Canada's policy on Vietnam. Our policy of Quiet Conspiracy. Quiet complicity. Oh, what is that word?

Economically, we are supporting the American policy over there, which is a policy of Bombing, Burning, and Pacification. However, we don't believe that Pacification will work. We tried that in Quebec. Bombing and burning, or B and B as we like to call it, has been much more effective over there in Asia. Due to the advanced technology of the U.S. Air Force, they have been able to wipe out entire fields of rice. So that now, a lot of Vietnamese people who are not dead are hungry. But those who are dead can rest assured that their ashes will never be owned by the state. As would have been the case under communism.

Yes, it is unfortunately true that sometimes the only way to save people from the horrors of communism is to get rid of them. But I believe our policy of quiet duplicity . . . what is that word? Because I believe the Americans will never give up fighting over there until they have made the Vietnamese people just as happy as they have made their own coloured people. And if this means a hundred years of war for them, it means a hundred years of contracts for us.

And what a terrible cost this war is. I'm not talking lives now, I'm talking dollars. Do you know what it costs to kill one Vietnamese? Three hundred and fifty thousand dollars. And that's a civilian. It costs twice that amount to kill a soldier. They have to kill some soldiers. And that's in American money. Now, in Canadian money, that would come to . . . plus eight percent

Portraying Prime Minister Lester B. Pearson

. . . seven hundred and forty-nine thousand, six hundred and fifty-four dollars and thirty-six cents. And more horrible than that, if the Viet Cong continue to steal American oil, the U.S. may be forced to escalate again and bomb Texas.

Now we have been subjected to the most cruel criticism for honouring our commitments to supply war materials to the U.S. at this time, but this is the true spirit of Canadianism. If we have a product to sell, we sell it, even if it's our country.

We had worked on material for *Squeeze* right up to the twelfth hour, and yet we didn't have to cut one number. Everything worked. Mother Martin's was a great place to be working. The establishment had a one-hundred-year history in Montreal, and at its current location it was owned and run by Roy Patterson, a Montreal realtor. With its beautiful big comfy chairs in the lounge, specialty roast beef from the kitchens, and a wide selection of malt Scotch at the bar,

Outside Mother Martin's,
waiting to get paid

Mother Martin's was a favourite Anglo hang-out. Roy thought it was a coup, to own a place with such a reputation and long history. He welcomed the journalists from the Montreal *Gazette*, which was next door, who lined the bar as early as three in the afternoon, and he particularly welcomed priests. If Roy could get a bishop in his restaurant, he was in heaven. It was as if Roy thought he could buy indulgences.

There was an edge to Roy, when he was sober, but as soon as he had downed the first Rob Roy, he would become the world's most charming, generous, delightful human being. Fortunately for those of us who worked with him, he was drinking most of the time, so he was almost always fun. Roy was a great fan of Glayva, which starts out as Scotch, then goes through a few more distilling processes for people who like their drinks chewable. Glayva is not meant to be drunk in volume, it is meant to be drunk at the end of a meal, but Roy liked to drink it in volume, before, during, and after a meal. It started to be a problem.

After we had done our bows one night, Roy asked the technician to bring the lights up. He walked out on stage. "Ladies and gentlemen," he began, "you've been a really nice audience, why don't you all come upstairs and have a nice lobster dinner." He was inviting the entire audience to have dinner on the house. It was madness, but Roy was feeling good, and he had decided to do something nice. It seemed to me that this generosity had the potential to become a major problem, but for the moment I had other things to worry about.

It was a Friday night and we were well into the opening number when I noticed to my horror that the person sitting at the centre of the front table was my cousin. I looked again. There was another cousin. The whole table was solid with relatives. Throughout all the years of my professional life, I've suffered with a mental disorder called "relatives-in-the-audience syndrome." I'm not sure whether the condition emerged from fear of offending or fear of disapproval or fear of distraction or just plain fear. All I know is that it's something I've worked all my life to overcome with absolutely no success. Whenever I'm aware that I have relatives out front, the liberating freedom I normally experience on stage disappears.

My reaction that evening was my usual reaction: to go promptly into shock. My concentration was completely shattered. My performance skills had left the building. I could feel all the blood leaving my body and heading up into my face. I had blushed a couple of times in my life, but this – you could have stood me on Cape Scott as a warning beacon to small ships. The hostess of the room thought she had done something really nice by seating my relatives as close as possible to the stage. Really nice? I couldn't remember my lines, my name, what show I was in, what city I was in, or why I was in it. My advice to other performers who may suffer from the same disorder: wherever you appear, always tell the staff that if people show up claiming to be your relatives, they are to be told, "All the seats down front may appear to be empty, but the people who booked them three years ago are on their way here right now on a big bus. Fortunately for you, we have a few very special seats right at the back of the room that are kept for the exclusive use of people likes yourselves. Walk this way."

Toward the end of my time with the show, Ted Zeigler said something which meant a lot to me. We were sitting quietly in the dressing room, waiting to go on. "You know," he said, "in all this long run, I looked forward to coming to work every night." It *was* a long run, but we had such good fun, Ted and Peggy and Jerry and I. I enjoyed it so much that I even contemplated producing a revue

Squeeze, 1968, with Peggy Mahon and Ted Zeigler at Mother Martin's

and touring it across the country, and wrote to the Canada Council to see what their response might be to the idea. "Without in any way anticipating the Council's decision," the bureaucrat replied, "it is my opinion in this period of financial austerity, the Council has to set up priorities and it would only support projects of very high artistic quality." Which, translated, meant: forget it.

Squeeze ended up running for a year and a half, although Barrie Baldaro replaced me a year into the run. When Barrie came in one day to say he wouldn't be there for the last week, I decided to close it. I didn't want to go back into it again. If I had, I am sure it could have gone on and on. But I was already planning a second *Squeeze*, which after I had wracked my brains for an original, catchy title, was called *Squeeze II*. My idea was to present a revue which I could lend my name to as director and producer, but not appear in.

I hired Roy Wordsworth, John Davies, Marthe Mercure, and Sophie Clement for the show. Rehearsals went along smoothly until Roy, who was commuting from Toronto, drove his car off the highway. He was quite badly hurt, and as it was only a few days before the show was due to open, I had to come in and take over his roles, while continuing to direct, since no one else could have prepared quickly enough. We made it, the show opened well, and drew good crowds. Then, after three or four weeks, Roy Wordsworth's bones were healed enough for him to come back into the production. As soon as I stepped out of the cast, the audience numbers dropped dramatically. This was a surprise – it just hadn't occurred to me that I was the only cast member who had a bit of a following among Montrealers. We got busy, promoted the show enough that the numbers picked up, and it had a substantial run.

I was at Mother Martin's one night, to see how a new cast member was doing, when owner Roy Patterson's son, Tony, came over to me. "Dave," he said, whispering as quietly as he could, "whatever you have in here that's yours, get it out of here tonight. The bailiffs are coming. There'll be a padlock on the front door by 6:00 a.m." So as soon as the audience had left, we went to work. We scrambled till two in the morning, taking carloads of stuff away, until everything of ours was out. Because the situation was so frantic, there wasn't time to feel angry, but I knew I was headed for problems, as there would be no money to pay off my cast. Roy Patterson had hosted one too many lobster dinners on the house.

The next day, I got on the phone to the manager of the Playboy Club. He said he would be happy to have us, but wanted the name of the show changed. So we changed it to *Squeeze 3*. Two weeks later, we were back in business. I was proud of being able to make the move – usually venues are booked six months in advance, so we were lucky. It went well enough at the Playboy Club, but we were by no means playing to a satirical revue audience. Some who came were francophones from out of town. Others were anglophones from *way* out of town. Others were American tourists for whom any Canadian references were completely meaningless. Not an easy assignment. I would call that run slightly less than a glorious triumph.

Diane and I had bought a house in Lower Westmount, and settled comfortably into it. The house was one of a row of houses that all tipped slightly backwards away from the street – our next-door neighbour used to joke that he could come home drunk, pass out inside the front door, and wake up in the morning rolled up against the back door. When we moved in, our house had already been renovated, and there were only a few finishing touches to be done. My old friend Walter Ikeda came and helped me tile the floor of the library room, and a young man whom I had met while working as a prison volunteer came and did a fantastic job on the plumbing.

I had met him when Diane and I had volunteered to be part of an organization known as ARCAD. I forget now what the initials stood for, but ARCAD was founded by volunteer Kay Lines, with the intention of trying to reduce recidivism by improving the lives of prison inmates. Professionals in the arts volunteered their time to teach in prisons – some taught painting, some writing. I taught comedy, and Diane recruited some francophones to teach and others to perform for the inmates. Comedian Yvon Deschamps, singer Robert Charlebois and Les Baronets, with then-singer René Angelil, and Les Cyniques were among those she persuaded to come and entertain.

We spent a lot of time at the LeClerc Institute, a medium-security prison where I helped the inmates put on shows. Some of them were tough, but they were also smart, and were often way ahead of me. They were also suspicious of why I was there. I would be, too, in their place. I'd be reluctant to trust someone who did that, when no one had shown much interest in me before. I'd think, "Why is he doing this when he doesn't have to? It must be to make him feel good." My reasons for doing it were simple: I did it because I hoped, in some way, that getting these guys involved in putting on a show might increase their sense of their own value, their own worth, and that in a small way it might help when they got out.

One day, I got talking to one of the guards about it. "Is this really important?" I asked, as I had my own doubts. He said that we were the only people the inmates saw who were not in uniform. I had never thought about it that way, but the only people they ever saw were people whose job it was to keep them in their place. If we gave them anything, it was a sense that they were more than people who needed to be kept in their place. The inmates turned out to be good performers and the surprising thing was that they were not self-conscious at all, which you might have expected. They wrote the shows themselves, and were always a great hit with the other inmates.

ARCAD was just one of the political activities I got involved in at that time. Looking back, it is hard now to recapture the ferment of those years – the late 1960s and early 1970s were an incredible time in Quebec. It wasn't just the increasing nationalism of the Québécois. The ferment seemed to be everywhere. When the Russians invaded Czechoslovakia, putting an end to the Prague Spring, Diane and I joined the demonstration in front of the Russian Consulate in Montreal. There were huge demonstrations against the war in Vietnam, and we took part in those, too. We also took part in the Hemispheric Conference to end the war.

After the October Crisis in 1970, there was an increasing bitterness in Quebec, both among nationalists and the left, about how the Canadian government had handled the situation with the FLQ. During the crisis, I attended a big ACTRA union meeting, at which Laurier Lapierre was the only person to speak out and question what had happened since the imposition of the War Measures Act. All kinds of innocent people were being arrested, basic civil rights were abandoned, and Laurier was pleading with the ACTRA community to get involved, and not let this go on.

It was a much-needed plea. Throughout that time, I was rehearsing a TV show, and would arrive at rehearsal to hear the most incredible rumours going round about the FLQ kidnapping and torturing women. People were buying into the hysteria. They seemed to have lost their senses, as though they were willing to let a handful of terrorists destroy the morale of the whole country.

I have one enduring memory of that time, and it involves the great Quebec comic Olivier Guimond. Olivier was the funniest comedian I have ever seen, in either official language. He was verbally very funny (even I could tell that), and physically he had no equal. At the end of the year, in the annual Quebec New Year's Eve television show, *Bye Bye '70*, Olivier did a sketch in which he was a soldier, on duty outside a big Westmount mansion. It is snowing, as the homeowner looks out at Olivier, the soldier on duty, and feels sorry for him. He brings drinks out to the soldier. At first, Olivier says he can't drink, he's on duty. But the owner persuades him. The two get talking, and drinking. After another drink, the owner invites him in. As he goes up the steps, Olivier gets his leg caught in the wires of the Christmas-tree lights, and slides back down. When he tries to straighten things out, he just gets more entangled in the wires. Eventually all the lights are wrapped around him. Between the tree lights, the ice on the steps, and the drinking, Olivier loses his footing. The homeowner grabs him. "It's all right, Monsieur," Olivier says to the homeowner as they both struggle to stay upright. "If we go down, we go down together." It was hilarious and profound.

The day I dreaded had come. My sister had called with the news we had all been expecting. My mother had died; she had no specific illness, it was just old age. She was eighty-three. After my father's death in 1965, she had for a short while lived with my sister Dorothy, then she had moved into a seniors' residence in East Vancouver. I had taken Diane there once, to meet her. They hit it off immediately but, when we were leaving, Diane caught a glimpse of her standing at the window, watching us go. It was as if, in her mind, she was saying goodbye. We had our lives back east, and who knew when we

My mother

might see her again. As it turned out, it *was* the last time Diane saw her. I saw her again when it came time to find more extensive care for her.

On my last visit with her, when I had walked into her room, her face lit up and she smiled in recognition. For a brief moment, my mother had mistaken me for my father. When I spoke, she realized it was me. We sat together for a long while, hardly talking, but I felt the same closeness I had always felt with her. She was still present for me, the same Beatrice Chappell who had taken me with her on her errands about the city when I was a young boy, the same Beatrice Chappell who had fed the unemployed when they knocked on our door, asking to work for food. Looking at some of the other residents, sitting in their wheelchairs, staring out with glazed eyes into infinity, I felt very grateful she wasn't so affected. Old age is not for cowards, I thought, as I looked around.

At the funeral service, my sisters and brothers-in-law were all together one last time. There was a caring gentleness about the ceremony which was absolutely appropriate for my mother. The cleric clearly knew her, and spoke movingly about her, which made me think of what my cousin Joe had once said to me: "I don't know anyone who doesn't like your mother." She is buried beside my father in the beautiful Capilano View Cemetery, overlooking the Lion's Gate Bridge, a bridge my mother and I walked across together the day after it opened. Beatrice Chappell lived a life of selfless devotion and service to others. No one could say that of her son, but I like to think that she may have influenced me in some small, subtle way. I would have been very happy if nature had made me more like her and less like my father. But who has nature ever listened to?

Unless you have a really strong and valid reason for not taking a job, a booking agent will not understand. In fact, the only strong and valid reason they can accept is that you already have another job. Anything else, to an agent, is irrelevant. I shouldn't blame my agent, though, for taking the job on my behalf at the Gatineau Club in Hull, Quebec. But to this day, I hate myself for not trying to unbook it. Diane was pregnant, and close to term. I should have been in

Montreal, with her, but instead I was playing the Gatineau, staying in a small motel, and driving back to Montreal to check that she was all right. Someone had just given us a small dog, which I took to Hull with me. I really liked the dog, but it couldn't have seemed that way. One of the waiters at the nightclub said, if I was looking for a home for the dog, he would love to have him. I checked the waiter's background, and then gave the dog away. I was not thinking straight.

Our daughter, Valérie, was born on June 29, 1970, while I was in Hull. I was only away that one week, but it was the wrong week to be away. I just didn't think – then – that my wife having a baby was a valid reason to turn down a job. Dora Mavor Moore's remarks on funerals echoed in my head. I could hear her saying "the only time an actor leaves the theatre for a birth is for his own."

Outside of the revue work, Montreal brought many other opportunities. I got the chance to appear in three Quebec movies – *Quelques arpents de neige*, *J'ai mon voyage*, and *Tiens-toi bien après les oreilles à Papa*. Unlike English Canada, at that time Quebec had a budding movie industry. Although I never saw myself as a movie star, I certainly enjoyed doing them, particularly *Tiens-toi bien après les oreilles à Papa*. Gilles Richer, who had written for *The Katimavik Revue* and *Moi et l'autre*, wrote the screenplay. It was a comedy

Tiens-toi bien après les oreilles à Papa, 1973 motion picture. With Gérard Poirier and Roger Garant

based on the idea of insurance fraud. People on the brink of cardiac arrest were getting insurance, and dropping dead the next day. I played Monsieur Thompson, the Anglo boss of Britannia Life, who spoke French with an atrocious accent, which was good type-casting. Dominique Michel was the lead, and again proved a delight to work with. The great Quebec comedian Yvon Deschamps also starred. The film itself did surprisingly well at the box office, becoming the biggest local success of all time, earning $400,000 in the first month of its release, which was a lot of money for a Canadian film at that time. Still is.

It was while I was in Montreal I met two people who later came to play a great part in my life, John Morgan and Martin Bronstein. They had created a very funny satirical radio show, "Funny You Should Say That," on which I made frequent guest appearances, often with new pieces for characters who were now well-established – Sergeant Renfrew, Bobby Clobber, and the Member for Kicking Horse Pass. We would do a read-through the night before taping, then the following day the show was recorded before a live audience at Sir George Williams College Theatre.

Counterfeit Maple Syrup

I'm Sergeant Renfrew. I was sitting in my lonely log cabin on the fourteenth floor of Mountie headquarters in Ottawa with my invincible canine assistant, Cuddles. He was recovering from a wild night at his favourite after-hours kennel club, the Purple Hydrant.

The Chief was on the phone. "Renfrew," he roared, "someone is flooding this country with synthetic maple syrup, presenting it as having come directly from the maple sugar cane, thereby undercutting the value of real maple syrup, which I have just been told comes from a tree. Get on this case, Renfrew. A whole batch of this phoney stuff has just been spotted in a petite village près de la frontiere de Québec et Nouveau Jambon Transparent."

I hate it when he switches languages on me right in the middle of an assignment. I quickly punched the words into my pocket translator. "Nouveau" means "new." "Jambon" means "ham," "Transparent" means "sheer," New Hamsheer.

In no time Cuddles and I were in a tiny aircraft winging our way to a tiny landing strip près de la border of Québec and New Hamsheer. We were met there by the most powerful Mountie I have ever seen. Somewhere between a fullback and a Sumo wrestler. Her name? Sergeant Leslie Bontemps Roulez. I punched it into my translator. Leslie Bontemps Roulez in English is "let the good times roll."

I wouldn't touch that with a barge pole.

I called her Sarge. She hustled us into her cruiser. Within minutes, we were on the highway. She turned off at a small village called Prochaine Sortie. As we made our way along its one street, I checked out the name. "Prochaine sortie" is "next exit." What a weird name for a town!

It's as strange as that one in Ontario, "Guelph." Punch that into a Polish translator and you get "barf." Many of our early pioneers were alcoholics.

As we moved along the road, we passed "Le Roi de Burger – Chez Whopper." We passed "Le Cloche Taco," "La Créperie Smitty," and "Les Beignets de Tim Horton." The sergeant stopped the car at a place called "Epicerie." I ran inside. It was no picerie. It was une store de grocery! And there, on the counter, was the phoney maple syrup!! Selling like hot cakes.

Quickly I looked at my Mountie wristwatch. Mickey's big hand was on the ten. His little hand was on Minnie. It was exactly coffee time! I bought four cans of the phoney syrup and Cuddles and I headed over to La Créperie Smitty. I asked Monsieur Smitty if he had a can of old-fashioned organic maple syrup around. He found one. I tied a napkin over my eyes and took the maple challenge.

When I regained consciousness, Cuddles was fighting off a big man in dark glasses and black gloves, swinging a baseball bat. Cuddles grabbed the bat in his powerful jaws! The man panicked and ran. Cuddles went after him like a pit bull pursuing a postal person.

I staggered to the door. And beckoned to Sergeant Bontemps Roulez to follow Cuddles. But she was holding four boxes of day-old Bits de Tim, and there was no way she was going to let go. Bits de Tim are Tim Bits – little balls of imitation concrete covered with sugar.

I ran, grabbed the sergeant, and followed Cuddles down the road. At that point a huge truck pulled onto the road and turned in our direction. It was heading right at us! The truck was loaded with cans of phoney maple syrup. The big man in the dark glasses and black gloves was at the wheel.

Frantically, we ripped open our boxes of Tim Bits and opened fire! The windshield shattered! These Tim Bits were TWO days old!!!

The driver jumped out of the truck holding a big can of his phoney syrup. But before he could hurl it at us, we hit him with a second barrage! He staggered backwards and fell on his can. His can split open, and he lay there prostrate in a pool of his own syrup.

As for Cuddles and me, on our wall, there's a plaque. Presented to us by the Maple Tree Tappers' Association. When Cuddles looks up and sees his likeness on that plaque he's as happy as a cochon in composte.

"Comedy Crackers," CBC television, 1971. Mauling the French language as well as any drunk could, but making no progress with sober francophone.

"Funny You Should Say That" moved from radio to television, as "Comedy Café." Later, when its name was changed to "Comedy Crackers," I became one of the regulars, along with Peter Cullen, Joan Stuart, Barrie Baldaro, George Caron, and Ted Zeigler. We recorded every other week, in front of a live audience in the Versailles Room at the Windsor Hotel, then the sketches were edited into half-hour shows, which aired on CBC, in a challenging time slot. We followed "Hockey Night in Canada."

It was another chance to work with Joanie Stuart, a comedienne I had long admired. She had appeared in the entire long run of *Up Tempo*, which established her, and in the McGill University smash hit *My Fur Lady*. On stage, Joan had a physical freedom that was a joy to behold. She was always the consummate professional, showing up on time, with all her lines memorized. Nothing was ever too much trouble for her, if it would improve the comedy. During one memorable taping, I watched in amazement as Joanie ad libbed her way through a sketch for which her fellow performer had not bothered to learn his lines. She blended her lines with his lines, and carried him through the entire sketch without the live audience knowing that anything was wrong. Apart from her professionalism and quick-wittedness, Joanie had exquisite timing. Mavor Moore once said to me that he thought her timing came from the fact that she was a highly trained dancer. Her sense of rhythm was built in.

I stayed with "Comedy Crackers" through its various name and time-slot changes for two and a half seasons. Martin Bronstein and John Morgan, who had originated the show, were not involved after the first season. They took the CBC to court, claiming ownership of the concept for the show, but it was a difficult case to prove. I wanted them to win their case, but the CBC lawyer kept asking what I did in the show that was unique to that specific show. I had to acknowledge that there was nothing that was unique – I had done Renfrew before, I had done the Member for Kicking Horse Pass before, and I had done Bobby Clobber before. Ted Zeigler said to me this just wasn't a case they could win. He was right.

I eventually decided to leave the show in the third season. The irritation of an actor who did not seem to want to work finally got to me. Dale Barnes, our producer, would come to rehearse the show, describing the action, which Joanie, Ted, Barry, and I would then block. Peter Cullen refused to take part. He would sit on a chair, at the side of the room, and read his lines from there. Dale never took him to task for this, but it was driving the rest of us crazy. To have an actor there, but not taking part in the physical staging, was a colossal waste of time. In the end I couldn't stand it, so I quit.

I think, if I had been bilingual, I could have worked in Montreal forever. Dominique Michel was always asking me to appear on her show, which I did not feel I could do, because of my lack of fluency in French. To perform comedy in a second language, you must be more than adequate, and my repeated attempts to learn *la langue française* were still to no avail. A dialectician, I am. A linguist, I'm not. By the end of 1972, things were changing. The October Crisis of 1970 had taken its toll. A steady flow of English Quebeckers was leaving the province, and they weren't coming back. As I looked around, I saw that many of the English-speaking performers I had come to know were also leaving. Ted Zeigler left and headed off to California, saying vaguely that he had opportunities to do research for a production company. He eventually ended up as the lead comic on the *Sonny and Cher* show. Martin Bronstein and John Morgan took their new *Jest Society* stage show on the road. There was a reason so many were leaving. The work opportunities just weren't there any more.

My first five years in Montreal had been great, but over the last year things had been getting slower and slower. I had always done well with bookings for banquets, but these also seemed now to be almost non-existent. If it hadn't been for the Jewish community, there would have been no banquets at all. The other religious groups were thinning out, and atheists don't hold banquets. With great reluctance, I felt the time had come to pack it in. Living in Montreal for six years had changed my outlook and broadened my cultural scope. It had been a great run – *Katimavik Revue*, Mother Martin's and *Squeeze*, movies, Ted Zeigler, Joanie Stuart, Dominique Michel – I had done interesting things and worked with some great talent. I had spent lots of time with the Ikedas. I had met and married a beautiful woman whom I loved more than anything. But things were not going smoothly for us at this point. I had moved out of the family home.

Diane and I were having our differences, to the point where she finally said to me, "You'd better go." I went – to a small apartment a few blocks from our house. It was from here that I began my sorties to Toronto in search of work. I knew I could no longer support a family as a comedian in Montreal. Worse than that, I worried that I might no longer have a family to support.

Chapter 8

ACCUSTOMED TO YOUR FARCE

You could say things were at a low ebb. In Montreal, I had acquired some status, but six years is a long time in show business, and back in Toronto, no one seemed to know or care who I was. I had been away from the city too long. I was forty-seven years old, and it wasn't just that I was starting from zero, I was starting from minus. Nonetheless, I felt there was no reason to panic. I had realized very early on that what I had chosen to do – to be a comedian making a living with Canadian humour in Canada – was not going to be easy. Knowing that, and feeling it deeply, helped a lot. I would just suffer through these setbacks without it becoming a big deal. I had learned, long ago, that there are four stages to a performer's career:

1. Who's Dave Broadfoot? Never heard of him.
2. I want Dave Broadfoot for this part.
3. Can you play this part the way Dave Broadfoot would play it?
4. Who's Dave Broadfoot? Never heard of him.

The first club date I did after getting back to Toronto was at a hotel on Kingston Road. The man who hired me thought he was doing me a big favour, offering me seventy-five dollars for a show, which was a lot less than I had been getting when I left six years earlier, and a quarter of what I had been earning in Montreal. I remember that engagement vividly. At the entrance to the dining room of the hotel was a sign saying "qualified medical personnel in attendance at all times." It suggested to me that they knew a lot about the quality of their food.

Re-entry into the Toronto scene was made a little easier by the Jest Society – the group of young writer-performers I had known in Montreal. In 1973, the company included the founders John Morgan and Martin Bronstein, along with Roger Abbott, Don Ferguson, Luba Goy, and Marty Doyle. John Morgan, whose home I was staying in until I found an apartment, invited me to join them as a guest comedian in a new show they were launching at the tiny Poor Alex Theatre, on Brunswick Avenue, off Bloor Street. They had developed a format that was a mix of scripted and improvised pieces. To aid with the improvisation, near the end of the first act, Martin Bronstein would go on stage and ask for suggestions from the audience. After intermission, the cast would return with sketches based on these audience ideas. Very few of the improvised sketches ever missed. A Jest Society performance was always a lively evening.

I did several scripted pieces, including a monologue of Conservative leader Robert Stanfield delivering a speech in French, which one reviewer said was even funnier than Stanfield himself. Bad French comes naturally to me. But the contribution I remember best was a special appearance by the Member for Kicking Horse Pass in a parody of a current television show, "Under Attack." The Member, as on television, was grilled, first by members of a panel, then by members of the audience. This free-wheeling question-and-answer technique can be unpredictable, but when it's working, and you are able to respond to what the audience asks, it becomes a kind of comedy ecstasy. The only way to be prepared was to read about every possible topic on which anyone would be likely to ask a question, find a humorous angle, and then file it away in the brain. It was there when I needed it. When I had absolutely nothing to say, the bluffing in the political character was as funny as any answer.

Unfortunately, the Jest Society run was over fairly quickly, and that was when the reality of being back in Toronto really hit. I made up my mind to work harder than ever to get my career rolling again.

First, I called my old friend Jack Fulton, and suggested we do a book together, a Frank and Fearless Political Testament of the Member for Kicking Horse Pass, a.k.a. the Honourable David J. Broadfoot. Over the years of performing as the Honourable Member, it seemed to me that he had developed a distinct point of view. We decided to call the book *Sex and Security*. It had, of course, nothing to do with either subject, but it seemed like a catchy title. We had recently been deluged in the Canadian media with news of a woman named Gerda Munsinger, who had had an affair with the Canadian minister of defence, and, because of her connections to men from the Communist bloc, was deemed a "sex and security" risk, an expression that had earlier been applied in the same situation to Christine Keeler in London.

Jack and I spent many humorous days elaborating on the Member's philosophy on a variety of topics. On the subject of sex education, he believed that professional sex specialists should visit schools two or three times to give intensive demonstrations; on foreign ownership, he felt that giant U.S. corporations were not raping our country, since we were getting well paid; and on marijuana, it was his opinion that it should be made less and less illegal over a period of years, until totally irrelevant. Other subjects we addressed included organized crime ("Those who insist there is no organized crime in Canada must be very deeply involved in it"); bilingualism ("In Canada, there are people who speak three languages. There are others who speak two. And then there are Anglo-Saxons"); and women's liberation ("Women should be free, or else they should be very expensive").

Advance copies of the book were sent to the press, and Jack Dennett, on his late-night show on CFRB, said it was the funniest book ever written in Canada. That made me wonder what the competition was, but I was still glad he had said it. I was glad, that is, until I found out that the publisher had neglected to supply the bookstores with any copies. This little oversight was not so very funny, and the fact that Jack Dennett had broadcast to the world that he had stayed up all night reading this Frank and Fearless Testament went for nothing. Needless to say, we made very little money, but we had a good time.

At the same time I was working on the book, I was putting together material for a long-playing record and for another revue at Old Angelo's. *Take a Beaver to Lunch* was my first revue in Toronto in almost eight years, and thankfully it was a resounding success. Part of that success was due to Susan Keller, a talented singer and actress, who was just right for the show. Although she was not a comedienne, Susan played straight well, in a relaxed way, not trying to prove herself to be a comedienne. *Toronto Sun* columnist McKenzie Porter described *Take a Beaver to Lunch* as the best Canadian revue since *Spring Thaw*, which helped us at the box office. Originally, the show was planned to run for six weeks, but it did so well that it was extended to six months. I was delighted with this, and was surprised to find, when I told Susan we were going to be extended, that she could not have cared less. She was waiting to move on to her next venture. The following year, I did a new version of the show, this time with comedienne Carol Robinson. We played at Old Angelo's for eight months, and also went on an Ontario tour.

I had moved into an apartment on Poplar Plains Road where my first visitor was my daughter, Valérie. I had spent time with her on my many trips back to Montreal, where we did all the things that dads do with their children: the park, children's theatre, the zoo. These visits were among my most precious times with her, but they

Valérie, aged 4, Montreal

were also a reminder of what I had lost. It was good to have her come and stay, and for me to get a three-year-old's view of Toronto. Again, we did the dad-and-child thing – Kensington Market, Centre Island, and Casa Loma.

I was settling back into a Toronto routine, when I got a phone call from Roger Abbott. He told me that the Jest Society was being given an opportunity to do some shows for CBC radio. "Would you like to join us?" he asked. I had worked happily with the group earlier in the year at the Poor Alex, and had only one question. Were the shows to be recorded in theatres in front of a live audience, or were they going to be done in an empty studio with only microphones to play to? I had some experience of the studio situation – Jean Templeton and I had done our radio shows without an audience – and nothing is less conducive to producing great comedy. When Roger told me the shows were to be done in a theatre with an audience, I told him to count me in.

That one call changed my life, and dictated much of its course for the next thirty years. It resulted in a regular radio home for my comedy and collaboration with the most stimulating, exciting, and supportive group of performers I had ever worked with, the members of the Royal Canadian Air Farce – in alphabetical order, Roger Abbott, Martin Bronstein, Don Ferguson, Luba Goy, and John Morgan.

"The Royal Canadian Air Farce" was not the original title for the show. Our first working scripts were labelled "Beaver Follies." Only now can it be revealed whose brilliant suggestion this was – but I won't embarrass him by giving his full name. His initials are Dave Broadfoot. Fortunately, John Morgan and Roger Abbott had a better idea. While driving to Buffalo one day, they were talking about what the CBC would be called if John Diefenbaker had his way. Royal Canadian Wireless Company or Royal Canadian Air Farce? they suggested. They looked at each other. "That's it," they shouted, and nearly drove off the road. The show had its name.

For that first show, we worked separately on our scripts, then spent a day of rehearsal in Roger Abbott's home. We critiqued and edited each other's material, which was an amazingly positive process, based on a trust in each other's judgement. We spent the next day on our own, editing and rewriting, coming together again on the third day. More rehearsals, more new material, and more editing. The fourth day of preparation, we got together with the CBC producer, the sound engineers, and the sound-effects technician. The fifth day, November 20, 1973, was the day of the first "Air Farce" performance.

We made our way out of Toronto, to the Curtain Club in Richmond Hill, a twenty-five-minute journey from downtown. There was enough time for a long rehearsal with the technical crew and a dinner break, before the audience began arriving. Ron Solloway, the CBC producer who had given us the opportunity, went out on stage and told the audience we would be taping material for three separate thirty-minute shows, the first of which would air on December 9, 1973, as part of "The Entertainers." Roger Abbott then did a warm-up, and introduced us all. Then the announcer came on: *From the Curtain Club in Richmond Hill, the Royal Canadian Air Farce*, followed by Luba chiming in, *Ici Farce Canada!*

The audience response to that first evening of tapings was everything we had hoped for, and the production attitude and working pattern established that week were maintained throughout all future

"Air Farce," 1974. What's missing is the chicken cannon.

programs. We were all thoroughly committed to making each and every show, no matter the time and effort involved, as funny as we possibly could. Would the show have succeeded if it had been done in an empty studio with only microphones to play to? I firmly believe the sound of those roaring audiences was a major factor in the show's success. Everything Air Farce ever did subsequently was done in front of a live audience. Soon we had a commitment to produce twenty-six original shows per year.

With the exception of Martin Bronstein, who left in 1976, we stayed together as a group for over fifteen years. In that time, I came to know the Air Farceurs well. They all have strong and highly individual personalities, which made the ease with which we worked together all the more remarkable. Roger is the unflappable one, always able to turn a negative into a positive. From day one, he was the cornerstone of the show. He was never actually called the "director," because he didn't want to be, but he is the key person, the one who makes the decisions. He has the same attributes I saw in Mavor Moore – he is capable, even-tempered, calm in a crisis, a good organizer. There were never any tantrums with Roger. On stage he could be a quick thinker, as I saw one night in a stage show. The costume changes were frantic, and at one point, Roger had to change quickly into a dress, to become Carol Lawrence, then wife of Robert Goulet. He was moving so fast, the dress got caught and was ripped before he got on stage. With his dress half off, Roger managed to stay in the character of Carol Lawrence while ad libbing, "Ohhh, that Robert. He's such an animal."

John Morgan I liked from the moment I met him. He had done many things before "Air Farce": he'd been in the air force, had taught school, had been a journalist, a fisherman, and a pub owner. A man with a wonderful sense of humour, he is the most prolific comedy writer I have ever met. On first read-through, John's writing was always the equivalent of fine potter's clay. His rewrites moulded that clay into fine sculpture. There were times on "Air Farce" when John would come in at the beginning of the week and surprise us by having written the whole show. It constantly amazed all of us how he would suddenly have an idea for a monologue, would still be writing it as we were driving to the taping, and yet be able to walk on stage and deliver that same monologue as if he had known it forever. I guess it didn't occur to him to be anxious about what he had written – which was so different from my own approach. I would want to have worked on it for days before being prepared to walk out on stage and perform. But then, John never had one-quarter of the anxiety I had. What he did have was an insatiable curiosity. When I was staying at his home, I was going downtown one day. "Which way are you going?" he asked. "Are you going by the Yorkville Library?" I was. "Wait a minute," he said. He ran upstairs and got two big suitcases, full of books. I couldn't believe it. I could hardly lift them. But John had read through them all in the two-week loan period. "That's the way it is," he said. "No output without input."

Don Ferguson had come to the Jest Society almost by accident. He had abandoned academia for more interesting extracurricular activities, and when I first met him, he was working as a photographer. He came to take publicity photos for the Jest Society, and stayed hanging around to shoot for his own portfolio. Watching the way the improvised material came together, he thought to himself, "I could do that." As is the way in show business, at that moment a young male member of the cast announced that he was leaving at the end of the week. It was extremely short notice and the Jest Society was desperate. They asked Don, since he had seen the show several times, if he thought he could fill in until a replacement was found. He went on stage for a week to help out, and never left. A brilliant man, and a very quick learner.

People refer to Luba Goy as "perky," which seems to me a huge understatement. Originally trained as a classical actress at the National Theatre School, Luba amazed me constantly with her extraordinary versatility. Give her any female character, and she can play it. Luba, as everyone knows, is short and, being originally from the Ukraine, is fluent in Ukrainian. She is warm, outgoing, able to make instant friends with almost anyone she meets, and is particularly adept with children. To get them going, she talks like a duck. I'm sure if she ever visits the land of her birth, the Ukrainian children will be thrilled to have a bilingual duck talking to them in their own language. When I am testing a monologue out loud for the first time, Luba can be counted on to provide genuine audible laughter, a response that gives the impression that my new monologue may be usable. She has only one imperfection. She is dilatory.

Roger, Don, Luba, and John. Working with these very bright, very talented Air Farceurs was exhilarating. I now truly understood the difference between working with people who only perform, and people who are writer-performers. This was a group of writer-performers, and I could see that the difference is huge. Writer-performers have sat at home, at the typewriter or computer, and worked things through, and through again. They have a profound respect for the written word, which is where it all begins. After all, you can have lots of wonderful people around you, but without the script, there is nothing. Writer-performers, more than anyone, know how difficult it is to produce this script. They know that getting on stage is only the end of a long process. The joy may be concentrated in the performing, but there can be no joy without the hard work of writing.

There is one characteristic that writer-performers do not have: I have never seen a writer-performer with an oversized ego. People who are purely performers often have terrific insecurities, which come out in arguments about the size of their name on the marquee, their place in the running order of talent, the size of the dressing room. All these things that are related to nothing but ego seem important to actors, but with writer-performers I have never run into any of this. I have never heard a writer-performer say, "There are no small parts, only small dressing rooms." I did hear an actress, who will remain nameless, say that.

At the beginning, the "Air Farce" writing was done by John Morgan, with contributions from Martin Bronstein, Roger Abbott, Don Ferguson, and myself. As we moved along, Rick Olsen and Gord Holtam came on board, first as back-up contributors, then as full-time writers. That gave Roger and Don more time to concentrate on the business arrangements and producing the show. Rick and Gord became responsible for half the show's material. As is to be expected of writers of zany, outrageous, bizarre, off-the-wall comedy, they are both solid, sane, normal, well-adjusted, happily married family men. Rick realized that aggression can be sublimated through comedy – even so, staunch Canadian that he is, he continued to be a part-time hockey player. Gord, when he started writing comedy, was a professional drummer. That built-in sense of rhythm is a godsend for a comedy writer. Gord can sense if the rhythm of a spoken line is right, and, if a punchline is correctly written, he can hear a drummer's rimshot after the line is delivered.

Another key member of the team was Alex Sheridan, our sound-effects technician. Throughout the years on radio, sound effects were key. Alex would be on stage with us, surrounded with the tools of his trade – coconut shells (for horses' hooves), cornstarch (footsteps in the snow), whistles, boxes of sand, celery, cellophane, paper, balloons – whatever was needed for that week's effects. Alex and John did not always see eye-to-eye, because John had his own original ideas about sound, which often involved what can only be described as lateral thinking. "John, it doesn't make sense," Alex would say when John suggested things that offended his sense of logic. An approaching train, getting louder and louder, until it comes right through a restaurant, might not make sense to Alex, and would definitely go against all his training as a sound-effects technician, but he would reluctantly give it a try. Whenever he did what John suggested, the audience would be in hysterics.

Most of what I did on "Air Farce" revolved around characters I had already developed – Renfrew, Big Bobby Clobber, and the Member for Kicking Horse Pass. They proved almost infinitely adaptable to topical situations. Politics was reserved for the Member, crime for Renfrew, and sports for Big Bobby – and this just about covered the Canadian scene. On "Air Farce," with the help of the entire group, Renfrew became a national celebrity and members of the RCMP seemed to love him more than anyone else. The character that seemed to get the biggest audience response, though, was Big Bobby Clobber. On "Air Farce," Roger Abbott was always Big Jim, Bobby's frustrated interviewer.

BIG JIM

[Roger Abbott]: *Good evening, hockey fans. I'm about to be joined here by my special guest, hockey superstar Big Bobby Clobber. Just before I bring Bobby out, here are tonight's hockey scores, 8 to 6, 5 to 4, 4 to 1, and 3 to 2 in overtime. Now let's bring out my special guest, Big Bobby Clobber.*

[Dave enters in full hockey uniform]

BIG JIM:	*Big Bobby, hi.*
BOBBY:	*How's that?*
BIG JIM:	*Hi.*
BOBBY:	*Not really. I only had three beers. But I feel like I could write a whole phone book in the snow.*
BIG JIM:	*Bobby, there's a rumour going around that you are part of a group bidding for a new hockey franchise. Is it true?*
BOBBY:	*Yeah, it is true. There is a rumour. I heard it myself.*
BIG JIM:	*Nobody can figure out which city you are trying to get the franchise for.*
BOBBY:	*On that, my partners said I have to keep my mouth shut or people will figure out what the heck is going on and find out we're getting a secret tax break if we get the franchise into the city I can't talk about because they already had a lot of trouble with another franchise bid for a team from a guy from out west who I can't mention his name because if, when it's like that, and you talk, eh. It's, you know, if you talk [pause] . . . What did you ask me?*

BIG JIM:	*I'm not sure. Tell me, have you found a venue for your new team?*
BOBBY:	*No time for that, Big Jim. We're too busy trying to find a place to play the games. There aren't many choices in Hamilton.*
BIG JIM:	*I think you just let the cat out of the bag.*
BOBBY:	[laughing] *My cat doesn't have a bag.*
BIG JIM:	*How about a name for the team?*
BOBBY:	*The other partners want a name with the word "puck" in it. They've got it, but I can't tell you what it is.*
BIG JIM:	*The Mighty Pucks!*
BOBBY:	[laughing] *The Mighty Pucks . . . No way. The Hamilton Puckers.*
BIG JIM:	*Do you have any fund-raising plans for the team?*
BOBBY:	*Oh yeah. The first one is a big fund-raising dinner with a lot of big stars. I asked the great goalie Patrick Roy to be the host. We'll have the whole epitoamy of hockey there, Bobby Hull and Brett Hull.*
BIG JIM:	*The Father and the Son.*
BOBBY:	*The Father and the Son and the goalie host!*
BIG JIM:	*So you're not worried about finding funding?*
BOBBY:	*Oh sure. I'm worried. I'm pretty sure I am. I try to be. As worried as the next guy. One thing I know . . . when you're fund-raising . . . to raise funds . . . there is only so much wool you could shear off the back of the goose who's laying your golden eggs before you're going to milk it dry.*
BIG JIM:	*And you never can tell where your next goose is going to come from.*
BOBBY:	[Doesn't understand] *Okay.*
BIG JIM:	*Bobby, before you go, how about a word of wisdom for the young sports fans out there?*

BOBBY:	*Oh that, I do have, Big Jim. It's a kind of a*
	prayer, eh? I learned it from the coach.
	Grant me the senerity to accept . . . the
	seniority to . . . Grant me the senility to
	accept the things I can't . . . The courage
	to accept the other things . . . I couldn't . . .
	and the wisdom to . . . see a doctor . . . if
	I can't go either way.
BIG JIM:	*There you have it, sports fans. You heard it*
	right from Big Bobby himself. A horse's
	mouth if ever there was one. If the hockey
	franchise goes, it will probably go to
	Hamilton. A city with a coliseum, a police
	force, and a Sheila, all called "Copps."

Re-established in Toronto, I kept commuting back to Montreal as often as I could to see Valérie. Although Diane, Valérie, and I vacationed together, making trips to Mexico and Guadeloupe, we were no closer to getting back together. I had more or less made up my mind that I had to get over the emotional turmoil and start to build a new life. I had to accept what had happened, I told myself. I had made enough money from the combination of all my activities to make a down payment on a small house. The house itself was a bargain, but the renovations to make it livable cost more than the home itself. Those renovations, which I helped work on, were about finished, and I was considering taking in tenants, when Diane called. She had agreed to continue living in our Montreal house until we had a buyer, and, at last, in 1976, we had one. During one of our conversations to sort out the details on this, she mentioned that freelance work in Montreal was drying up. "Maybe you should try Toronto?" I suggested. She agreed. Timing, I thought, perfect timing. This time, Diane's. And so began the next chapter. The best chapter. We were together again.

Valérie and Diane,
by the Thames, 1978

I was committed to a tour to entertain UN peacekeepers in Cyprus, the Middle East, and Germany. When the tour was over in early 1976, Diane and Valérie packed up their belongings, drove down to Toronto, and joined me in the new house. Diane quickly found freelance work as a producer, and Valérie settled into the Toronto French School preparatoire. We were a bilingual household, with a unilingual member. Diane spoke in French to Valérie – and only in French. "To you," she told Valérie, "I will never speak English. My father would disown me if he had to speak to his grandchild in English." To me, Diane was forced, by my continued inadequacy in French, to speak English. Diane did not know Toronto at all back then – she missed her friends in Montreal, and she missed the culture, so we visited Montreal a lot in those early years. She now knows the city better than I do, and has made a lot of firm and lasting friends here. But to this day, even a simple thing like buying a greeting card in French requires an expedition. There is still not much of Quebec culture available in the most multicultural city on earth.

We acquired a dog, Sheba, a border collie, a much-loved addition to the family, but, as it turned out, less than adequate as a guard dog. One evening, Diane and I were watching television downstairs, with Valérie upstairs, when Diane thought she heard the sound of a door knob turning. I hadn't heard anything but thought we should investigate. The front door was well locked. We went to the back door and, as I tried the knob, Diane let out a blood-curdling scream. In the dim light of the dining room, she saw a man standing partly covered by a window curtain, smiling at her – smiling, as psychiatrists say, "inappropriately." It was a neighbour from a few doors away. I didn't know if he was stoned, or drunk, or dangerous, but I ran in and grabbed him. Never before have I felt so murderous. I kept telling myself to stay calm, as I manhandled him out the back door. Diane called the police, who promptly showed up and arrested him.

Diane was traumatized by the incident, and refused to stay in the house. We spent the first weekend after the break-in at a Muskoka resort, following which we began the search for another house, far from our old neighbourhood. The one we found was in Don Mills. Quickly, we negotiated a deposit, a mortgage, bridge financing, and a moving van. It was months before the break-in came to trial. When it did, the defendant testified that there was no break-in. I had invited him in for tea, he said. The way the judge rolled his eyes made it obvious that he did not buy a word of it. Unfortunately, the wrong charge was laid, and the case was thrown out. At the trial, we learned that our breaker-inner was a psychiatrist attached to a mental hospital. We also learned never to go to court without a lawyer.

We stayed in exotic Don Mills for several very pleasant years. I would drive back and forth from downtown quite happily until one year, during ragweed season, disaster struck. I am hyper-allergic to ragweed pollen, which if I inhale too much puts me promptly to sleep. One day, I was driving home after a long meeting at the CBC. The ragweed was so potent that day that I had all the car windows shut tight, the air conditioning going full blast, and the car radio turned up to deafening. All designed to keep me awake. It didn't help.

When I regained consciousness, I found myself lying in the front seat of the car, with my nose almost ripped off, from intimate contact with the steering wheel. The pollen was so strong it had put me to sleep, and nearly killed me. I staggered out onto the road and over to the car I had hit to see if the driver was all right, which thankfully he was. I then turned back to my car, where I collapsed in shock. My beautiful Lincoln was a write-off. The car I collided with wasn't much better. Lying on the operating table as a doctor tried to save my nose, I was vaguely aware that he was talking to me. "Don't worry," he said. "I know who you are. I know what you do for a living. I know you need your nose." Thanks to him, I still have it.

It was clear that driving was a dangerous occupation for me. I have vivid recollections from Montreal days, driving west along Boulevard Edouard Montpetit, hitting a patch of ice, and in a split second heading east. I have driven south along Decarie Boulevard, hit ice, and suddenly found myself heading north in the south lane. Most of all I remember one Christmas leaving Diane's family home in Hull, and heading to Montreal along Highway 17, with all our fragile Christmas presents. When the car ahead appeared to be moving slowly, I decided to overtake it. As I did, we hit a patch of ice, flew off the highway and into the air, coming down to earth at the bottom of a concrete gulley. We landed so hard, the top half of the car was almost completely detached from the bottom half. We sat there in shock, the car a total wreck, our Christmas gifts shattered. A priest, headed for Montreal, pulled over and took pity on us. He helped us load our luggage and our broken Christmas booty into his car, then, being a really good Samaritan, he drove us all the way to our front door in Lower Westmount. Without a word being spoken, I knew that I would never be allowed to drive a car again if Diane was in it. To this day, no matter what vacation tour we go on, no matter how arduous the driving, my hands are never allowed near the steering wheel. Diane is an extremely competent driver. This I find to be a female characteristic. That may sound sexist, but I am old enough to say what I want.

After the ragweed incident, as Diane could not drive me everywhere I needed to be, we decided that driving should be eliminated. From Don Mills, we moved to Rosedale, to a street that was only two blocks from a subway station.

Meanwhile, "Air Farce" continued to tape at the Curtain Club in Richmond Hill. One winter day, Roger, Don, John, and Luba were driving out to a taping, when their car slid off the road. (Clearly I wasn't the only accident-prone Farceur.) This shook us all up, and someone suggested that maybe we should find a way to tape closer to home. That led us to a brief encounter with a facility known as the Adelaide Court Theatre, in the heart of downtown Toronto. Suitable venues were hard to find at that time. Personally, I felt as comfortable at the Adelaide Court as an Inuk in the Sahara. We were obliged to do our stuff in the set of whatever play was running there at the time. You could find yourself entering the stage between a refrigerator and a dishwasher, with an ironing board between you and your microphone.

From Adelaide Street, we made the trek eastward through the concrete jungle to Cabbagetown, which was where the CBC studio theatre was located. Cabbagetown has the perfect ambience for a comedy show. It is filled with irony. You find there every strata of society living side by side, from the down-and-out drunks to the elegant alcoholics, from subsidized houses to sand-blasted mansions. I know the respectable residents in the southern section are not thrilled to waken to the daily discovery of worn-out syringes and previously enjoyed condoms lying prostrate on their doorsteps. On the other hand, as you move northward among the less colourful Cabbages, you'll find it little different from the Forest Hill Highlands or Mainland Rosedale, in that there are filthy rich living next door to the disgustingly affluent.

The CBC theatre was located on Parliament Street just north of Carlton Street, which is still a fairly mixed area. During one of our rehearsal breaks, I ran out to a nearby convenience store to buy some Scotch tape. I heard the store clerk apologizing to a customer for having run out of Aqua-Velva aftershave lotion. He said all he had left was Mennens. The customer sneered. "I wouldn't drink that stuff if you paid me."

After we had done several tapings in the Parliament Street studio-theatre, the weather turned very cold. I began noticing that, week after week, the first three rows of the audience were always filled with the same people. They were extremely loyal, but not very responsive. I couldn't figure it out. Slowly, it dawned on me that, since there was no admission charge, many of these good people were in the theatre to keep warm. They were happy to be inside any heated building. What we performers were doing there was beside

"Air Farce," radio days. Left to right: Luba, me, Don, John, and Roger

the point. We didn't need to worry about their lack of response – the explosive enthusiasm of the majority carried us. Not only that, there was a marvellous performer residing in that theatre to keep us all inspired: Tuffy, the cat. He was always on our side. Even though he rarely took the opportunity to go on stage himself and perform for the audience, they loved it when he did. His act was to walk proudly on stage, then run quickly up and down the fabric-covered movable walls that were used to hide several pieces of office equipment, which had mysteriously begun to appear in the theatre. If Tuffy's act had been backed by appropriate music, he would have been a smash hit on television. He was far more interesting than anyone ever introduced by Jenny Jones or Jerry Springer, and far more intelligent.

We all enjoyed Cabbagetown – it was convenient, and the audience there loved us. But then some nameless person inside the Canadian Broadcasting Corporation decided to un-theaterize the theatre. The raked floor, where the audience sat, gradually became terraced and sectioned off. Each new section became an office. Every time we arrived for work, we found more and more office equipment on stage, as well as out front where the audience used to sit. Soon, the performance space had almost disappeared, and the audience space had been cut in half. The theatre had become an executive's heaven, and a performer's nightmare. This, at a time when Toronto was enduring a glut of empty office space. The uncomprehending executive, with little more than contempt for what we were doing but an abiding lust for administration space, had decided that the theatre was irrelevant. How do I know? He told me so.

One night, we were taping the show in front of the ugliest green curtain ever hung before an audience in the history of entertainment. The curtain had to be there in order to mask all the new desks and fax machines, computers and printers and other office paraphernalia we had managed to shove out of the way. I was making an entrance around the curtain as one of the others was making an exit. Trying to avoid a crash, I bumped into a desk, tripped over a cable, got trapped in the curtain, finally got on stage, then tripped over an electrical outlet protruding from the stage floor, and dropped my script, all fifty pages. It was not a splendid moment of inspired comic invention. It was not even amateur night in Portage La Prairie. I glanced at Roger. He glanced at me. In that moment, we both knew, without saying a word, that we would never do another show in that building. We never did. By the way – no offence to amateur performers in Portage La Prairie. My father only set foot on stage once in his life. It was during an amateur night in Portage La Prairie.

"Air Farce" was homeless. It was then that we began accepting all the invitations to tape our shows out of town. Where we went depended on who wanted us. Charitable organizations used "Air Farce" as a fund-raiser, and in effect became our sponsors, selling tickets to the event at whatever price they felt appropriate. The charity received all the admission revenue, less expenses. What we got was an excited audience and at least two hot radio shows. After each taping, one of the shows was broadcast within hours. The other show was held for future broadcast, with the content planned so that it would make sense that way. The second show tended to be less immediately topical.

We had done quite a number of out-of-town tapings in the past but now we were permanently on the road, which I enjoyed. I've always liked travelling. I've never considered, as many people do, that life on the road is a hardship to be endured. I was travelling with friends. We played good halls. In the evenings, the restaurant meals were fine. John, who loved cheap food, would go off on his own, to find a really good cheap Chinese meal, while Roger, Don, and I would look for an expensive restaurant, and give them the opportunity to exploit us. The three of us always ate together. I loved being with them, they are so full of ideas and points of view on everything.

An example of how sympatico we Farceurs were came one night when Roger, Don, Luba, and I were driving home from a performance in London, Ontario. Our fatigue gave way to a kind of creative craziness. Roger had been reflecting on recent news about a nasty bit of work named Helmut Buxbaum. Helmut B. had just been sent to prison for life for arranging to have his wife dispatched from here to eternity. Helmut was a wealthy man, who could afford to

This hybrid version of "Air Farce" was a cross between a radio and a television show.

hire the dispatchers with the profits he made from overcharging seniors for their care and feeding while they were residing in one of his chain of rest homes. As we were heading home along the 401, Roger suddenly announced that we should produce a musical based on the life of the said Helmut B., and that it should be called *Hey, Buxbaum!* (A recent production at the Charlottetown Festival had been called *Hey, Marilyn!*) Don, Luba, and I quickly jumped into the spirit of the thing. We worked out the plot line, with songs, dialogue, and production numbers. Roger insisted that the lead role had to be played by Tom Kneebone, a small, very thin actor with a Joe Clark-style chin. Someone else voted for Al Waxman. Roger would have none of it. "If I can't have Tom Kneebone," he said, "I'm not going to go ahead with this project." The part of Mrs. Buxbaum, we decided, should be played by either Barbara Hamilton or Rita McNeil. The finale was to take place in one of the Buxbaum seniors' residences. One of the semi-invalid elderlies hears on her Walkman that Helmut B. is going to prison. She shouts it out, at the top of her lungs. With the music building, the lights slowly come up as we see very elderly patients shakily emerging from their beds. As soon as all the elderly feet are touching the floor, the music changes into a pulsating rhythm, and all the elderlies go into a salsa victory dance of wild abandon. They dance their way up on to the tables, and oxygen tanks and gurneys, as the music becomes frantic. The music suddenly stops and the seniors give a loud victory shout in unison: "Helmut is kaput!" If you see a musical production coming to town based on the life of Helmut Buxbaum, remember Roger Abbott thought of it first.

With the success of "Air Farce" on radio, CBC decided that it would give it a try on television. We had built our audience by being extremely topical. This particular television concept, which was not our idea, was to make shows that would be anything but topical, since they were to be broadcast several months after they had been taped. The material would have to be timeless. We would have to become Wayne and Shuster. It was the wrong approach for "Air Farce," and I said as much, which upset the producer, who had actually come from the Wayne and Shuster show. "Let's do TV, but let's do it the Air Farce way," I suggested. "Let's make it topical. Let's not

(Left) King Louis: Vous êtes dans la rivière, ma chère. You are in Seine. Air Farce TV special, 1980. (Right) Bugsy and Beaver. With John Morgan as Beaver and me as Bugsy. Smiling to distract pest controllers.

get carried away with sets and costumes." But carried away with sets and costumes we were. There were twenty sets on the first super-special, plus over two hundred costumes and a mountain of props, among them mashed potatoes, croissants, chocolate éclairs, and French bread, all for a culinary Battle of the Plains of Abraham.

Our feeling was that this was all unnecessary. Wayne and Shuster were extremely capable, extremely successful, and didn't need a second unit. But then we were also mindful of our cherished Canadian tradition of making things as difficult as possible. So, reluctantly, we Farceurs all agreed to give this un-Air Farce concept our very best effort. Complicating matters, we were being asked to produce, in two nights of tapings in a theatre, sketches that would fit into ten different television shows. It was an idea, which, not to put too fine a point on it, seemed insane. Nonetheless, like the Fraser River arriving at the Fraser Canyon, we poured ourselves into it.

The CBC audience-relations department insisted that they would handle the arrangements for the theatre audiences, which meant we had to turn our radio fans away. At showtime, we discovered that the critically important studio audience for the first night in the theatre was to be composed of five busloads of hearing-impaired senior citizens. Two of the bus drivers were directionally impaired. They never did show up. I have absolutely nothing against hearing-impaired seniors. I am about to join their ranks. But I will never volunteer as an audience member for the recording of a comedy show. Bewildered smiles don't do the job. The response has to be audible. When a comedian's livelihood depends on audience response and there isn't any, it can be disconcerting. Comedy timing rides on the waves of laughter, the performer always cutting in to start the next line before the laugh dies away. That's what creates momentum. Curiously, despite all the problems, those television shows garnered healthy audience numbers. But it was years before the right opportunity to do TV again presented itself to "Air Farce." By then, I had left the show.

I was taking part in the Merryposa Comedy Festival in Orillia in 1980, when Diane and I checked the real-estate ads in the Orillia *Packet and Times*. We had decided it would be a good idea for us to have a small place in the country to escape to. One of the first ads we read described a "secluded" property. "That sounds like it," I said. So Diane, Valérie, and I drove out to take a look, following a long serpentine path off a concession road in Medonte township, through thick woodland to a farmhouse. Here the forest gave way to open land. It was a beautiful property, truly secluded, and we all loved it. So we bought it, and made an agreement with the next-door farmer, Klaus Andersen, that his cattle could graze on our land. Now we were pretend farmers. I did some minor upgrading on the house myself, and we installed a swimming pool. These minor changes accomplished, every morning I was there I swam in the pool, while the neighbour's cattle came over to the fence to puzzle at this strange activity, and look longingly at the great expanse of beautiful blue water they could only drink from in their dreams.

It didn't take us long to learn that real farmers, like our neighbours, Klaus and Connie Andersen, have remarkable self-sufficiency in the country, whereas dilettantes like us have none – but they

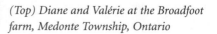

(Top) Diane and Valérie at the Broadfoot farm, Medonte Township, Ontario

(Centre) Valérie at the Broadfoot farm

(Bottom) John Morgan and his son Christopher, visiting the farm

always came to our aid when needed. Klaus would plough our long, curving driveway in winter. He had the right-sized plough, plus, the bonus, he knew how to use it. The whole area in winter was an absolute wonderland. Every night, to look up at the sky was a thrill. We never got tired of seeing the myriad stars in the night sky. I also never got tired of walking in the woods in the snow. During our first winter there, I made a circular trail on our property, which meant that we city slickers were not in danger of getting lost in our own woods. Coming back into the warmth of a blazing log fire after a walk on this trail was one of the great joys of Medonte.

Summers, when "Air Farce" was not taping, I would often perform at the Orillia Opera House. Away from the theatre, time off was spent digging wild garlic on nearby Crown land. We'd go off with our buckets and shovels, and once we had a bucketful, the hard part began, rinsing and rinsing and rinsing the garlic until the tenacious

Merryposa Comedy Festival, Orillia Opera House, 1977. Left to right: Tony Molesworth, Steve Smith, Morag Smith, Tommy Sexton, Greg Malone, Jim Carrey. I'm in the middle.

earth had been removed. Once the garlic was clean, Diane, who is a wonderful cook, would start the pickling process. Bottled, chilled, and labelled "Lonely Log Cabin Pickling Corporation," the wild garlic became the perfect memento for visiting friends. We were happy that we had decided not to have a place on the water – nearly all the places we had seen on nearby lakes seemed very noisy with all the Sea-Doos, Jet Skis, and power boats. Here, in our secluded farmland, we had lots of space – forty-three acres – wonderful neighbours, and no noise. Just the occasional whistle from a distant train, and the odd moo.

We had been enjoying the property for almost nine years when one midwinter day I arrived there to find a bill tucked between the doors for a substantial delivery of fuel oil. When I went down to the basement to check the oil tank, it showed "empty." I was at a loss to understand this, and, as it was a Sunday, we were about to have a serious problem. I called our neighbour, Klaus, and he was able to bring over a few gallons to keep things going. Next day, I called the fuel company. They were happy to bring more fuel, and were completely unconcerned about the tankful that had disappeared.

I thought no more of it, until the following spring. I was working in the city, and Diane had gone ahead to Medonte to have the pool man come to open the swimming pool and top up the water in it. They were both shocked and horrified to see that, instead of water flowing out of the hose and into the pool, there was thick chocolate-brown fuel oil. The missing oil had been delivered not to the basement fuel tank, but to our deep well. From that point on, every spare minute I had was spent trying to rectify the disaster. A tankful of fuel oil was sitting in our well of drinking water. Getting that oil out of the well became my whole life. I had nightmares about it. In retrospect, I should have enjoyed it more. It was as close as we'll ever come to owning an oil well.

Shortly after this disaster, I noticed a young man, accompanied by an attractive girlfriend, checking out the area. Across the concession road from the entrance to our property was an abandoned quarry, which seemed to have caught his eye. Soon he was bringing in building supplies, and a house was taking shape high on a granite hill at one end of the quarry. I introduced myself to him. We would often stop to say hello. Then, without warning, he disappeared. There was a lot of gossip in the area about his well-built house, sitting high on the hill, empty. Nobody seemed to know where he had gone, and after a while we forgot about him.

A couple of years later, Diane was in the house by herself waiting for me to get back from a trip to Toronto. Suddenly, she heard the sound of motorcycles roaring toward our house along our long winding driveway. She ran inside, locked all the doors, and, rather than call the police, who would have taken over half an hour to get there, phoned our nearest neighbour for help. He jumped into his pick-up truck and headed on over to our house. Meanwhile, the bikers arrived and Diane could see they were highly skilled – they were all steering with one hand, and drinking beer with the other. The lead biker began yelling my name, and telling the others he was my friend. He was a bald man, with a long, white beard, and though Diane thought back over some of my more unconventional friends, she had no idea who he was, nor did she recognize any of his gang. But she could hear he was trying to convince the other bikers that Dave Broadfoot was a good friend. The doors to the house remained firmly locked, and I disappointed all by not making an appearance. Some of the bikers gave up on their fun and began to leave. As they did, our neighbour with his pick-up truck came flying up the drive-way, forcing the bikers off the road, and into the woods. It was a few weeks after this that we discovered that the lead biker was our neighbour who had built the home at the quarry and disappeared.

These two incidents – the misdelivered oil and the uninvited biker gang – took the joy out of being in the country. We decided to sell the farm, and our home in Toronto, and move to a location that would be the best of both worlds. That's what we did. As I like to say when I meet people in my travels, "If you're ever in Toronto, try and find me."

Chapter 9

HEARTBREAK HOTELS

Through all my years with "Air Farce," in fact, throughout my fifty years as a professional comedian, I have spent a huge amount of time on the road. It's a life that, unlike many entertainers, I actually enjoy. I once heard Maureen Forrester singing a song about the poignant sadness of spending time in the lonely guest rooms of strange hotels. As I listened, I realized that I couldn't identify at all with the sentiments expressed in that haunting lament. To me a lonely room has always been a perfect setting in which to be productive. Whether the need is for undisturbed rehearsing or undisturbed writing, a lonely hotel room is a perfect escape from distraction.

I produced the first four chapters of my first book, *Sex and Security*, in a lonely hotel room. It was during a layover in Winnipeg between engagements. Instead of going home, I stayed put in my lonely hotel room and got a lot of writing done that wouldn't have been done amidst normal domestic distraction. I'm the type of person who will actually take a flight *earlier* than necessary in order to have extra time for rehearsal in a lonely hotel room.

It's true there can be some problems with hotel accommodation. The extraordinarily dry air in wintertime in some prairie hotels can mean walking dreamily along a carpeted hallway from the elevator to your room, putting the key in the door lock, and receiving a jolt of static electricity that will not just focus your mind, it will also straighten your hair. To combat the dryness of the winter in a prairie hotel, I learned to do a couple of things before going to bed. I herewith pass them on to you. Fill the bathtub with very hot water and keep the bathroom door open so the evaporation spreads into the bedroom. Then take the largest towel from the bathroom, get it soaking wet, and spread it out on the carpet near the foot of the bed. Don't worry about getting the carpet wet; by the time the chambermaid shows up, it will be bone dry.

I did face a minor hotel challenge during the time that I was the owner of a diaphragmatic hiatus hernia. I was obliged to carry large books in my suitcase, so that in each hotel I could place the books under the head end of the bed. This was necessary so that I could constantly sleep on a slight slope. Pillows simply do not do the job. The whole body has to be on a slope. By the time my touring was finished for that year, the symptoms of hernia had disappeared and I had acquired a whole new respect for books.

Today, hotels are a far cry from what they were when I first started touring. In a Regina hotel, in the late forties, a guest had been requested to comment on the quality of his accommodation. "My room was fine," he wrote, adding, "I was a prisoner of war." The only time you run into inferior accommodation these days is when you are driving late at night, trying to get to the next town, but you are too tired to go on. Just when you can't drive another kilometre, you come across a small highway motel. If it looks neglected, it probably is. I once pulled into one of these motels by necessity, checked in, and went to my room. I went to take a bath, turned on the tap, went back to the bedroom, took my clothes off, went back to the bathroom. No water. I called the front desk. "I've got a leak in my bathtub," I said. "Go ahead," the guy said, and hung up.

Big hotels can be just as quirky. I was once performing at a hardware convention, and was booked into the hotel that was holding the event. "Hi, Mr. Broadfoot," said the woman at the front desk. "We did have a room for you, but with the Rotary convention and the hockey playoffs, we got overbooked. Don't worry, we're working on a room for you at a hotel down the road."

"But," I said, pathetically, "this is the hotel I'm doing my show in."

"Do you have an actual reservation?"

"Yes."

"You have confirmation of the reservation?"

"Yes."

"May I see it?"

"No."

"Why not?"

"I'll need it as evidence when your breach of contract comes to trial."

She gave me the bridal suite for less than a single room. I was in for a great night's sleep. There was no bride.

After I finished my performance that night, and got back to my splendid accommodation, I decided to have a nightcap before turning in. I grabbed the ice bucket and ran along the hall to the ice machine, successfully locking myself out of my room. In my pyjama top and jockey shorts, carrying the little ice bucket at groin level, I made my way down ten floors in the elevator to the front desk to ask for a duplicate key. Feeling utterly mortified, I got back on to the elevator as a kid of about ten got off, with a big grin on his face. The little terrorist had pushed every single floor button, giving me the longest elevator ride and the most excruciating four and a half minutes of my life. Back in the suite, my mind turned to the mini-bar. It almost made up for the humiliation. I was able to buy a bottle of soda water and a bag of potato chips for under forty dollars.

It wasn't my only hotel embarrassment. At one of the larger hotels in Winnipeg, an inexperienced desk clerk handed me the wrong room key. I unlocked the door to my assigned room, and couldn't help but notice that the bathroom door was open. A naked man was about to take a shower. At that point, the phone started to ring, so, naturally, I went to answer it. It was the desk clerk, calling to let me know what I had already discovered; she had given me the right key to the wrong room. As I ran back to pick up my suitcases and headed out the door, the wife of the naked person in the bathroom arrived. Standing there, holding luggage – even though it was my own luggage – I started to feel awkward. "Don't I know you?" she asked. "No," I said. "I've come to get my luggage . . . I'm taking it . . . to another key . . . to another room." I stumbled through the door, into the corridor, and made my way back to the front desk.

The clerk did find me another key and, best of all, another room. I used it to go and hide.

Through all the years of my performing career, appearing as an after-dinner speaker at banquets and conventions has been – and continues to be – my economic mainstay. There were times when I was doing as many as 150 of these performances a year. I have performed for all the major political parties. Prime ministers Jean Chrétien, Brian Mulroney, Joe Clark, Pierre Trudeau, Lester Pearson, and John Diefenbaker have all had the opportunity to laugh at my version of them. "I'm not sure whether I'm Lester Pearson," Lester Pearson interrupted himself giving a speech one

(Top) With one cabinet minister and two police chiefs (John Clements and Chiefs Marks and Ackroyd). No escape.

(Bottom) Turning it on for a Palliser Hotel banquet, Calgary, 1964

day, "or whether I'm being Lester Pearson being Dave Broadfoot being Lester Pearson."

I've also done my share of galas. I've performed twice for the Queen, and once, memorably, for President Ronald Reagan. It was at a National Arts Centre gala, celebrating his first visit to Canada as U.S. president. For Ronald Reagan, the Member for Kicking Horse Pass threw a lot of American references into his monologue. After the performance, the head of the U.S. Secret Service told me that the President, who had been sitting in a box seat, had been laughing so hard while I was on that he moved some of his men into place directly under the box seats, in case the President fell over the railing. He wasn't being facetious. The President wasn't just laughing, he was rolling around, pounding his knees at the punchlines. I could see him throwing himself around from the stage.

Prime ministers, presidents, and queens were the high end of the banquet circuit. Usually, they presented few problems to the performer. That wasn't the case with all banquets and conventions. Some, while not as bad as nightclubs – where hecklers are a major hazard to be contended with – provided their own particular challenges.

There I was, trying to come up with something that might please a client. In this case, the Marine Safety Association, who were holding their banquet at the King Edward Hotel in Toronto. Trying to be relevant, I had got dressed up as a frogman, complete with wetsuit, goggles, snorkel, helmet, and flippers. Because of the layout of the venue I was forced to hide from the audience on the fire escape outside the top-floor ballroom. Finally, after an interminable three-hour wait on the fire escape, my introduction came. "Ladies and gentlemen," the master of ceremonies began, "I'm sure none of you have forgotten the entertainment we endured at this event last year. It was, I think we all agree, pretty awful." This was not promising. "Some on the committee felt we shouldn't bother having any entertainment at all this year," he went on as I stood there in my frogman suit, wondering why I bothered. "I suggested we give it one more try. I have no idea what this fellow is going to do, but here he is, Don Bradfort . . . Braidford . . . I'm sorry, David Braidfood." When someone buries you that deeply during the introduction, unless you've had years and years of experience, it's next to impossible to claw your way back out of the ignominious grave you've just been buried in. If you are wearing a wetsuit, goggles, and flippers, there is no possibility of recovery.

Another challenging engagement took place in the civic arena in Victoria, B.C. I was in shock when I saw the physical set-up. The arena stage was built so high there was no possible eye contact with the audience. Beyond that, the entire area in front of the stage was a vast half-circle of sales booths, which continued to operate throughout the stage performance. One booth was particularly noticeable – it featured demonstrations of vibrating lounge chairs – La-Z-Boys that bounce. I made the mistake of looking down to where the audience should have been, and was transfixed by the sight of all these vibrating human bodies on the demonstration chairs. As I performed into the oblivion of the arena air, nobody paid any attention. The acoustics were such that no one could understand a word I was saying, anyway. What made the experience unique was that nobody, not even the booking agent, seemed to care.

I've always been very wary of accepting "25-year-club" dinner engagements. There is a great spirit of camaraderie at a 25-year-club get-together, and on this particular occasion, during an open-bar reception that lasted for over two hours, the camaraderie was growing by leaps and bounds. During the dinner itself, the complimentary magnums of wine on each table added even more to the warm fuzzification. During my performance, the camaraderie was louder than I was. "Charlie, you old son-of-a-bitch, where the hell you been keeping yourself?" was the kind of line that was covering my punchlines and obliterating my laughs. Then, just when I thought I had a breakthrough, someone at the back of the room shouted "Norwegian!" I struggled on to the next punchline, which was again drowned out by a shout of "Norwegian!" From then on, each punchline became "Norwegian!" shouted by an anonymous person whom I couldn't see because of a lighting problem. The audience was illuminated solely by alcohol. The inexplicable use of the word "Norwegian" made this particular disaster one I remember with a certain fondness. Those of my friends who know of that Vancouver calamity have only to shout "Norwegian" while I'm performing, and I come undone. It takes a lot to break me up, but that will do it every time. My dream is someday to sit in an audience in Oslo, Norway, and every time a comedian gets to a punchline, I'll shout "Canadian!"

One of the worst venues I have ever played in is the Winnipeg Convention Centre – not the banquet room, where I have had many happy experiences, but a gigantic, cavernous concrete hell-hole, above the banquet room, where farm machinery is normally on display. I was booked to do an event for the Winnipeg Art Gallery at this location, and it was instantly obvious to me that the whole thing would be a fiasco. The stage was way too high, there was a huge gap between the stage and the tables, and huge clusters of balloons at face height on the tables meant that I could not see the audience, and they could not see me. It would be like trying to perform in the middle of a jungle of rubber. It would be and it was.

The organizers were not prepared to compromise with the physical set-up, and so I pleaded with them to let me out of the engagement. I offered to pay *them* double my fee, and cover my hotel and air fare myself, if only they would let me go. "We can't do that," they said, "you're in all our advertising." To make things worse, there were friends and fans in the audience to witness the awful event. One of the fans saw me at the side of the room immediately following the show. "Dave Broadfoot," he said, "I can't believe I'm actually talking to Dave Broadfoot. You won't believe how long I've been a fan of yours. Man oh man. I love your stuff. I never miss you when you're on TV. You always do a fantastic show. Fantastic." Then he paused for a brief moment, and looked me in the eye. "What the hell went wrong tonight?" was what he said.

A much less devastating, but equally exasperating, experience occurred in Thompson, Manitoba, at an event known as Nickel Days. The show took place three times a day in the local arena, a building with a corrugated metal roof, metal walls, and a concrete floor. Try to imagine the echo. To add to the noise, on the right side of the stage were people selling noise-maker balloons, the kind that when released fly around in circles emitting the sound of someone giving a raspberry at the top of their lungs. On the left side of the stage was a booth selling Molson beer. Facing it, on the opposite side of the arena, was a booth selling Labatt. As I came on to start the first show, before I could open my mouth, a young man in the audience yelled out at me, "You're an asshole!" As I began my warm-up, I realized this engagement could become a challenge.

The second performer in the line-up was a comic juggler, who had developed some extremely funny lines to cover anything that could possibly go wrong with his juggling act. The arena echo meant that no one could understand a word he was saying. At one point, he ran across the backstage area, shouting, "Dave, do something, I'm dying out there." I went over to the sound man to get him to fix the sound. He smiled confidently and gave me the thumbs-up salute. Nothing changed. The juggler came flying by again. "Dave!" he yelled. "The sound! I'm dead already." He was dead, and so was I. Later I told the manager of the arena how off-putting it was to be called an asshole before even getting started. "Why should you be offput?" he asked. "That was the mayor's welcoming address." I'm still not sure whether he was kidding or not.

Nothing, however, *nothing* can beat my experience with the Independent Loggers' Association annual banquet, at a hotel in downtown Kamloops which shall remain nameless. All right, it was the Stockman Hotel – no need for it to remain nameless forever. Many banquets are preceded by an open-bar reception that might last as long as an hour and a half. The Independent Loggers' Association open-bar reception held some kind of record. It lasted for three days. My introduction to the audience was handled by the inebriated organizer who had hired me. "All right . . . gentlemen . . . here he is . . . Gordonnnn Lightfoot." It was not a good beginning.

I could tell right away that the loggers were puzzled by my lack of guitar and by the absence of back-up musicians. None of them had ever seen Gordon Lightfoot in person, so they couldn't know he's much older than I am. No, I can't say that. I promised to tell the truth. Not knowing what else to do, I plunged into my first joke, which was about a deceased cabinet minister, Paul Martin, Sr., and the debate over capital punishment. The problem was, the audience were waiting to hear me sing "The Wreck of the Edmund Fitzgerald." They didn't realize I was doing jokes. A member of the audience sitting up front shouted defiantly, "Okay, Lightfoot, you brought up

the hanging business. Are you saying we should be using rope?"
"Only if it's between two consenting adults," I quickly replied. Then
the audience participant called me the expression that had not
only become popular in Thompson, Manitoba, but had now obviously become popular right across the country. "You're an asshole,"
he shouted. My response to that was just as loud: "So we can speak
as equals!" Things were not going well.

Soon, for reasons I did not understand, the loggers were punching each other. Gold neck chains were flying through the air. Just as
a wristwatch zoomed by my head, a man built like two jukeboxes got
up out of the audience, came on stage, locked his arm around me
like a vice, and said, "Now you're going to sing." Speaking as quickly
as I could, I explained I was not Gordon Lightfoot. "Gordon is a
singer," I said, "I'm a comedian. I don't sing. It's all a mistake."
Immediately, as his knee connected with my groin, a miracle took
place. A Gordon Lightfoot song, "If You Could Read My Mind," in
Gordon Lightfoot's voice, came floating from my throat. It was not
very loud, but it was quite heart-rending. Meanwhile, the rest of my
body limped its way offstage, backwards. Luckily, earlier in the day,
I had acted very professionally and memorized the location of the
fire escape.

Clearly, my name was a problem. It was too similar to too many
others. Besides Gordon Lightfoot, there was a less-famous singer,
Jimmy Lightfoot. Then another singer, on his way to semi-fame,
Dave Bradstreet. There was the writer Barry Broadfoot. Then foot-
ball gave us a great player by the name of Tony Proudfoot. Already,
there was a well-known sportswriter by the name of Jim Proudfoot.
In Alberta, there was a comedian whose name was Randy Bigfoot
(unrelated to the Sasquatch who bore the same last name but no
family resemblance). There was a leader of a political party by the
name of Broadbent, and in Toronto a comedian named Kneebone.
All this has led to me being thanked profusely for my stories of the
Great Depression (Barry Broadfoot). I've been complimented for
my moving musical tribute to the builders of the CPR (Gordon
Lightfoot). I've been lauded for my fearless opposition in the
House of Commons (Ed Broadbent) and criticized for unnecessary

roughness at the line of scrimmage (Tony Proudfoot). And just when the confusion was starting to ease off, I walked into an advertising agency in Toronto to be greeted enthusiastically as Peter Appleyard.

To help people understand who I really was, I did interviews. The more I travelled, the more interviews there were to do, and the more questions to be answered. It wasn't long before I noticed the same questions were asked again and again. I felt sorry for the interviewers, because there was only so much they could ask. I realized that I had to give some time to working out some thoughtful answers. I tried. I really tried.

Q. *How was your flight?*
A. *I'm the only survivor.*

Q. *How do you stand all the travelling?*
A. *I think about my luggage. It's lost. At least I know where I am.*

Q. *Is Dave Broadfoot your real name?*
A. *No. I had to change it because of professional duplication. My real name is Sigourney Weaver.*

Q. *Do you write your own material?*
A. *Only if I can't rewrite someone else's.*

Q. *Where did your characters come from?*
A. *Hallucination. I'm pretty sure it was something I ate.*

Q. *What prompted you to become a comedian?*
A. *Initially, I saw it only as a stepping stone to becoming a full-time waiter but then I allowed myself to become sidetracked.*

Q. *Any regrets?*
A. *I could have been an evangelist. Evangelists don't have to pay their writers.*

Q. *Looking over your career, what is the greatest lesson you've learned?*
A. *Drunks don't appreciate satire.*

Q. *What was your most embarrassing moment?*
A. *When I discovered I was not adopted.*

Q. *What is the bravest thing you ever did?*
A. *Outshout a drunk.*

Q. *If you had only six months to live, where would you live them?*
A. *Wasaga Beach. Six months would seem like twelve years.*

Q. *Do Canadians have a sense of humour?*
A. *How could I have made a living doing nothing but comedy for Canadians if Canadians had a sense of humour?*

The fact that, after spending three-quarters of my time on the road, I still have a marriage is remarkable. Fortunately, Diane, very early on, had carved out a life of her own. She was always there for me, when I returned, and never complained when I wasn't there. At one of my after-dinner speaking engagements, I remember the head of a large corporation paying tribute to his wife. "Without Thelma," he said, "I wouldn't be standing here today. She went way beyond the call of duty of any wife, and she made my trains run on time. Stand up and take a bow, Thelma." After the reference to the trains running on time, it was a bit of a disappointment when Thelma stood up. She didn't look at all like Mussolini.

Saying thank you to one's spouse publicly always seems awkward and out of place. Except maybe at a birthday party. But birthday parties can be problematic, too. Diane's birthday falls on December 24. This is a perpetual challenge. No way to avoid being upstaged by the Lord, whose birthday celebration falls the following day. My own birthday is December 5, and even with that three-week separation, one can feel a bit crowded, birthday-wise.

*(Left) At home, with
Diane and Valérie*

*With Diane, receiving a
honorary doctorate at
Athabasca University*

To have Diane show up at her own sixtieth birthday party, then, was a major accomplishment. I did a lot of lying to convince her that the party she was coming to was nothing to do with anyone's birthday. It was, I said, just a mid-day drop-in reception our good friends, Joan and John, were having in their home. Quite a few of our best friends happened to drop in while Diane, Valérie, and I were there.

I knew making a speech honouring Diane at that event would embarrass her. I had to find another way to embarrass her. This is it. I have been married to her for thirty-five years. I'm where I am today because having a partner who believes in me has made me want to excel. Through thirty-five years, she has been consistently outgoing, hard-working, cheerful, and compassionate. She has been the best of travelling companions in the dozens and dozens of places we have visited together. She has helped run my business life through the years, and has managed always to separate business from personal life, and maintain a balance. On countless occasions, I've seen her tenacity and I've seen her compassion. When her mother, Lucienne Simard, was dying of Alzheimer's and received less than the proper care from the hospital, Diane fought to set the situation right and won. She also made sure that no one else would again suffer in the way her mother had. In the years we have been together, she has volunteered countless hours of her time to organizations like Amnesty International. She has sat on the boards of numerous non-profit arts organizations and charities. She deserves to be toasted, and this is the toast I raised to her on her sixtieth birthday.

> This is the day
> To honour our Diane
> This is the day
> Her splendid life began
> A toast to mark this special day
> Before her hair starts turning grey
> With a heart full of joy, I say
> Long live Diane.
>
> When she was born
> They threw the mold away
> A noble human cause
> *Elle toujours chercher*
> Her heart is big, her heart is true
> She made her hubby's dream come true
> And so with pride, he says to you
> Long live Diane.

I was on the road with "Air Farce," on my way to Calgary, when during the flight a public-relations officer for a symphony orchestra approached me with the suggestion that I put together a stage presentation that could be done with Orchestra London. The real London. Not the one in England. It occurred to me that it would be a great deal more fun to do this as a group, so I asked my "Air Farce" colleagues if they were interested. They eagerly agreed. It was a new challenge, so we put our ideas together and quickly came up with a more-than-adequate supply of music-related comedy material.

Welcome to another Masterpiece Opera, today being broadcast live from the stage of the magnificent world-renowned Toronto Opera House.

Today's masterpiece opera is the delightfully obscure "Le forza del bravo castrati" by Martello Monteverdi, or as we say his name in English, Marty Greenberg.

The story revolves around the Bravo half brothers, who are both heirs to the same throne. The first aria we hear is from the younger brother, Vittorio Bravo, "Sprigiti la presto" – "Hurry up in there. I have to go."

Unable to use the throne, Vittorio, in his frustration, stabs the King. With his sword now warmed up, Vittorio decides to strike while his iron is hot, and proceeds to run it through his mother, Mama Bravo, as she sings "Ay Vittorio Oo OoOo AhAh Ah un furtiva lagrima, cough, cough, cough, Arrivederci."

Overcome with remorse, Vittorio heads to the grand hall, and stabs Valentina, an innocent serving wench, who has the misfortune of also being a soprano. This prompts Valentina to intone her mournful swan song, "Perky, Perky."

[Look closer at text.]

Excuse me. "Perque, perque."

Just moments later, Vittorio finds his lover, Gladys, the scullery maid, with her fleas.

[Look closer at text.]

No. And with her, flees.

Reluctant to leave the castle with Vittorio, Gladys explains why she cannot marry him. "Io non so cucinare, prego."

Translated. "I don't know how to cook. I'm pregnant."

Vittorio replies, "Non posso sposarti. Sono impotento." I can't marry you anyway. I was wounded at the front, and rendered incompetent.

Then, suddenly, Vittorio's brother the Grand Duke Carlo, who all this time has been hiding in a closet, comes out of the closet and stabs Vittorio. But Vittorio refuses to die. As we hear the dramatic duet.

> Morto.
> Carlo.
> Morto morto
> Carlo Carlo
> Morto morto morto
> Carlo Carlo Carlo
> Morrrrrtoe
> Si si sono morto ay
> Right, right, I'm dead, Okay.

As he dies in the Grand Duke Carlo's arms, Vittorio incantates the tragic lamentation, "Lascia che me tomba per terra."

Translated: "Though you are closer than a stepbrother, and truer than the truest two-edged sword, and long have been fondest in my thoughts, there is nothing you can now do to change what fate has willed for me this day. For God's sake, please let me . . . turn the page . . . Oh. For God's sake please let me . . . [Turn to next page.] fall down."

Then, clutching the lost documents of birth, Vittorio's full-bodied cleaning lady, Valpolicella Folonari, rushes in with the lost documents of birth. The documents reveal that both Bravo brothers are impostors, and actually members of a rival family, the Boyardees. And with anger swelling in her beast . . . her best . . . her breast . . . both her breasts . . . her basoom . . . bosom . . . Valpolicella, the fat lady, sings, as she points to the Grand Duke Carlo.

[Spoken very deliberately.]

"He is an impostor."

One by one the chorus join the refrain.

He is an impostor.
He is an impostor.
He is an impostor.
Impostor. Impostor. Impostor. Impostor.
He ee ee ee ee is an im im im im im
Paw paw paw paw

Storrrrrrrrrrrrr!

    Finally the real Carlo Bravo returns from the Crusades just in time for the Grande Finale and in a haunting, timeless aria, he banishes himself forever to a distant Italian city. "You can stay here if you want toe, I am leaving for Toronto."

"Air Farce" as symphony concert guests

After a few appearances with Orchestra London, requests began coming in from symphony orchestras all over the country. The calibre of the orchestras we played with varied considerably. I will always treasure the memory of standing with Roger Abbott, watching the end of an orchestral rehearsal in Timmins. I was impressed they would tackle such a complex, avant-garde composition, filled with strange atonal effects and dissonance. At a break in the rehearsal, I talked to a young woman violinist, who was seated in front of where Roger and I were standing. I asked her the name of the piece they were rehearsing. "'Rhapsody in Blue,'" she replied cheerfully.

"Gershwin's 'Rhapsody in Blue'?" I asked, in shock.

"That's right," she said.

"*George* Gershwin?" I asked.

"Yes," she replied.

"*The* George Gershwin?"

"Of course," she said. "Who else."

I didn't dare look at Roger, but as if by instinct we both began moving quickly toward the fire escape. As we left the building, we dissolved into hysterical laughter. That night, when the playing of "Rhapsody in Blue" was over, the full house gave the orchestra a huge round of indifference. Roger and I had only been confused. The audience was completely baffled. In retrospect, maybe that was what the conductor was trying for. It could have paid off if the concert had ended with a quiz contest.

Most of our performances on the road were done as fund-raisers. We began many of the shows with Luba and Roger, disguised in raincoats and hats, as two latecomers to the audience, who would begin annoyingly to struggle through row after row of patrons, trying to figure out where they were supposed to be seated. I suddenly appeared out of nowhere, as the most abusive, loud-mouthed usher the world has ever seen. I loved my role, screaming abuse at the latecomers, calling them every horrible name in the horrible-name book. The least offensive moment was when I referred to Luba as a snivelling bag of rat hair. As there were no empty seats on the main floor, I had to seat them up on the stage with the orchestra. Whereupon, the two of them started on a coughing orgy. Everyone who had ever attended a symphony concert, or had played in one, could identify with the whole episode.

Whether performing with symphony orchestras, or in our live theatrical productions or making shows for our loyal radio listeners, I loved being with "Air Farce." I loved the work we all did. I also loved the directors we worked with and I loved being part of an aggregation that helped me win a Juno award, a bunch of ACTRA awards, a couple of honorary doctorates, and the rank of Sergeant-Major in the Royal Canadian Mounted Police. Despite all this, in the summer of 1989, I decided to leave "Air Farce."

(Above) Thunder Bay, Ontario, being promoted to Honorary Staff-Sergeant, RCMP

(Right) With Diane, in front of the RCMP display, Thunder Bay

Because "Air Farce" began as a radio show, it never had a stage manager, someone to keep us in line. As the enterprise progressed, we had become involved in many different endeavours – radio productions, stage productions, television productions, and symphony concerts. All the theatrical productions or films that I had been involved in previously had always had a strict stage manager or assistant director. No one was allowed to get away with anything. If you came to a theatre rehearsal late, it was understood that a fine would be levied against you. In filming, the assistant directors are just as tough. When the word "Action" is called, you had better be in place, on the set, on your mark, in costume, in make-up, lines learned, focused and ready to go. I noticed that, from the a.d.'s perspective, the fact that one of the actors might be a star meant absolutely nothing. That was because, whether the person holding up the filming schedule is a star or not, thousands of dollars a minute are flowing out of the budget. The assistants are tough, because they are paid to be tough.

And so it is in theatre. In my early days, I can vividly remember working in my third stage production with the same stage manager. Her name was Grania Mortimer, and she was highly regarded by all who knew her. By the time of our third show together, a strong bond of mutual respect had developed between us. On this particular production, as a writer-performer, I had been working day and night during the rehearsal period. I rehearsed all day, then went home and wrote for a good part of the night. On this one day, I had been up until 2:30 a.m. writing, had gone to bed, then got up and started writing again at 7:00 a.m. At 8:50, I flew out of my apartment to a nine o'clock rehearsal. I arrived at 9:07 a.m.

As I made my way up the long staircase carrying two heavy briefcases full of scripts, there, glaring down at me, was Grania Mortimer. I could see the fury in her eyes. "This rehearsal was called for 9:00 a.m.," she said, in a quietly ominous manner.

"Grania, please," I replied, "I was working until 2:00 in the morning. Couldn't you rehearse a number I'm not in?" It was the wrong thing to say. She gave me a calm, expressionless look.

"This rehearsal was called for 9:00 a.m.," she said. "We are staging the opening number. You are in it." She took my briefcases, and I flew into the rehearsal hall. My reputation for punctuality meant absolutely nothing. This time, I was late. This very professional stage manager, who happened to be a beautiful woman with gorgeous hazel eyes that you might easily get lost in under other circumstances, had made me feel like a dropout from kindergarten, but a dropout from kindergarten who would never ever be late again, no matter what. And what has all this to do with leaving "Air Farce"? you ask. Read on.

For an early-morning stage appearance in Ottawa, it was arranged for the Farceurs to check our stage set-up and props at 6:30 a.m. Roger Abbott, Don Ferguson, and I checked everything out, put our props in position, and then left the stage. We decided, between us, that the missing member of our cast had probably not come to the set-up because she wasn't going to be using many props in her sketches, but just to be sure that everything was all right, Roger called the front desk of our hotel and asked to be put through to our missing person's hotel room. He was told by the operator there was no one by that name staying in the hotel.

We were taken aback by this news to say the least, but assumed that our talented cast member of the opposite sex had made her way to Ottawa on her own and had gone to sleep at her mother's home. When her mother told us she had not heard from her daughter recently, we were dumbfounded. Roger quickly got on the phone to our missing person's home in Toronto and asked her son if he knew where his mother was. "Sure," he said, "she's in bed." Her son gave her a message to fly out of her bed to Pearson International Airport and jump on the next magic carpet to the nation's capital.

We other cast members made an emotional shift from "dumb-founded" to "thunderstruck," as we began going over material in our show trying to think who could take over which of her parts and realizing there was no possible way this could be done. It would make no sense. What else could we do? Eliminate all the sketches that Our Lady of Perpetual Tardiness was to be involved in and had diligently rehearsed for? This would give us a very short show.

During this panicky period, I kept trying to think which of my own material on file in my brain I might summon up to help fill out our time. We were standing backstage, in the midst of this mental turmoil, when we heard the master of ceremonies preparing to intro-duce us. "Now, the next event in today's program, the comedy relief you've been waiting for . . ." Our brains switched from the panic of desperation to the calmness of inevitable disaster. At that moment, to our utter amazement, a door behind us opened, and there stood our missing cast member, all smiles and ready to make her entrance.

On another occasion: over two thousand people were sitting in the National Arts Centre, in Ottawa, waiting for an Air Farce per-formance to begin. All of us backstage were also waiting to begin. All of us but one. When everyone involved in the production was getting ready to go on stage, Our Lady was doing her customary, lengthy chit-chat with one of the NAC crew, a compulsion that could not be overcome. We had already gone through the last-minute ritual. From her dressing room came the panicky call. "How much time do I have?" and the response, "Ten minutes," followed by her inevitable, desperate cry, "I can't make it." It was a standard routine. Wherever we were, it never varied. It made the possibility of start-ing on time unthinkable.

Others could cope. Unfortunately, I couldn't. I had been trained in the Grania Mortimer school of punctuality. Anxiety from late starts turned me into the Sir Edmund Hillary of the world's highest ulcer, with no sherpa to help me get over it. I consulted my nervous system. "Dave," it said, "if you don't leave this situation, the anxiety will affect your attitude to the entire enterprise, to 'Air Farce' itself." "Dave," I said to myself, "if you can't trust your own nervous system, you don't deserve to have one."

And that is why I left "Air Farce." As you may have noticed, I'm very reluctant to reveal the name of the person who caused my anxiety because, apart from that small problem, we get along very well. She is a good friend, a brilliant comic actress, whom I have no desire to upset. Anyone born in the Ukraine and raised in Ottawa deserves only sympathy and understanding. Looking far into the future, when her fans, friends, and admirers, have gathered to witness the funeral of Our Lady of Perpetual Tardiness, I can picture the cleric, in all his embarrassment. "The funeral is on hold," he is saying, "Our Lady is going to be fifteen minutes late."

Chapter 10

OLD ENOUGH TO SAY WHAT I WANT

Although I had left "Air Farce" as a regular in 1989, I continued to perform in the show as a guest. Roger Abbott showed a remarkable grace with me over this – he had not wanted me to leave at all, but he never carried a grudge about it, and was happy to invite me back. With radio and television appearances, banquets and conventions, it was still a busy life, but not busy enough for me. I decided to go back to something I had dabbled with in the sixties, the one-man show. *Dave Broadfoot's Comedy Crusade*, which opened at the Bayview Playhouse in Toronto in June 1989, was the first of the one-man shows that have now become a mainstay of my performing life. The coffee houses of the sixties had disappeared, and I felt the club circuit was for younger comedians, so my shows are now back in the theatre. My first love.

To this day, standing alone in an empty, dark theatre evokes in me a feeling of awe, a feeling of comfort, of solace, of reassurance – from knowing I'm standing where so much has been accomplished by so many playwrights, directors, composers, lyricists, musicians, actors and singers, dancers and choreographers, not to mention comedians and audiences. For me, the older the theatre, the more intense the feeling. I can't express it any better than Johnny Wayne did. "When you come in here," he said, "you take your hat off. You are in my church." Every other year, I set off on a tour of the country that takes me to thirty or forty towns and cities. It can be gruelling work, and many friends ask why, at my advanced age, I still do it. I don't spend much time thinking about it until people ask, but I was musing on it one day recently with my agent, Paul Simmons. "I'm thinking about retiring," I said to him. "You can't do that," he shot back. The appalled look on his face made me stop thinking about it at once.

It was only a passing thought. Why would I give up doing one-man shows when I love them? They are unlike any other theatrical form. You are up there on stage, on your own, for two hours plus, and you have to carry everything with your performance. A lot of the time, I am just Dave Broadfoot, but I also do a lot of character comedy, because I love to act. In my case, a "one-man show" really means what it says. My tour manager, Terry McRae, deals with the itinerary, and my publicist deals with publicity, but I do everything else. That means writing the scripts, with a little help from friends like Jim Foster and Nicholas Pashley, working out the lineup, collecting the props, organizing the sets, and rehearsing and directing myself. From this, you can see that, if something goes wrong, I have no one to blame but myself.

I have tried to keep the productions simple. A sparse set, just a few props, and a few costumes, no more than I can pack into my car. I use a lectern, which I designed myself – it's constructed so that it neatly folds down to fit into the trunk. The perfect coffee table for the set was available at Goodwill Services, for a very reasonable sixty bucks. Unfortunately, it turned out to be too long for my car, so I had to cut off a large chunk, and refinish it. The fine trim was hard to match perfectly, but I worked hard at it, and now, I am proud to say, you can't tell it has been shortened at all. Goodwill Services – a big help to my career – also supplied me with the perfect overcoat for a new character, an old homeless man, Bartholomew. Actually, the coat was a bit too classy and new, so I had to distress it. First, I ripped all the lining out, then made a few tears, and dyed it a dirty beige-brown to get the exact look I wanted.

But my biggest triumph, in the prop department, was the fibre-glass lobster. On one of Her Majesty's visits to Prince Edward Island, she had been presented with a fibreglass lobster. Asked "Why the fibreglass lobster?" the man in charge of the event said it was because they found out she didn't have one. This seemed to me to be an outrage. I just couldn't picture it. A Queen without a fibreglass lobster is no different than a king without a Styrofoam beaver. It's not right.

As I was about to do a number involving a whole suitcase of mementos, I was determined to open with this reference, and close the sequence by producing the fibreglass lobster from my suitcase. "This was found in England, in a small pawnshop close to Buckingham Palace," I planned to say. As I had not checked out the ready availability of fibreglass lobsters, this was a foolhardy piece of writing.

I set out on a search for the elusive lobster. Home Hardware was out of them; Canadian Tire was out of them. Other hardware stores did not seem to stock them. Every toy store and joke store I passed had never heard of them. I hunted and hunted, to no avail. I had given up all hope, when, one day, while appearing in Barrie, I was walking down the main street. As I passed by the Salvation Army Thrift Shop, there, in the window, was a huge, perfect fibreglass lobster. It was exactly what I had in mind. I went in. "Is that lobster in the window for sale, by any chance?" I asked the clerk. She told me to come back the following Monday when Helen would be in.

When I returned the following Monday, Helen was curt. "We're not selling anything in our display," she replied to my query. "Well," I said, "what if we start at sixty dollars?" Helen stopped dead. She looked stunned. "Sixty dollars?" she said. "Are you serious? You want to give us sixty dollars for that thing? I'll have Betty wrap it up for you." The lobster was a steal at twice the price. It was a little bulky, and almost filled my suitcase, but it gave me the funny moment I needed to end the routine.

Writing has always been the trickiest part. All through my performing career, I have never really considered myself a writer, but I have been forced to become one out of necessity. The need for new material never goes away. Back in the fifties, when I was appearing at Number One Fifth Avenue in New York, I hired a young writer to produce material for me. I paid him a fairly substantial sum of money for what he did, because I thought he would be more in tune with what a Manhattan audience might like. His writing turned out

*Proud owner of the
fibreglass lobster*

to be serviceable, but it was not a great improvement on my own. To make it viable for me, I had to rewrite it. I've found that with all the writers I have worked with since, I always rewrite, to make it fit my delivery. I have a need to make it my own. For my shows now, I write almost all the material myself. Then, if there is a piece I am not sure of, I send it to my friend Jim Foster, a writer with the Orillia *Packet and Times*. If he can make improvements, he does. Nicholas Pashley, who has a day job at the University of Toronto bookstore, and a night job writing his own books, helps out too, when he has any spare time. In radio days, Rick Olsen and Gord Holtam did considerable writing for me, but they have such heavy schedules now I haven't the nerve to ask them. The key, when all the individual pieces are done, is to get enough variety in the show lineup. It is more fun for the audience, and it is certainly fun for me.

With the one-man show, I wanted to keep a select group of the characters I have performed over the years. Bobby Clobber presented

Bobby Clobber waltzing with Governor General Adrienne Clarkson

a problem. He had always been interviewed (usually by Roger Abbott). I tried to do it playing both the parts, but it never really worked. The differentiation wasn't strong enough. I then tried doing it as a monologue, but that didn't work either. The joy of Bobby Clobber is the way he responds to the people interviewing him. That's how we have all seen his type so many times on TV – all those endless interviews with sports stars who have absolutely nothing to say. For a while, I was forced to drop Bobby from the show. It was a long time before the solution occurred to me. Get a volunteer from the audience to interview him. It worked so well that people always thought the volunteer was not a volunteer at all. Everyone said they were very well rehearsed, which was something they never said about me.

Another idea, to bring variety into the one-man format, was to get the audience to ask questions. I installed a question box in the theatre lobby, and every night at intermission I had just enough time to select the fifteen or so questions that were the least obscene.

Q.　*What can you do if you're in the bath and the doorbell keeps ringing and you get out of the bath and go to the door and find two smiling people there determined to talk to you about eternity?*

A.　*Be honest. Say, I'm a pervert. I'm lonely. I have nothing on under my bathrobe. Whenever I hear the word eternity, I get very horny. Come on in and let's get naked.*

Q.　*Ramses II of Egypt had one hundred children. Why are condoms named after him?*

A.　*It's based on irony. It's the same as naming the peace prize after the man who spent his life inventing explosives. Nobel.*

Q.　*Why do men have nipples?*

A.　*The nipples are there to remind a man that no matter how powerful he may become, there will always be a part of him that is totally useless.*

Q.　*How come a man can learn to run a computer in ten minutes but takes a lifetime to figure out how to iron a shirt?*

A.　*That's because, in the beginning, men were hunters. In those days, there were sizable dragons roaming the earth. When they breathed, they produced clouds of steam. That's why, to this day, asking him to handle anything that produces steam can traumatize a man.*

Q.　*How come Canada is still a monarchy?*

A.　*Because people would rather pay allegiance to a monarch they have nothing to do with than an idiot they voted for.*

Q.　*Why did Humpty Dumpty have a great fall?*

A.　*Humpty was Canadian. His great fall made up for his lousy summer.*

Q.   How are we going to keep Quebec in Confederation if they hold
     another referendum?
A.   Same way we did the last time. Wait until the last minute, and
     then say "I love you." Actually, that may not work. I tried it
     with my first wife.

Q.   Why does a man refer to his sex organ by name, like Willy, Dick,
     Peter, Charlie, Wang, Dong, Schlong, Weinie, Wazoo, Percy?
A.   The reason for giving it a name is because a man doesn't want
     ninety per cent of his decisions made by a stranger.

Q.   How many government workers does it take to change a light-
     bulb?
A.   One. But he gets upgraded three levels by the time it's all
     screwed up.

Q.   If there are further cuts in public-service funding, won't our
     firefighters be hitchhiking to fires?
A.   Yes. But first we'll need a campaign to persuade drivers to pick
     up hitchhikers carrying axes.

Q.   My dad got his social insurance number mixed up with his
     answering code number. Will he have to wait until he is sixty-
     five to get his messages?
A.   Yes.

Q.   Why do humans have pubic hair?
A.   What would you rather have, pubic teeth?

Q.   Dave, if I step out of my house and I see a fire truck in the
     street with all its lights flashing while my dog is trying to take
     on a skunk just as a woman who looks like Céline Dion comes
     walking by with two weasels on a leash, what does it mean?
A.   It means your present medication is not working.

Keeping up the level of the performance through a long tour is critical. I do it through sheer doggedness. Nothing is going to stop me. Not lack of food, lack of sleep, or lack of time. No matter what, at 3:00 p.m. I'm in the theatre checking the light, sound, props, and continuity. After a meal break, I'm back in the theatre at 7:00 for the performance at 8:00. I clear my mind of everything except what I am about to do. I may go over some lines if they are not as locked in as they should be. I might vocalize, if I am not sure of my voice. Sometimes I exercise before I walk on. If I have really rehearsed, there is no problem with nerves. It's always the same – if I have rehearsed and rehearsed, there always comes a point where my body just says, "That's enough. You're ready." The nerves vanish. That's important, because when I walk on stage, it has to be as if I just bought the building.

When you are this ready, out there on stage, you just fly. I imagine it's the way a jazz musician feels. The audience gives you your rhythm. When you are tuned in to them, and when it's going well, it's very, very exciting. The rhythm is there, you work with it, and try to build on it. I learned very early never to let a laugh die – I always cut off the end of the laugh, and push on forward. John Morgan is the only person I know who is prepared to stand on stage and let a laugh die. He makes it work, but I can't do it, to me it's like fighting the music. I learned long ago to shape monologues so they build to three crescendos: they hit a first crescendo, then start again and build to a second crescendo, and from there they go to a third. That way, you can finish in a blaze of glory.

After the show, if I meet any of the audience who come backstage, there are always two favourite questions. The first – "Where do you get your timing?" – has no answer. Timing is innate; there is no explaining it. You have it or you don't. It's not something you learn, although, curiously, it is something you can improve. The second most-asked question is "How do you memorize all that stuff?" I think every actor or performer develops his own method. For me, the first thing is to be aware of where I am going, the basic ideas. If you learn by rote, and go blank, it's a disaster. If all you have in your mind are the words, and not the flow of ideas, you can get into very

Visiting after a show with Barry Humphries, a.k.a. Dame Edna. I've always enjoyed meeting other comedians.

deep trouble indeed. But with the flow in mind, at least there is a structure you can work your way through till you find your way back to where you are supposed to be. Fortunately, although I've mangled words badly, I've never dried up. Not completely. Not yet.

At the end of the evening, I pack my costumes, and go back on stage to help pack the props and sound gear. Everything is loaded into the vehicle, I thank the theatre crew, and head back to the hotel. Then it's up early the following morning, and off to the next venue. I spend about two to three months on the road, in as few as twenty and sometimes as many as sixty venues. Toronto, Vancouver, Regina, Halifax – the major cities – but also everywhere from Prince Rupert to North Battleford to Wawa to Baddeck and Pictou and Corner Brook. I have travelled the length and breadth of Canada, and I've loved almost every minute of it.

I was sixty-nine years old when, in June 1994, I went with a group of entertainers to perform for Canadian peacekeepers in Bosnia and Croatia. Depressingly, it seems peacekeepers will always be needed to keep people from trying to kill each other, and entertainers will always be needed to help entertain the peacekeepers. Korea, Cyprus,

Gaza, and now Bosnia and Croatia. I have seen my share of the wars of the twentieth century from the entertainment sidelines.

We arrived in Zagreb, to be reminded instantly of the dangers our peacekeepers face in the region. A young Canadian soldier had been blown to pieces by a land mine shortly before we got there. One consequence of this was that the officer in command took the trouble to demonstrate these nightmare devices to us, just in case we should encounter one. More and more plastic was being used in their manufacture, he told us, making them harder and harder to detect. They were also being layered underground, one on top of the other, making them all the more lethal when detonated. Fortunately, we never encountered any, although the damage they caused was visible all around us, in the maimed bodies of civilians.

After our performance for the Canadians based outside Zagreb, our group was flown to Sarajevo in a full-sized Russian commercial airliner. We were surprised and delighted to be travelling that way in what was otherwise a totally military environment. At Sarajevo, the temporary steel-and-sandbag walls around the airport perimeter were higher than I could ever have imagined – from the tarmac, you could see absolutely nothing. Leaving the terminal building, we were escorted to a military van and whisked away. As we passed through the heart of the city, we could hear sniper fire, and were told that a sniper had just fired at our vehicle and missed. As we sped through the streets, towering stacks of burned-out cars and buses lined the sidewalks, with sheets of metal leaning against them. These stacks gave civilians something to hide behind, when snipers opened fire. We passed the burned-out remains of the Olympic stadium, which not long ago had been the focus of the city, a city that was then acclaimed as a model of tolerance for the world to emulate.

We drove on to Visoko, where the main body of Canadian peacekeepers was based. All along the route, we could see what one always sees in the aftermath of battle: miles and miles of pointless, wanton, gratuitous, non-strategic destruction. In Visoko, the accommodations were unique. All the troops were situated in a very large, rough building the UN had taken over. The building was several storeys high, with all the windows missing. Each floor was a military encampment, with rows and rows of tents set up within the exterior walls.

(Above) Bosnia, encampment at Visoko

(Right) With some of our tour musicians, Visoko, Bosnia

(Below) Ready to leave Visoko, Bosnia, for Primosten, Croatia

Our entertainment unit was assigned to the fifth floor, women in one tent, men in the other. Nearby, there were several other abandoned buildings, one of which contained a large room on the ground floor. It was here that we were to perform.

I began my show with a joke about officers, always a sure-fire hit with enlisted soldiers. "We need always to challenge ourselves; to be always ready to put ourselves at risk," I started, "for instance, after a long lecture from your commanding officer, tell him you'd like to sum up everything he said, but you don't have a shovel! Take that chance! Take that risk!" On the second night of the performance, just after I had said that line, out of the darkness a giant six-foot-six soldier emerged from the audience, carrying a very large rocket launcher with a shovel hanging from it. The soldier moved into position on the corner of the platform I was on, faced me at an angle, and aimed the rocket directly at my head. I was totally surprised at this, but quickly made him part of the act. I looked over slowly at him, looked back, then looked again, looked back, before carrying on. The audience roared. The slow, uncertain, fear-filled reaction to him was all it took. The rocket-loaded soldier remained in position, at the ready, for the rest of my presentation, and got the biggest laughs of the evening. After this, the commanding officer, Colonel Wlasichuk, emerged from nowhere and took over the microphone, to say that he was going to overlook conduct unbecoming a comedian, and went on to commend me for volunteering to come to Bosnia. It was a unique moment – especially with the rocket still aimed at my head. The show ended without casualties. The next day, after observing from an outpost the horrendous damage being done to civilians by Serbian snipers hidden in trenches behind the trees on the hills, we were ready for our next performance.

We left Visoko on a very obscure, one-lane gravel road, over very rough terrain, for Primosten, on the Adriatic coast of Croatia. This rough, abandoned logging road was taken in the hope of avoiding any military action. I was absolutely amazed at the skill of the transport personnel, driving very large vehicles over very narrow gravel roads, and in some cases no road at all, having to manoeuvre past oncoming convoys with no inches to spare. We experienced some delays en route, such as trees lying across the road – by accident or design, we'll never know. The only really tense moment in the journey occurred when some paramilitary types with rifles suddenly appeared on both sides of the road, walked out, and stood directly in front of our convoy. We were not allowed to pass. I looked at our driver. Sweat was pouring off him, and not from the heat. At that point, an officer from another vehicle approached the paramilitaries. I have no idea what he said to them, but they finally decided to back off, and allowed us to proceed.

We passed Mostar, and from the highway, this large, modern city appeared absolutely dead and uninhabited. It had been bombed and shelled, and there was no glass left in any of the windows. Many of the buildings and houses had been reduced to rubble. We were told that there were people living there, but as we passed by, we could see no signs of life. In Primosten, our performances for the transport regiment were done in the open air. After the second performance, we were invited to a tent where an enterprising soldier had laid down plywood, turned down the lights, and created the ambience of a dance club. I walked onto the plywood for a bit of hip-shaking, and was startled to be grabbed from behind by two big strong arms. "Holy mackerel," I thought, "these guys have been here too long." But when I whirled around, I was facing a beautiful woman. Another soldier, seeing my surprise, yelled out that she was the best driver in their unit.

I had just finished bumping around the plywood with her, when I bumped into another woman from the transport detachment. She was from Nain, Labrador. I asked her what she felt like the first time she drove in convoy through the region. Mostar, she said, was the most devastating sight. When she went through the first time, it had just started raining. A little boy, about five years old, came out of one of the bombed-out houses and just stood there in the rain. A small girl, about three years old, came out and stood next to him and, as she did, he reached down and took her hand. At that point, the lady from Nain said, she lost it. Her tears were falling faster than the rain, as she thought of her own two small children back home.

After our final show at Primosten, we had a free day before heading back to Zagreb, and home. I will always be thankful for the conducting officer who had the foresight to arrange for a boat to come to Primosten harbour, to pick up our group and take us on a cruise along the coast among the nearest of the Adriatic islands. We were guided by a Croatian captain, his wife, and daughter. We anchored off one of the islands, and all dove off into the warm Adriatic water and swam to our hearts' content. Then the captain weighed anchor, and moved the boat to tie up at the dock of the small island village. On the waterfront, we found a good restaurant in the little hotel. Our lunch was prepared while we wandered around the village – a sumptuous seafood lunch, fit for an emperor or a Canadian entertainer. Whichever shall leave the bigger tip.

Between the cruising, the exploring, the swimming, the lunch, the weather, the company of the Croatian captain and his family, and his homemade Schlivovitz, it had been a magnificent final day, and I, of course, was feeling guilty. Guilty, because not far away people were coping with land mines and snipers. And guilty because Diane and Valérie, who would have so loved this, were so far away.

It was only when all of our troupe were back in Canada, safely settled into our respective grooves, that we heard that the Visoko building, inside which we had comfortably been billeted in army tents, had been shelled.

An anthropologist, whose name I can't remember, had a theory that comedy originated in the pleasure human beings derived from observing the misfortunes of others. Comedy, he said, was initially sadistic. If that is true, we human beings have come a long way. I have performed comedy for Canadians now for half a century. That's not sadistic, that's miraculous. When I started out, I wanted to be the best English-speaking comedian in Canada, but also to remain anonymous. That's the way it pretty well worked out – the anonymous part. It's part of being Canadian.

"Our first allegiance must be to where we live." I think Thomas D'Arcy McGee was right. Our first allegiance must always be to where we live. Not long after the broadcast of the TV special "Old Dogs, New Tricks," a fan was complimenting me on the show. "Let's face it, Dave," he said, "you've got the talent. You could have gone to California years ago, become a comedy star, made a ton of money, and by now be coming out of the Betty Ford Clinic. I guess you didn't want it badly enough." I guess he was right. Frank Shuster put

Receiving the Order of Canada from Governor General Ed Shreyer, 1983

the whole thing in perspective for me, very early on. When he was young, he said, he had dreamed of going to Hollywood. When he got there, he found himself sitting beside a mansion pool. His wife, Ruth, walked by. "You know, Ruth," he said, "this isn't it." There it was, and he didn't care about it at all. Somehow, I knew that was true for me, too.

Canada/U.S. Comparisons

American politicians can be bought.
You can't buy Canadian politicians. You have to rent them.

Americans are plagued by organized crime.
We have the Human Resources Department.

American evangelists talk about life after death.
We have an appointed Senate.

Americans have always been scared of political jokes.
Canadians go out and vote for them.

American athletes pray before a game.
Our athletes pray during a game. I heard a Canadian hockey player call on Jesus Christ six times in one game.

Americans look at things as they are and say, "Why?"
Canadians look at things as they could be, and say, "There's no way."

Americans fought a war against unfair taxation.
Canadians say, "What other kind of taxation is there?"

Americans ask, "What is Stockwell Day?"
I tell them: stock-well day is the day Canadians go to the liquor store to get ready for the long winter.

Even the attitude to the weather is different.
You say "Nice weather!" to an American, and he'll say, "Uh-huh."
You say "Nice weather!" to a Canadian, and he'll say, "It's too nice. We're gonna pay for this."

Even Thanksgiving is different. We celebrate it a whole month before they do. We have that much less to be thankful for.

Americans are never sure their leader is telling them the truth.
With our leader, there's never any doubt what he's telling us.

Americans call their political opportunists "favourite sons."
We go all the way and say what they're sons of.

We have the Mounties.
They have the CIA, and the CIA has an image problem, because they have never taken the trouble to produce a musical ride.

The authority above the government here is the Governor General.
The authority above the government there is the National Rifle Association.

A big event here is getting into the Order of Canada.
A big event there is getting out of the Betty Ford clinic.

As soon as Francis Scott Key finished writing the "Star Spangled Banner," he became an American hero.
As soon as Calixa Lavallée finished writing "O Canada," he moved to Massachusetts.

A great American said, "Give me liberty or give me death."
A great Canadian said, "Give me liberty, or if you'd rather not, hey, that's okay too. Is there any more beer?"

I've made occasional forays south of the border. Even after I was well-established here, I occasionally went down to New York, and played a number of clubs where you could go on without being paid. Getting in front of a different audience with different interests is always a challenge. After one performance, I was standing at the bar of a small club in the Village, talking to the guy beside me. "I don't know why I do this," I said. "It's madness, to do this. I don't need it." But in a way, that wasn't true. I did need it. I wanted to see what would happen. The last time I did it, it was very exciting. One of the pieces I performed was a parody of a review of a book that had been censored, and when I left, the young audience were yelling "right on" and giving me high-fives.

There have only been a few occasions when I worked in the United States for any length of time, and I was always happy to come home. Those U.S. occasions became so rare that I eventually gave up my green card. My work was here in Canada, and the comedy I cared about came from where I live. I did not want to do Americana – we have enough of that, our media are saturated with it. Over the years, the characters that I have developed – Renfrew the Mountie, Bobby Clobber the hockey player, the Member for Kicking Horse Pass – have all been solid Canadian citizens. The key to their acceptance has been finding an approach that does not give offence, and in that I think I've been successful. The biggest Renfrew fans are the Mounties themselves. Hockey fans love Bobby, and politicians seem to love the Member.

Not giving offence doesn't mean being politically correct. I am not politically correct. I appropriate voices, and I am not afraid to talk about subjects that others think are risky. Is it right to take on the voice of an East Indian? Yes, as far as I am concerned, if it is done with respect, affection, and accuracy. Nothing is more disrespectful than a poorly executed accent, and I pride myself on a good ear, and getting accents right. John Morgan and I performed a sketch about an immigration officer and an immigrant that reversed the expected roles. The immigrant was very English, wore a bowler hat, carried an umbrella, and spoke with an Oxford accent. The Canadian immigration officer was an immigrant from India, wore a turban, and spoke with a heavy Bombay accent. The immigration officer tells the arriving Englishman about the present unemployment situation in Canada.

ENGLISHMAN: *I've been unemployed for four and a half years.*

OFFICER: [Brightening] *Ohhh. So you have experience. Tell me, do you have a criminal record?*

ENGLISHMAN: *Just one. Englebert Humperdinck singing "Please Release Me."*

OFFICER: *No problem. Here are your documents. You will have to work very hard here. And you will become very homesick. You'll miss all the sights of home. The little boats, the men climbing the craggy cliffs to meditate. The animals wandering in the street.*

ENGLISHMAN: *I see you still miss India.*

OFFICER: *I'm not from India.*

ENGLISHMAN: *No? Where are you from?*

OFFICER: [Amazed] *Can't you tell by my accent? I'm from Newfoundland.*

It was always the audience members of East Indian background who laughed the hardest.

Fashions in comedy change over time. I performed a sketch in 1971 that was, I thought, a very clever interview with a rapist. The rapist complained throughout about the public not being able to see things from his point of view. It seemed funny then, but it would be unimaginably offensive now. One day, after I had done a joke that used the word "rape," a woman approached me. "Do you realize what it is you are tossing off in such a nonchalant way?" she asked. It made me think, and once I did, that joke was gone forever. Fifty years ago, comedians called a psychiatric hospital a nut-house, homosexuals were "faggots" or "fairies." I remember a comedian singing a parody of the song "Love and Marriage."

> John loves Mary
> John loves Mary
> She's a diesel dyke
> And he's a fairy.

None of this is acceptable now. As for mother-in-law jokes, even when they were not considered offensive, I hated them, because they were always based on the same tired cliché. No surprises. Anything that involved stereotyping people or dividing them has always been anathema to me. Watching the "Just for Laughs" comedy festival in Montreal, I have at times been nonplussed at how willing American comedians and comedians from other parts of Canada have been to engage in negative, stereotypical put-downs of Quebec. They speak as if it is a great revelation to them that Montreal is a place where French is spoken, and how irritating and annoying this is. This kind of comedy plays to bigotry and, for me, playing to people's bigotry has no place in comedy. As comedians, we have a freedom to be as outspoken as we want, but I see no point at all in pushing people apart. We have the golden opportunity to unite people in laughter. We all have a right to be here. And we all have a right to laugh.

I believe laughter is to the mind what jogging is to the body, and when you can look at a mistake you've made or a hurt you've sustained and laugh about it, you have found the key to sanity. Groucho Marx told of an incident in which he had taken his son to a swimming pool, when the pool manager approached him and told him Jews were not to use the pool. "Listen," Groucho said, "the kid's only half-Jewish. Let him in up to his hips." Most people would not be able to respond that way. They would be so hurt and insulted, they would just walk away. But Groucho gives this brilliant rejoinder, making the pool manager look like a nickel when he thought he was a dollar. I witnessed a similar incident on a London bus. The driver was asking the passengers to move back. "How can I move back when I got a big nigger blocking my way?" an angry Cockney voice yelled out. "Big nigger *gentleman* blocking my way," the black man calmly responded. It was almost asking too much for someone to respond with such grace.

Such occasions are rare. There is all too much predictability, cliché, and stereotyping in humour. So that when a young black man approaches you on the street at Eglinton and Yonge and asks, "Do you have any spare change to help fight off the white man's oppression?" you are delighted to give over your spare change. Or walking along Sherbrooke Street in Montreal, when an old man asks, "Anything for the Beer Foundation?" you are eager to support the cause. Good lines deserve good money.

Throughout my career, I've worked hard, to keep producing new material. That is a matter of survival. If word got around that I was doing the same old stuff, who would hire me? If you are juggling, you can do the same act you did five years ago, and people either want it, or they don't. The act doesn't change much. But a verbal performer has to keep updated.

I believe that comedy is a very serious business – for me it has been a vocation – so it is always a surprise to find that not everyone views it this way. A young theatre apprentice once asked me what I really wanted to do in the theatre. I wanted to do what I was doing, I said, I just wanted to do it better. That didn't seem to satisfy her. "Yes," she said, "but don't you want to do something important?" "I think it is important," I said. Later, I mentioned the incident to Dora Mavor Moore. "Pay no attention, David, to the youthful enthusiasm of misguided *amateurs*," she intoned. Amateurs, maybe, but the attitude has come up again and again over the years. At the National Theatre School, I went to give a talk to the students. They were indifferent and arrogant, and at the end the questions were all very patronizing. "Why did you choose to become a comedian?" one of them asked. I had the feeling that they thought what I was doing was far beneath what they were already achieving.

In case anyone reading this is an aspiring comedian, please don't be discouraged by misguided amateurs. A life in comedy means constantly developing fresh material, whether you ever get to perform it or not. If you are a genius, you may be able to walk on stage and perform without any material at all, but I have never met anyone like that. I have heard of it, so such a person must exist. It may be you. If it isn't, you'll have to buy, steal, or, if there is no other way, write your own material. If you are lucky, like me, you will have been raised as a fundamentalist Baptist, and will soon have a filing cabinet full of evangelical sketches and monologues. You're a lucky up-and-comer if you have relatives to try your new jokes on. Relatives know, if they don't co-operate, you can cut them out of your will. If all else fails, you can speak your exciting new humorous bits into a tape recorder and then force yourself to listen to yourself in playback.

"Our first allegiance must be to where we live." Thomas D'Arcy McGee was assassinated shortly after he said this – by a Fenian who did not like his allegiance, the only such political assassination in our history. In Canada, a comedian, like everyone else, does not live in danger of losing his life for what he says. I've spent most of my career getting laughs at the expense of the federal government, the same federal government that then made me an Officer of the Order of Canada. In the rest of the world, things are not always so benign for the satirist. In Myanmar, Thu Ra, a humorist who satirized the government, was arrested and imprisoned. In the days of the Soviet Union, when a Russian humorist defined a string quartet as a Russian symphony orchestra that had just returned from a tour of the West, he was sentenced to two years' hard labour. Palestinian humorist, Naji Salim, drew a cartoon showing a dove pecking its way like a woodpecker through the upright pole of a gallows. For this impertinence, he was murdered. In Guatemala, Jose Rolando Pantaleon wrote a satire on Guatemalan labour problems. He disappeared. When he was found, his jaw had been broken, all the skin had been ripped from his back, and there were five bullets in his body. In Egypt, Faroud Fouda made fun of some Islamic fundamentalists. He was shot in the street in broad daylight. As he lay dying, his best friend arrived to tell him that he had discovered Faroud was number three on the Islamic jihad hit list. "I was too easy on them," he said, "I should have been number one." In Colombia, a Colombian comedian had made fun of the government. He also made fun of the rebels who were fighting the government. Later, while driving in Bogota, he was stopped at a traffic light. A car pulled alongside him, and he was shot dead. No one knows which side the killer was on, rebels or government. This list could go on. One thing is certain. There are too many countries where the government tortures comedians. We can celebrate the fact that in our country, comedians torture the government.

One day in January I looked in my book for 2001 and thought, What's going on here? Where are all the bookings for banquets and conventions? Where are all the one-night stands I usually do? They seemed to have evaporated. So using Dave Broadfoot's first rule of career development, Make Your Own Work, I decided to do something about it. It had been three years since I did my last tour, and I'd been working on new material throughout that time. Even though I had more than enough to mount a completely new show very quickly, it felt like a lot of work putting it together for only two bookings. I remarked on this casually to Terry McRae, who has organized my tours for the past several years. "It's all new material?" he asked. When I said that it was, he said, "Let's do a tour." So we did. He decided we should call it *The First Farewell Tour*. Why? The first reason is there is so much of Canada to say farewell to, we didn't think we could do it all in one tour.

The second, more serious reason, is that people are now *constantly* asking me when I am going to retire. I answer that I don't really know, which is true, but the question always starts me thinking. Why are they asking? Maybe I should? I'd like to be remembered at my peak. I don't want to go on when I can barely make my way across the stage, can't remember my lines, and my delivery is shot.

There are some world-famous comics who have done that. Nothing like they used to be, and yet there they are, still performing. I hope that I will have the good judgement, or at least good enough friends, who will tell me in no uncertain terms, "Quit, already." But it's a tough thing, knowing when to walk away from it. For one thing, I love doing it. I have slowly over the years come to realize that all I ever really wanted to do is what I am doing. How addicted am I? How hard would it be to live without that adrenalin? I think maybe I can live without it, but I'm not sure. I haven't made plans. I could perhaps work as a semi-amateur freelance carpenter. On the other hand, the insurance premiums for my assistant would be astronomical. It's probably too late to go back into selling men's clothing. Flogging Harris tweeds may not be as easy as it once was.

I think, ideally, a stand-up comedian should die standing up. On the punchline. Believe it or not, it has happened to a few people. Tommy Cooper, the British comic, for one, and Jack Wasserman, the Vancouver columnist, who slumped over the lectern after delivering a joke at a roast. He got double the laugh, because everyone thought he was making a physical comment on what he had just said. His last comment was really "I just died." That timing, to me, is absolute perfection. It doesn't get any better than that. No suffering, no disease, no protracted illness, just a lot of laughter on the exit. So, in the interest of promoting this as a possibility, at the age of seventy-five, in February 2001, I set about putting together an extensive cross-country tour.

Over the years, people have come to expect to see Sergeant Renfrew, the Member for Kicking Horse Pass, and Bobby Clobber in my shows. They had become like old friends to the audience. They expect them to have new stories to tell and new things to say, but they would be disappointed if they did not make an appearance. There is another ongoing character who has emerged in recent years, Bartholomew X. Bartholomew X was actually inspired by elderly men I saw and visited with many times during my childhood. We had a number of Bartholomew types living in North Vancouver; they seemed to have no visible means of support, but somehow managed to stay alive. The adults called them eccentrics. One of them lived in a tiny wooden house not far from us, one lived in an old rundown clapboard bungalow, and one lived in an absolute shack. He was the most outspoken. He talked about anything and everything that was on his mind. In fact, they all did, and as this was the Depression, they had plenty on their minds. Something they all had in common was a respect for children. They spoke to us as if we were adults – which is probably why they made such a big impression on me, and why, all these years later, the respect and affection I had for them still lives on.

A Grate Life – Bartholomew

I criiiiiied because I had no shoes.

Then I thought, Why the heck am I crying? I got no shoes because I burned them to heat up my potato. It's my own fault. My old man always told me, Bartholomew, no matter what happens to you in life, never set fire to your shoes.

My old man was a farmer. So was I. Till the five crop failures in a row, then the big fire, then the flood. That was a bad month. Bein' a failure is okay but you can't make no money at it. Unless the prime minister puts you in the Senate.

So I made my way into the city. Tried to get onto skid row, but it was booked solid. So I moved into a cardboard refrigerator box. The old timers was always referring to me as nouveau poor. Whatever that is. But I knew lots of poverty stuff from the farm. Like, when it's really cold, if you sleep with a pig, you get two-point-five kilowatts of heat comin' at you all night long. I tried it in the city, but my neighbours complained about the oinks.

[Pulls cup out of pocket, with a dead teabag in it.]

I'm gonna have to invest in a new teabag. Teabags is like politicians. You can't tell if they're any good until they're in hot water.

Speakin' of hot water, I had a lady woman of the opposite sex with me for a while. Desdemona. She was quite a looker. If you could get past the cold sores and the broken teeth. She was a natural. Never used no soap or that shampoo stuff. She told me, if she wanted, she could grow mushrooms in her hair. They say beauty is only skin deep. Well, Desdemona had really thick skin

I says to her, Desdie, why don't we put our two boxes together? She says, "Poorkwah paw?" When I heard them words, I knew she was from Hawaii. I put the boxes together and scrounged a tin can and a couple of pieces of pipe and made us a little oil heater.

When Desdemona seen the heater, she went nuts! "You're just like all the others," she screamed. "Tryin' to get me hot." And she took off.

I miss her of course. I miss everything from them days. Everythin's changed. They even makes movies down here now.

I seen Nicole Kidman down here last week. She says "Hello." I don't think nothin's gonna come of it, but that's what she said, "Hello." Just by the way she said it, I could tell she's bored with Tom Cruise.

[Pulls bottle of water from other pocket and pours water into cup.]

Yeah, everythin's changed.

All the squatters' hangouts is being condominyized for rich folks. One or two rich folks is okay but when you start lettin' whole families of them move in, they destroy the character of your neighbourhood. And they're lazy. Don't even count their own money. Lazy. But you can't say nothin' or you'll get called a bigot.

The only other problem we got is a drug dealer who's hangin' around. He says to me, "You're in my space, move out of here you ugly old bastard or I'll shoot yuh."

I hate that, when they call me old. I looked him right in the eye. I says, "I got gout, a cataract in one eye, ringin' in my ears, hardenin' of the arteries, chronic dermatosis, insomnia, ulcers, heartburn, hemorrhoids, gingivitus, arthritis, bursitis, and I find it hard to pee . . . go ahead and shoot me." That stopped the arrogant son-of-a-bitch.

[Raises his teacup in a toast.]

To us!

Most of the material for *The First Farewell Tour* I wrote myself, with some help from Jim Foster. Before asking a paying audience to sit through it, I needed to try it out. Normally, when I'm doing a banquet, I put a new piece of material into the middle of the show, to get the feel of the audience reaction. It would have to be only a short piece, because I never like to use a paying audience as guinea pigs. This time, though, as I had no banquets booked, I decided to do a reading at the Cabbagetown Community Arts Centre. I expected about twenty people to show up, but the place was packed when I arrived, and I could hardly get in the door. I gave everyone forms to fill in for comments, and they were very useful. I think it's very important what a cab driver or a schoolteacher has to say – they are the people who are going to show up eventually in your audience. I did a second tryout for a private club of single-malt Scotch connoisseurs, who threw themselves into the business of asking questions of me in my role as the evangelical Pastor Hugo Gabortnik.

Pastor Hugo Gabortnik is another character in the show. He started life as an Anglican cleric, responding to written questions from his parishioners, but that seemed too low-key, so I converted him into a TV evangelist, which was better because it gave him a lot more fervour. To get the mannerisms right, I sat down and watched a lot of evangelical shows on Vision TV. The faith healers are the scariest. *"Oh, friends, welcome to our moment of healing. Let the Holy Spirit come into this room, and into this woman's body, and bless her and cure her sciatica."* I don't even have to takes notes, the cadence is so firmly etched into my brain. The phoney solicitousness, the manner of walking across the stage. I heard one evangelist say he had been influenced by Mick Jagger's performances. I thrive on getting even for my childhood guilt, and I have a drawer full of scripts to prove it. Diane came in one day, and caught me in front of the TV set, mesmerized by Benny Hinn and Peter Popov. "Why are you watching that?" she asked. "How can I perform them without watching?" I replied. "This is the new breed of faith healer. I have to keep up." The last thing I want is to get out of date in my evangelical style. After all, this is satire. It's important to get it right.

We opened at the Markham Theatre, and what I discovered there, and at subsequent venues, astounded me. There was something going on between me and the audience that I had never felt so strongly before. Touring through Ontario, everywhere we went, the venues were sold out, and every evening ended in a prolonged standing ovation. I was on stage alone, for two hours, each night, but at the end I was never tired. I was elated: I loved it. I was amazed at the packed houses. Everyone wanted to shake hands – there was a remarkable warmth. I don't remember this much fervour when I was younger. It was obviously something that had to be earned.

It was a busy schedule and the biggest difficulty throughout was finding time to eat. Jennifer Kasper, my driver and production manager throughout Ontario, has remarkable staying power at the wheel. We had things down to the simplest possible set-up. Just costumes and the bare minimum of props – a couple of chairs, a tripod, a flip chart, and my collapsible lectern. The only real problem on the tour, and it can be a serious one, is when the cast comes down with a cold. A one-man show is a one-man show – no one else can do it for you. I only had a problem once. It was when I was performing at the Thousand Island Playhouse at Gananoque, and I woke up to find the sound of the Broadfoot voice was rough to the point of being non-existent. Theatrically useless. I had a show to do that night. The Thousand Island Playhouse was sold out. Busloads of U.S. ticket-holders would be coming over the bridge from New York State.

There are moments in life when there is no one to tell you what to do. This was one of them. I drove east along the Thousand Island Parkway until I came to a thickly forested area on the St. Lawrence River side of the road. Just past this, I pulled over and got out of the car, and waited until I could see there was absolutely nobody around. Then I walked into the trees and went to work. Slowly, I tried to vocalize my way up the scale, while I paced back and forth among the sound-absorbing Scotch pines. I knew I could easily have been mistaken for a birdwatcher who had lost his grasp on reality, but that didn't stop me. At first, no sound came forth at all, but I kept at it. Gradually, the voice began to emerge, which surprised me. By mid-afternoon, it had grown strong enough for me to drive back into town, and on to the theatre. During the performance that evening, the voice seemed stronger than usual. It made me think how lucky I have been through a long performing career never to have had a major health calamity.

The head usher at the Thousand Island Playhouse later told me that there had been extra curtain calls that Sunday night. I have no recollection of that, but I do recall my ecstatic relief at having the voice return to the throat and remain there for the entire run. It made me think of Stephen Leacock explaining his "luck." "The harder I work," he wrote, "the more I have of it."

Out west, Terry McRae was my tour manager, production manager, and driver. Terry is a wonderful person to tour with. He'll drive eight hours at a stretch, then do the set-up with me and the local technical crew, as well as organize countless interviews, everything needed to make the tour work. But Terry's sense of direction is not great. We were off to do our first television interview at a TV station outside Regina, and were heading in the wrong direction. We were going to be late, and it was making me nervous. "Let's not fool around with this," I said. "I'm going to ask for directions." We stopped the car outside Tim Horton's. A young Aboriginal boy was fixing his bike. I went over to him. "Could you . . ." I began. The boy looked up at me. "Dave Broadfoot," he said. "What are you doing here? I was watching you on TV last night. Where do you get off charging people twenty-four dollars to come and see your show, when I saw you last night for nothing?" Then, with a big smile, he promptly gave us very exact directions to the TV station.

In Saskatoon, I had come into the theatre lobby after the show, when another young native boy, Leon, aged eleven, came up to me. "Mr. Broadfoot," he said, "I've got to tell you, yours is the coolest show I've ever seen." He then introduced me to his seven-year-old sister, Max. "Is your full name Maxine?" I asked stupidly. "No," she said, looking at me as if to say, Why would you ask such a dumb question?

The tour showed me, for the first time, a much younger audience, people who have seen me on the Comedy Network, which endlessly replays my specials and old episodes of "Air Farce." I had expected the silver-haired crowd, but this was new. Everywhere I went, the

Returning to my Grade
One classroom, at
Ridgeway Elementary
School, North Vancouver

response was friendly and welcoming. The next morning, as I was crossing the street in downtown Saskatoon, an approaching bus slowed down, and the driver opened his window. "Dave," he yelled at me, "get on the bus, let me give you a lift, even if it's only one block." He pulled in to take on passengers, jumped out, and shook my hand, and introduced me to all the passengers.

In Lethbridge, I was walking past a place with a sign "sourdough pizza." A young man who had been standing in the doorway ran over, and asked if he could shake my hand. "This is my place," he said proudly.

"That's interesting," I said. "What an original idea. Sourdough used to make pizza."

"Oh, no," he said. "It's not original. It's a franchise. From the States."

In Edmonton, I was amazed when, after doing a television interview, the interviewer ran all the way down the street to catch up with me to say thank you for coming on his show. That said more about him than it said about me – I'd never had an interviewer chase me down the street to say thank you before. You don't get any cool, detached aloofness in Alberta. They're still proud that they give the rest of us gas.

You could say it was all ego-boosting, which Diane did, when I returned home, but it was beyond that. I have never felt such pure affection from audiences before. Fortunately, to stop my head getting too big, there were some not-so-ego-stroking moments. At the airport in Brandon, I was in a crowded waiting room, uncomfortably aware that many of my fellow passengers were staring at me. I moved to a nearby room, and took a chair as far away from the door as possible, took out a script and started to work on it. A big, elderly farmer came in, walked all the way over to me and sat down so that he was touching me, clearly aching to talk, but I went on working on the script. The plane was delayed and the room filled up, and soon they were all back at it again, staring. Finally, the farmer found the courage to strike up a conversation. "I know who you are," he said. "You're on 'This Hour Has 22 Minutes.'" "Close," I said. "That's close." At that point, one of the crew came over to speak to me. "Gordon Pinsent," he said, "how are you?" In the U.S., celebrities need security guards. In Canada, we need name tags.

In a recent radio interview, I was asked how I would like to be remembered. I replied that I would like to see my name somewhere I feel I've made a contribution, a liquor store maybe, or perhaps a parking lot. I was always impressed, I said, with the way in which the people of Kingston, Ontario, honour their departed citizens by putting their names on parking facilities. That prompted a young Kingston radio listener to write to the mayor, suggesting they name a parking lot after me. The mayor responded by explaining that, to obtain this honour, you had to be deceased. He said, as far as he knew, Dave Broadfoot had not achieved this status.

I thought nothing more of it, until about a year later. I was preparing to tour eastern Ontario, when I received a phone call from a writer, Jack Chiang, of *The Kingston Whig-Standard*. "Did you know you are about to have a parking lot named in your honour?" he asked. "Come on," I said, "I'm not dead yet. I'm not even sick." He was serious – they had made an exception to the rule for me. The ceremonial event was to occur the next day. Jack Chiang met me at my hotel in Kingston, and drove me out to the parking lot outside the *Whig-Standard* building. The assembled crowd heard speeches from the publisher of the paper, then from the mayor of Kingston, and finally from the member of Parliament for the area. Then it was my turn. I was asked to climb a ladder and unveil the sign, which was attached to a high steel pole. I wondered, if I slipped and fell from such a height, would I fulfill some astrological plan and become dead just in the nick of time to properly receive this memorial honour. But, no, I managed, against all odds, to unveil the sign without losing my footing. There it was, for all the world to see – DAVE BROADFOOT MEMORIAL PARKING LOT. I was immensely gratified. To have a memorial bearing your name while you are still alive is, I consider, the absolute ultimate in timing.

Some of My Favourites

Member for Kicking Horse Pass – Canada Rant (2002)

INTRODUCTION: *If you're depressed about where you've been, focus on where you are. Here to describe where you are is the Honourable Member for Kicking Horse Pass.*

[Music: Establish "State Occasion" by Robert Farnon.]

MEMBER: Canada . . .

[Music: Reduce volume, till barely audible. Sustain throughout until the punchline, then segue into "O Canada" play-off.]

MEMBER: *. . . how can we take it for granted? When all other Commonwealth countries have voted to become independent republics, which country will still be voting "undecided!!!!"?*

In which country do people celebrate a dead Queen's birthday in the middle of May, so they can go north to become lunch for blackflies? Canada.

Not a country with a big army, but a huge force of volunteer reserves . . . who are ready to defend their country on the second Thursday of each month!

A safe country. How many Canadians have been bitten by a Canadian shark? How many of you are sitting here tonight with no arms because of Canadian sharks? How many? Let's have a show of hands on this!! [Pause]

Exactly.

Canada! One of the three best countries in the world! Why? Because we are free! Free to turn right on red. Slow down for green. And go like hell on amber!

Canada. Home of The Bluenose. *The only ship ever named after an alcoholic.*

Canada. Where you hear people say, "The ice on the lake is too thin to walk on. I'm goin' out there in my pick-up truck."

Canada! As you drive across it, you see signs that say "Moose! Night danger!!" What other country warns its moose not to go out after dark?

Canada. Where washrooms are called "rest rooms." Yet how rarely we hear anyone say "Hurry up in there, I'm tired. If I don't get some rest pretty soon, I'm gonna burst."

What is Canada? It's a newly married couple staring at Niagara Falls! Their third disappointment!!

It's a country where you have the right to gather up every piece of useless junk you've acquired throughout your life . . . put it all outside on tables and make other people pay for it.

Canada. Where there are people who insist that safe sex means adding a railing to the side of the bed.

And others who are sure a penile implant is a stool pigeon in a federal prison.

Still others who claim "innuendo" is the Italian name for "Preparation H."

And then there are those who insist that "genitals" are people who are not Jewish.

And yet, wherever a Canadian person goes in the world, when it's time to come home, you'll hear that Canadian say, "How many ounces of liquor can I bring with me?"

Canada . . . a country facing just one great, over-riding question . . . "If Quebec leaves . . . what's going to happen?" I'll tell you what's going to happen! Newfoundland is going to gain a half an hour!

Member for Kicking Horse Pass – Air Safety (1987)

INTRODUCTION: *In these days of runaway patronage, galloping corruption, and triple-digit prime-ministerial extravagance, we are proud to present a man who stands above all that. A man admired for his candour, respected for his credibility, revered for his integrity. Unfortunately, such a man doesn't exist. Instead we present the highly questionable though authoritative opinions of the Member of Parliament for Kicking Horse Pass.*

[Member: "Maple Leaf March"]

MEMBER: *An anxiety-ridden world. That's what we live in today. And what do Canadians have to worry about?*

     Exactly.

     But that's not the whole story.

     We live today with a renewed fear of flying. Because of terrorists, and hijackers, and ordinary psychopaths who can't resist seat sales.

     It's difficult when you're out at the airport and you see a man there who, because he has to fly, is taking lots of pills and knocking back the booze in order to calm himself enough to face the flight. You have to ask yourself . . . "Why would he become a pilot?"

     It's not reassuring when you ask your pilot how long he's been flying and he says, [drunk] *"All night."*

It's not reassuring when the security person demands to see your boarding pass and *your* dental records.

It's not reassuring when your plane has to be jump-started by a Volkswagen.

Or when you see a man out on the wing with a paintbrush trying to cover up the name of the airline.

It's not reassuring when the building you leave from is called "the terminal *building*."

Going through the security gate is traumatic enough.

On my last trip through security, an incident took place that left me speechless. The security person frisking me with her hand-held frisker stumbled on the carpet in the middle of her frisk.

I wasn't going to have any more children anyway.

Why can't these employees be trained to recognize terrorists?

The terrorist is the one cleaning his nails with a machete!

He's the one carrying the basket of pineapples with little triggers on them.

He's the one whose boarding pass bears the name "Abdullah Abba Dabba Dabba Du Mad Dog of God."

He's the one who enjoys *the in-flight meal!!*

There has to be a better way of handling security. And I believe I have the answer.

Fly naked!!

Imagine how a passenger would feel going through security naked *and* making the alarm go off.

What could he be carrying?

Mind you, as a naked passenger, you'd have to be very careful when fastening your seat belt.

And you'd have to find another place to stick your boarding pass.

You can't blame people for worrying.

I was flying on one of those small independent airlines . . . the Flin Flon Water-Bomber, Crop-Dusting, Ambulance, Freight, and Passenger Service Airways Incorporated. I asked the clerk if it was a no-smoking flight. She said, "Oh sure. We haven't had a fire in three weeks."

The plane left the terminal building and then we sat on the tarmac for a good three hours – three hours – waiting for clearance to take off.

A woman passenger began yelling, "I'm going to have a baby!"

The flight attendant said, "You should have thought of that before you boarded this plane."

The woman said, "I wasn't pregnant before I boarded this plane."

[Looks at watch.]

My time has run out.

I have to attend an international air-safety symposium in Mexico City next week. If I don't leave now, I'll miss my train!

[Music: Play-off.]

Sergeant Renfrew – Neo Nutzi Skinheads (1986)

I'm Staff Sergeant Renfrew of the Royal Canadian Mounted Police. The story you are about to hear has been taken from Mountie files, and until now, has not been missed.

I was sitting in my lonely log cabin on the fourteenth floor of Mountie headquarters with my indestructible dog Corporal Cuddles, when suddenly the Chief burst in, in an absolute lather. "Renfrew," he said, wiping off the lather, "last night a gang of Neo Nutzi skinheads broke into Mountie headquarters, got into the men's showers, and spray-painted swastikas on several naked Mountie bums. You're on this case, Renfrew. Before we can act, we need a lot more intelligence. So take your dog."

Skinhead . . . swastika . . . Second World War . . . long time ago . . . out of date . . . ignorant . . . bitch . . . bitch on wheels . . . turning . . . stomach . . . liver . . . kidney . . . kidney . . . kidney . . . k . . . k . . . k . . . Ku Klux Klan . . . white sheets . . . blankets . . . Hudson's Bay Company . . . That's it! Cuddles and I are going shopping.

When we got to downtown Ottawa, the streets were full of buskers. I noticed the busker doing the magic act had a shaved head. And she had a beautiful body. She was wearing eight-inch-heel shoes in red alligator vinyl . . . a black imitation leather mini-skirt three and a half inches long. No, three and three-quarter inches long . . . In fact, nine and two-third millimetres long . . . with stainless steel rivets. She had a strapless silver Spandex halter . . . Cantilevered . . . Dazzling emerald green earrings . . . [Drifting into dreamland] Gorgeous blue eyes . . . [Stiffen back to attention] But we were looking for a male suspect . . . So I paid no attention to her.

But then . . . she interrupted her magic and asked me if I wanted to do a trick with her. I wasn't about to fall for that old trap. Five times is enough.

I asked her if she knew any males with a similar full head of skin. She came close and whispered in my ear, "Go to Hull."

Hull is a city across the river from Ottawa.

I thanked her for the clue and was heading for the bridge, when I noticed another young busker with a shaved head up on top of a xylophone singing and tapdancing the National Anthem.

He had all the right words. Immediately, I was suspicious. Then I noticed he had a clarinet protruding from his pants pocket. Or maybe he was glad to see me.

When I got closer, I saw it wasn't a clarinet. It was a piece of lead pipe. I would have to keep an eye on this suspect.

Luckily there was a clothing store right behind the busker. I ran inside, climbed into the window, and posed as a dummy.

Nobody noticed.

The window dresser came in and took off all my clothes. There was nothing to do but keep up the pretence. Then she took that off too. The ensuing fight of the window dresser with the window dummy attracted a bigger crowd than the busker. But at least I got my bikini shorts back.

And just in time. The busker had packed up and was heading into a strange-looking building. A former restaurant that had just been converted into a rundown warehouse. Cuddles and I followed the busker inside. We found ourselves in a big room, filled with young men with shaved heads.

On the wall there was a chart of two heads with measurements. Drawn up by a professor from London, Ontario, the chart proved beyond a doubt that a skinhead has a larger brain than a woodpecker.

All of a sudden a door opened and in walked a big bald man in a chain-link vest, steel-toed boots, Tilley endurable pants . . . and a patch on one eye. As he got close, I saw it wasn't a patch. It was a jock strap. The man was a genius. You couldn't look him in the eye without feeling guilty.

As he began thanking the men for the successful spray painting of naked Mounties, one of them grabbed my hair. "Take this ugly wig off," he snarled. When my hair refused to come loose, I showed him my Mountie identification.

To no avail. Cuddles and I were grabbed from behind, taken into the street and thrown onto the back of a pick-up truck, driven by the skinhead boss himself.

On the highway we were lucky. There was a traffic cop in the next lane. I pranced up and down like an hysterical baboon to get his attention. The officer slowed down, blew me a kiss, and turned off into the Tim Horton's parking lot.

In desperation, I shoved Cuddles along the outside of the truck. He got to the window . . . leaped in . . . landed on the boss . . . knocking his foot onto the brakes.

When I regained consciousness, Cuddles was holding the boss by his endurables. Suddenly, I heard a yell, and the boss dashed out the passenger door.

Not a good idea. You don't dash very far with an Alsatian the size of Cuddles hanging from your groin.

The case was such a success, the Chief promised there would be a little extra money in my pay envelope. And there was. But so far, I haven't had the time to get to Canadian Tire to spend it.

Sergeant Renfrew – Contaminated Anti-freeze (1985)

This is Sergeant Renfrew. I was sitting in my lonely log cabin on the fourteenth floor of Mountie headquarters with my incredible dog, Cuddles, playing with a P.C. junior – that's the Prime Minister's kid – when suddenly the Chief burst in. "Renfrew," he said, "we have just uncovered a horrible crime. Government inspectors have found white wine in several brands of anti-freeze."

I couldn't believe it. Contaminated anti-freeze. In no time, Cuddles and I were buying three litres of the stuff at a large hardware store, which must remain nameless. After we paid for it with our Canadian Tire charge card, I checked the label. It read "Château-neuf-du-Welland-Canal Sparkling Anti-Freeze."

With the suspicious anti-freeze in our possession, we raced back to headquarters and our top lab technician, Torban Bragstock. "I want an analysis," I said.

"Here's an empty bottle, Renfrew," he said, "go in the next room and think about Niagara Falls."

"No," I corrected, "I want you to test this anti-freeze. I think it has wine in it." Bragstock took a healthy sip of the anti-freeze, let it swirl around his tongue and palate. He slurped. gargled, and finally gulped it down. I still remember his last words. "Not too bad."

But how to find the source of the tainted product? The only clue we had was the address. It turned out to be a beautiful restaurant that someone had converted into an abandoned warehouse. On the wall was a sign, "Trusspressers will be persecuted." Trusspressers will be persecuted? Could this be a misprint, or was the owner a bigot with a hernia? Through the window, we could see a lot of shady-looking characters standing on platforms around huge vats of wine. It looked exactly like a defence attorney's victory party.

Suddenly, I knew we had been spotted. Standing right behind me was the famous winemaker, Humboldt Dornflartz, a former European duke and cab driver. "I'm warning you, Dornflartz, you're giving the anti-freeze industry a bad name."

"You're wrong, Renfrew, I'm giving the wine industry a good name. I was the first Canadian to prove that wine could also be made from grapes. I'm saving the wine industry by finding new ways to use the stuff. I put it in anti-freeze and now I'm putting it in this." He brandished a bottle of Cold Duck. By now I was furious. Why would anyone want to tamper with Cold Duck, my favourite stain remover?

"Give me that bottle, Dornflartz," I said, "I'm arresting you for misrepresentation and there's absolutely nothing you can do about it."

When I regained consciousness, my hair was parted sideways and Dornflartz was gone. But we knew he would be back, so Cuddles and I quickly set a trap. We set a plank on a box like a teeter-totter, on a platform beside a vat of fermenting grapes.

When Dornflartz returned and stepped on the end of the plank, I leaped onto the other end. Dornflartz flipped straight up, spun around, and landed on his grapes.

As he floundered on the fermenting mash, desperately trying to stay sober, I swam out and put the cuffs on him. Cuddles unbunged the bung from the bunghole, drained the vat, then finally pushed a ladder down for us two drunks to stagger up. By the time we got to the top of the ladder, Dornflartz and I were bosom buddies. He was calling me Sarge and I was calling him Flartzie.

Today, Dornflartz is a free man. The law has been changed and anti-freeze that contains wine is no longer considered contaminated.

As for the wine industry itself, it's doing better than ever because of a new game that is sweeping the country. It's called wino roulette. The way it works is three people sit in a doorway and each one has to drink a full bottle of the cheapest available wine. Then one of them leaves. The remaining two have to guess which one left.

Sergeant Major Renfrew in San Francisco (1991)

I was sitting in my lonely log cabin on the fourteenth floor of Mountie headquarters with my indestructible four-legged canine assistant, Corporal Cuddles, who was busy laundering himself.

All of a sudden, the Chief came bursting in. "Renfrew," he said, "the Prime Minister is leaving for trade talks in San Francisco with the Governor of California. You and your dog are about to volunteer for security duty."

When Cuddles and I arrived in San Francisco, the local police were waiting with open arms. When they saw me, they put their arms away.

I told them, "Don't be misled by my fancy uniform," as they escorted us to the exclusive hotel where the Prime Minister would be staying. A Comfort Inn on the waterfront. Inside the VIP suite, I immediately began the security checks. First, the washroom. I was going to try the bathtub, but the water wouldn't stay in the tub. I phoned and spoke to a woman on the front desk. "I've got a leak in my bathtub!"

"Go ahead," she said. "Everybody else does."

In the little time that I was on the phone, a graffiti protester had entered the suite and was painting slogans on the walls. I noticed she was wearing a T-shirt emblazoned with the logo "Protecting Endangered Californians P.E.C." PEC!

When she saw Cuddles, she panicked and fled. Cuddles and I gave chase. We followed the culprit down the street. She jumped on a cable car. We jumped too! I missed! My foot went down the slot by the track. By the time I got my foot out, I'd been dragged 16 blocks and picked up 72 dollars in fares. Not enough to pay for a new pair of pants with one leg 16 blocks long.

When I got inside the cable car, it was wall to wall with passengers. Chinese people, Koreans, Filipinos, Italians, Portuguese, Greek, Vietnamese, Ukrainians, Tamils, Croatians, I couldn't believe it. What were all these Canadians doing in San Francisco?

And where was our suspect?

In seconds I was on the roof. But I could see nothing except a huge banner stretching right across the street. "San Francisco welcomes Canada's prime minister, Gene Christine."

People were shouting at me. It sounded like "Pluck" or "Yuck" or "Muck." Why were they shouting? Did they think the big banner was going to engulf me and become a giant slingshot?

When I regained consciousness, I was hanging by my Sam Browne from a flagpole outside the Comfort Inn. The word the people had been yelling at me was "duck."

When the woman from Protecting Endangered Californians, P.E.C., returned to the scene of her crime, Cuddles and I were waiting for her.

As she climbed over the balcony railing with her fresh cans of graffiti paint, I grabbed her right arm with one hand and her left shoulder with my other hand.

But then I realized she had another shoulder and another arm, and I had already used up all my hands! I grabbed her chest with my nose. And held her for questioning.

Because of how I held her, I couldn't think of any questions. So she asked me a couple:

[In a woman's voice] "Have you ever done this with another woman?"

"Are you presently in a relationship?"

"Would you like to join my protest group, P.E.C. Become a P.E.C.er?"

Today, that graffiti protester is a changed person. She moved to Canada and is now a full-time energy activist, a belly dancer in Mississauga.

As for me, the Chief apologized that he could only reward me with money. But as I explained to the Chief, "If it's good enough for Canadian Tire, it's good enough for me!"

Big Bobby Clobber – Switching Seasons (1981)

BIG JIM: *Hi there, sports fans. Fans, when you're talking*
              sports, you just have to talk about a guy who's not
              only a great sport, he's a man for all seasons.
              Here he is, fresh from an incredible season of playing
              baseball all summer. Our own hockey superstar . . .
              Big Bobby Clobber.

[Music out.]

BIG JIM: *Hi, Big Bobby.*

BOBBY: *Hi, Big Jim.*

BIG JIM: *Well, Big Bobby, how do you feel now that the base-ball is over and you're back into hockey again?*

BOBBY: *Well, let me say, on that, when you come to the end of the season, which we* are *at, and you've played full out and given it everything you've got, and you've been able to take the good times with the bad, and each time you had to dig a little deeper . . .* [Pause]

BIG JIM: *Yes?*

BOBBY: [Sotto voce] *What was the question?*

BIG JIM: *Does the switch cause you any difficulties?*

BOBBY: *The switch . . . Sometimes. If it's been installed wrong. But if you get to know which way is which when the lights are still on . . . it's no problem.*

BIG JIM: *I meant the switch from baseball, during the summer, back to hockey, now.*

BOBBY: *Going from baseball back to hockey isn't nearly as tough as switching from hockey over to baseball . . . I don't think.*

BIG JIM: *You find that tricky?*

BOBBY: *Yeah. You go into your first few ball games and you find out you're not stealing bases the way you could. Your slide sort of stops dead, and then you realize what's wrong.*

BIG JIM: *Your co-ordination's rusty?*

BOBBY: *You've still got your skates on.*

BIG JIM: *So it's important to remember to take your skates off before the baseball season starts.*

BOBBY: *Not only that. You never body-check a base runner. Only, on the other hand, in case of if you have to, of course, except in the case of a bunt situation.*

BIG JIM: *Well, Bobby . . . uh, the baseball game I saw you play, it seemed you had forgotten something when you came up to bat.*

BOBBY:	*Well yeah. When you're going to hit the ball and your bat has got the tape at the wrong end . . . it's got to be one of three reasons for that.*
BIG JIM:	*You're holding a hockey stick.*
BOBBY:	*One of* four *reasons.*
BIG JIM:	*Did you ever play hockey with a baseball bat?*
BOBBY:	[Laughing] *Did I ever play hockey with a baseball bat?* [Laughing] *That's funny . . .*
BIG JIM:	*Well, did you?*
BOBBY:	*Yeah. A couple of times. I couldn't figure out how come my stick only reached up to my knees.*
BIG JIM:	*That must have told you something right away*
BOBBY:	*Not* right *away. At first I figured I'd grown a bit.*
BIG JIM:	*Well, Bobby, an awful lot of kids were playing baseball last summer and now, like you, they've all made the big switch to hockey. Do you have any advice for them?*
BOBBY:	*Yeah, kids. You can always tell which game you're playing if you look at the letter on your sweater.*
BIG JIM:	*How do you mean, Bobby?*
BOBBY:	*Like me. If there's a big letter "B" on my sweater, I know I have to be playing hockey for the Bruins.*
BIG JIM:	*Or baseball for the Blue Jays.*
BOBBY:	*Uhhhhhh. Well . . . anyway, uhhh . . . it's the letter that tells you. In fact, I made up a poem about it.*
BIG JIM:	*Really? A poem! Can you read it to us?*
BOBBY:	*I don't have to read. I can say it to us.*
BIG JIM:	*Let's hear it.*
BOBBY:	*If you look at the letter*
	Sewn on your sweater
	Front
	You won't be high-sticking
	the pitcher
	When you should of made
	a bunt
	Keep your eye on your sweater
	And you'll have no disgrace

> *Like spearing the catcher*
> *Or icing second base.*
> *It don't being . . . It don't . . .*
> *doesn't . . . bring you luck*
> *If you fit a powl . . . hit a*
> *foul puck*
> *So hockey or ball*
> *You'll play lots better*
> *If you check out the letter*
> *That's stuck to your sweater . . .*
> *That's all.*

BIG JIM: *Thanks very much, Big Bobby Clobber.*

Big Bobby Clobber Gets Fired (1999)

INT: *Welcome, fans. The big story today is hockey star Big Bobby Clobber. He has been let go by his team. We've invited him here to get his reaction to the news. Here he is, my special guest, hockey superstar, Big Bobby Clobber.*

[Dave enters as Bobby.]

INT: *Hi, Big Bobby! Hi.*

BOBBY: *How's that?*

INT: *Hi!*

BOBBY: *That's okay with me, I'm pretty high myself. I think it's the time-release Sudafed.*

INT: *Well, Bobby, we're certainly shocked to hear your employment contract with your team has been terminated.*

BOBBY: *Right now, I've got bigger problems than that. I just got fired!*

INT: *How did you react when you found out you were fired?*

BOBBY:	*I started thinking about as of my age and that. As on the other hand, some people say the older I get . . . But it's no good if I get, you know, like . . . distracted or that . . . and I lose my . . . lose the uh . . . What did you ask me?*
INT:	*I can't remember. So . . . what are your immediate plans?*
BOBBY:	*I've been working on a book deal with a publisher.*
INT:	*A book deal! That sounds wonderful. Will you be doing the writing yourself or hiring a ghost writer?*
BOBBY:	*Not that kind of book deal. I send the publisher three dollars and ninety-nine cents and they send me six books. If I do it right away, I also get a tote bag.*
INT:	*So, we shouldn't expect your biography any time soon?*
BOBBY:	*It's my next iron on the fire. My unauthorized biography.*
INT:	*Unauthorized?*
BOBBY:	*So if I make a mistake, I won't get sued?*
INT:	*Will the book be the story of a hockey player or a human being?*
BOBBY:	*That's right. I want it to waver back and forth? Between the both? Because, you know, when you're too busy living your life, well, you know, sometimes it seems that that's what life is all about. Right?*
INT:	*I think so. Bobby, when you look back on all that hockey, what do you miss most?*
BOBBY:	*[Pause] My teeth?*
INT:	*So, do you have any regrets?*
BOBBY:	*The only regret is when you're not winning any home games and you're not winning any away games and all you can think about is some other place to play. And there isn't?*
INT:	*Bobby, have you ever thought about retiring?*
BOBBY:	*I can't afford it. I loaned all my money to our last goalie for his plastic surgery. He took a bad hit in the face.*

INT:	*That was a very nice thing for you to do. I'm sure he'll pay you back.*
BOBBY:	*The hell he will. He disappeared. And after all the surgery they did on his face, I don't know what the son-of-a-bitch looks like.*
INT:	*Well, Bobby, at least you've got your health.*
BOBBY:	*I'm pretty sure so . . . on that. Although sometimes I'm seeing double.*
INT:	*Seeing double? Isn't that serious? What if you see two pucks?*
BOBBY:	*I figured it out. I go after the puck on the left.*
INT:	*What about at other times? Say you're in the washroom and you're in a hurry to zip yourself up.*
BOBBY:	*I have nothing to say on that. And I'm only going to say it once. A washroom is no place to see double.*
INT:	*So how is the double vision right now?*
BOBBY:	*I'm holding my own.*
INT:	*So . . . no other physical problems?*
BOBBY:	*Sometimes I see spots in front of my eyes.*
INT:	*Are you seeing an ophthalmologist?*
BOBBY:	*No. Just spots. If I start seeing opolominous, I'll go to a doctor.*
INT:	*Before you go, Bobby, do you have a word of wisdom for the kids out there?*
BOBBY:	*When it come to that, I do have. Kids, you got to be careful on the wisdom business. Think about it a lot, eh . . . And later, when you think about what it was you thought, it can be that the thought you thought you thought, might turn out to be not the thought you thought you thought when you first thought it . . . and the next thing you know, you're back to square one. I know. I've been there.*
INT:	*Thank you, Big Bobby Clobber.*

Big Bobby Clobber – Pig Detector (1985)

INT: *Hi, sports fans. Let's bring out our number-one sport right now, hockey superstar, Big Bobby Clobber. Welcome, Big Bobby.*

BOBBY: *I am, Big Jim.*

INT: *There is a question I've been wanting to ask you, Big Bobby. What's your opinion of fans who throw things on the ice while you're playing?*

BOBBY: *That's right. I think you can get upset on that. Very so. Like two weeks ago, somebody threw a live squid on the ice. There's no way anybody can eat a big snack like that while you're playing.*

INT: *That same night, somebody else threw money on the ice.*

BOBBY: *That's nothing. At one of our games someone chucked a real live pig out onto the ice. You could get a real bad injury from a trip over a pig.*

INT: *Oh, come on, Bobby, what hockey player couldn't see a pig coming?*

BOBBY: *Our goalie? He might miss it.*

INT: *Well, you've got a good point, Bobby. I've got to join you on that. Anyone throwing objects onto the ice should be chastised.*

BOBBY: [Cringe] *Oh, I wouldn't go that far. Oh boy oh boy. He could pay a fine maybe. But not chastised. The guy might want to have kids someday.*

INT: *Bobby, tell me what you think could be done to stop the fans throwing things onto the ice.*

BOBBY: *Okay, Big Jim, I've thought on that. And like, they should set up a pig detector. Like they have those metal detectors at airports only like this would be for pigs. And the ushers could have some of those trifles in their pockets . . . or truffles . . . in their pockets . . . or stuff like the cats go for only made for pigs . . . pig nip. And then like you're a hockey fan, and come in and*

	you've got that pig hid under your coat . . . and the
	pig gets wind of the truffles . . . or trifles . . . of pig
	nip . . . he's gonna like . . . he's gonna jump out of there
	and uh . . . and run . . . and run to . . . for the . . . for
	the . . . [pause] *What were we talking about?*
INT:	*The behaviour of hockey fans. Do you have a final*
	word on that?
BOBBY:	*Okay on that. Fans . . . don't throw stuff onto the*
	ice . . . like pigs or even especially pennies. Because a
	player can break his leg on the money, even though
	he might pick it up. The money. And spend it. We
	don't need it. Money is not what hockey is about.
	I don't think. In sports it's like anywhere else. There's
	only so much wool you can shear off the back of the
	sheep that's laying your golden egg. (And then you'll
	milk it dry.)
INT:	*Thank you very much, Big Bobby Clobber.*

The Wendell Weirdsly German Crusade (1982)

Based on a newspaper article about evangelist Ernest Angley's crusade in Hamburg, Germany.

[Music: "Oh Happy Day," Gospel Organ]

ANNOUNCER: *It's the Wendell Weirdsly Tower of Power Evangelical Happy Hour! And today, we're coming to you via satellite direct from the Wendell Weirdsly European Crusade, now in Hamburg, Germany. Brother Weirdsly's message today is simultaneously translated from American into German by Brother Helmut Schlichenfrich. Now here's Brother Weirdsly.*

WENDELL: *Ohhhhhhhh, thank you, my friends.*

SCHLICH:	*Ohhhhhhhh, danka schoen micht froynds*
WENDELL:	[Walking on the spot] *I was walking the streets of Hamburg last evening.*
SCHLICH:	[Same walking movements] *Ich bin walkenzie der Hamburg strassenbahn letzt nacht.*
WENDELL:	[Mime] *I saw people drinking the potent German beer.*
SCHLICH:	[Mime] *Die Hamburgers vast gulpen zee energisht foamy bloatin.*
WENDELL:	[Spread line out] *I saw fine young women . . .*
SCHLICH:	*Ich bin watchin die jung schnookie pootsen . . .*
WENDELL:	[Mime pointing to woman and back to Wendell] *One of them said to me, "Good day, my love."*
SCHLICH:	*Sie sprachen zu mir, "Guten Tag, leibchen."*
WENDELL:	[Hands on hips] *And I said, "Young lady, what is love?"*
SCHLICH:	[Hands on hips] *"Fraulein, vos ist du liebe?"*
WENDELL:	*And she replied . . . "Fifty dollars."*
SCHLICH:	*Sie sprach, "Ein hunert und funf Deutschemarks."*
WENDELL:	[Point to self on "I," and point to "you," hands on heart "love," Italian gesture for "priceless"] *I said, "Sister, I offer you a love that is priceless."*
SCHLICH:	*"Schwester, Ich givenzie ein lieb dot iss uze lezz."*
WENDELL:	*She misunderstood and said, "Bye-bye, sweet doggie."* [Wave]
SCHLICH:	*"Buggenzie auf, schweinhund."* [Wave]
WENDELL:	[Point straight down] *That woman is lost!*
SCHLICH:	[Point straight down] *Dot frau isht geschnookered!*
WENDELL:	[Point straight up] *She will not fly. She has no wings.*
SCHLICH:	[Use arms as wings] *Zee habbenzie nein flugel!*
WENDELL:	[Looks bewildered. Holds up nine fingers. Looks at Schlichenfrich] *Nine flugel???*
SCHLICH:	[Shakes head] *No. Nein!!*

[Music: Gospel organ music (sneak under)]

WENDELL: *Friends. We are warned in the good book what happens to those who are content to sit around slurping beer . . .*

SCHLICH: *Froynds.* [Does delayed-reaction take.] *Vas iss dass? Knockin der sudsy slurpin???*

WENDELL: *Beer is the nectar of Satan.*

SCHLICH: *Nein. Bier iss goot vor der korper!!*

WENDELL: *Oh, friends. I feel a need to heal my interpreter's tongue.*

SCHLICH: *Ich haben ein lode su gag mein ausleger's lickenstick.*

WENDELL: *Pray with me as I lay my blessed hand on my interpreter's throat . . . and command the devil to come out. Come out, Satan!!!*

SCHLICH: [Angry] *Ausfahrt. Luft ihr fingerdigits auf mein gurgle shaft!* [Pushing Wendell away.]

ANNOUNCER: *The Wendell Weirdsly Evangelical Happy Hour has been coming to you live from the Weirdsly Crusade in the Reeperbahn Stadium in downtown Hamburg, Germany.*

WENDELL: *Praise be to Glory!!*

SCHLICH: *Yah! Glory . . . Preis bin zu Glory Floor WaxUnd Shine!!!*

Satan in Music (1987)

An evangelist has burned recordings that he says contain messages from Satan. Among the records put to the torch was one containing the theme song from the television show "Mr. Ed." The cleric charges that, when the record is played backwards, the satanic message is crystal clear. Here, tonight, is that evangelist.

Friends, as I have travelled across this country I have been struck. I have been struck . . . by many things . . . by a porter on Via Rail, by a beverage wagon on Air Canada . . . but most of all I have been struck by the monstrous evil conspiracy that is engulfing us today. Yes, friends, I'm talking about the way Satan is using popular music.

What is the dominant instrument in popular music today? It's not the harp. Not the bugle. Not the zither. Not the kazoo. Not the piccolo. Not the ukulele. Not the sweet potato. Not the spoons. Not the bagpipes.

It's the drum!

And what does the musician do to his drum?

He beats it!!!! With sticks!!!!

Ooooo ooooo the violence in music!

How about sex? [Pause]

That's a rhetorical question.

Don't answer it. Please.

What about Madonna, who sang that classic "Like a virgin, touched for the very first time." Who but Satan could make her be so dishonest!!!!

What about the song "To All the Girls I've Loved Before"? The person in question loved so many girls he sang the song with another man.

Oh yes . . . I hear you shaking your heads . . . "But, Pastor," you say, "these songs are all about love."

Satan knows that.

Satan is clever.

That's why you have to play these records backwards.

To get the real message.

What is love in reverse?

It's E.V.O.L. Evol!!.

What is sin backwards?

N.I.S. Nice!!!

Satan knows what he is doing. Even if he's a bad speller.

The very instrument he mentioned . . .

"Drum" backwards, it's "murd."

Oh yes. Satan can speak French.

But the most satanic message that ever was, comes from the theme song of the old television show "Mr. Ed." "A horse is a horse of course of course." When you play that song backwards this is what you hear.

Someone sang this song for Satan
The Devil wants you high on grass
The choice is yours . . . so go and kill
Or stay at home you horse-faced wimp.

I had to destroy that record.

Oh yes . . . oh yes . . . The man who wrote that song says we evan-gelists are wrong! But he doesn't say that he also wrote "Que sera sera" and "Buttons and Bows."

You write "Que sera sera" backwards and you get "Ares ares euq." And even more disgusting . . . "Buttons and Bows" backwards is "Snot tub and Swob"!!!!

Oh friends, if you support me in my crusade to destroy Satan's music . . .

Send me your prayers.

It doesn't matter how you send them. Visa or Mastercard. They are both blessed.

When you write, you can address me as "preacher" or "brother" or "reverend" or "holy one." But please don't call me "pastor."

"Pastor" backwards is "rot sap"!

Bless you. Victory is mine . . . sayeth the Rotsap!

Bartholomew – Culture (2000)

A lot of people think livin' on skid row is worry-free. No way is it free. I'm not sayin' I'm payin' off no mortgage on my cardboard box or that. No way. Paid that off a year ago.

I got to say, when things was goin' good, I sure spent a lot of money . . . on wine, women, and wine. But I also wasted money. Mind you, when things went bad . . . . I wasn't wastin' nothin'. I was givin' my used shirts away to the Salvation Army. They cleaned them, and I was buyin' 'em back at thirty-five cents apiece.

I kept thinkin' I was gonna make a fortune with my "invention" but I could never get a patent for it. The idea was a talking washing machine. *After the rinse cycle, the machine tells you where your missing sock is.*

When that fell through, I was desperate. So desperate, I sent my obituary in to the newspaper. They printed it, and I sent copies of it to everybody I owed money.

By the time they found out I was alive, they'd already written me off.

Dyin' don't bother me anyway.

When things was good, I got myself a deal on a previously enjoyed casket with a silk linin'. The undertaker told me I was lucky to get the silk. He said, "With the rayon, your arse'll be through in no time."

What's worryin' me is not that. It's what's happenin' to our culture.

I worry about it every year when it gets to be July and I start to think about Christmas gettin' close.

It gets worse every year. Like last year . . . a bunch of us geezers was over at the shelter. We was all sittin' around a roarin' fire. Which was pretty damn scary. They don't have no fireplace over there.

Once we got the flames doused, we turned on the TV and waited for Alistair Sim to come on in Dickens's A Christmas Carol. We tried every damn channel, and may God strike me silly . . . Alistair Sim did not come on!

The greatest Scrooge ever to walk the face of the earth has been replaced!!! Replaced???

Some guys in Hollywood remade the picture and dumbed it way down.

Scrooge showed up as a truck driver.

Imagine what's comin' next.

When they remake Hamlet, Ophelia won't drown herself. She'll marry her lady-in-waitin' and they'll open an aroma-therapy boutique. In Beverly Bloody Hills.

When they redo Pygmalion, Professor Higgins will be teaching Whitney Houston how to sing without sounding like Preston Manning getting a vasectomy!

With no anaesthetic!

I tell you we have to do something about this cultural thievery.

Look what's happening to our Canadian magazines. All three of them's in trouble.

Turns out three magazines is too many for a population of only thirty-three million. Not all of us is readers.

And now . . . the Americans has got hold of the Montreal Canadiens, the Montreal Expos, the Alouettes . . .

Americans has got hold of Eaton's.

They've took over Tim Horton's.

They got Laura Secord . . . This woman who used to be a patriot!

I don't know how she ended up in the ice cream and the chocolates, but it's been downhill ever since.

As soon as the Disney people get their mitts on her, she'll be turned into an American hero!!

America's Dairy Queen! As unpredictable as her chocolates!! She's plain, she's semi-sweet, she's half-raisins, she's half-nuts! She taught her cows to sing and dance to distract America's enemies!

In the movie, she'll be secretly on her way across the border to have sex with an American GI when her cows catch sight of a patriotic American bull and Laura gets trampled to death!

There's another word that goes with "bull" that I will not use!

The word is DOZER!!!!

I've had enough of this cultural bulldozin'!

I'm hitch-hikin' down to Washington, D.C., to protest!!!

Yes!

> *I'm on my way to demonstrate*
> *In Washington, D.C.*
> *I'll raise our flag*
> *I'll praise our flag*
> *I'll wave it proud and free*
> *I'll buy it when I get there,*
> *And save the G.S.T.!!*

Bartholomew's Eight Weeks (2002)

[Dave, in cheap bed-sitting room.]

Last time I was sittin' in my doctor's waitin' room, I was readin' an article about an old doctor who was bein' honoured 'cause he was one of the few who brave the elements to go out and visit his patients.

What I want to know is when do they honour us old geezers who brave the elements to go out and visit our doctors? Most of us is dead!

So I was sittin' readin' from the doctor's library. He had one People *magazine and one* Maclean's. *The* People *magazine was pretty up to date for a waitin' room. The letters to the editor was askin' how to get ready for the Y2K crisis.*

When the doc finally calls me in to show me my X-rays, he says, "Here's your stomach, Bartholomew. As you can see, it's quite a junkyard in there. Don't worry about the shot glass. You'll pass that in no time. Your medication is workin' just fine. Take a seat in the waitin' room. My assistant, Melatharalina, will tell you when to come and see me again."

This time in the waitin' room, I grabbed the brand new Maclean's, *and got readin' a news story about a waitress. The doc's assistant, Melatharalina, must have thought I left the buildin' 'cause she never did come out and see me, but I could hear her tellin' the doctor, "Old Bartholomew's got about eight weeks left at the most."*

"Holy crap," I says to myself. "If I've only got eight weeks left on this planet, I'm goin' to steal this magazine."

I finished readin' the story of the waitress back at the shelter. You probably read it too. She was in a restaurant, servin' her customers, when all of a sudden, this biker guy is standin' in the restaurant doorway, wearing a ski mask and holdin' a gun.

Suddenly another biker sittin' at a table jumps up, grabs the waitress and hides behind her. The biker in the doorway opens fire. The waitress takes four bullets. And get this, she's not only not dead, she's suin' the son-of-a-bitch of a biker who used her like a human shield.

When I read that the biker's scumbag lawyer said the waitress don't have a leg to stand on, I went into a deep think about how these biker thugs got no respect for nothin'. The only time they pay attention is when one of their fancy club houses burns to the ground.

So I ask myself, "Bartholomew, if you've only got eight weeks left, why don't you take a quick course in arson? What's the worst thing the bikers can do to yuh? Kill yuh? And shorten your life by maybe a whole week?"

So I look in CAREER OPPORTUNITIES *under* ARSON FOR BEGINNERS *but no luck. You can't get no degree in it. You have to teach yourself. So, that's what I done.*

Two days later, I'm about to do my regular obituary check to see which of my friends is freshly dead, when what do I see? I made the front page!

The headline is BIKER HEADQUARTERS A SMOULDERING RUIN. GANG MOVES TO NEW LOCATION.

Then, three weeks later, more headlines. BIKER CRIMINALS FACE REIGN OF TERROR AS NEW HEADQUARTERS BURNS TO GROUND. ARSONIST LEAVES NOTE "I'M STILL LEARNIN'. YOU AIN'T SEEN NOTHIN' YET."

Yesterday, there was a message for me at the shelter. My doctor's nurse, Melatharalina, wanted to see me. When I got there she said: "You were supposed to get this prescription last time, Bartholomew. I remember tellin' the doctor about your supply of medication. I told him you had only about eight weeks left at the most." Then she waves her finger at me.

"I hope you're not back on cigarettes, Bartholomew. I can smell smoke."

PICTURE CREDITS